ELEANOR
OF
AQUITAINE

ELEANOR
OF
AQUITAINE

*Queen
of the
Troubadours*

JEAN MARKALE

Translated by Jon E. Graham

Inner Traditions
Rochester, Vermont

Inner Traditions
One Park Street
Rochester, Vermont 05767
www.InnerTraditions.com

Originally published in French under the title *La vie, la légende, l'influence d'Aliénor* by Editions Payot
Second edition published in French under the title *Aliénor d'Aquitaine* by Éditions Payot
First U.S. edition published in 2007 by Inner Traditions

Library of Congress Cataloging-in-Publication Data
Markale, Jean.
  [Vie, la légende, l'influence d'Aliénor, comtesse de Poitou, duchesse d'Aquitaine, reine de France, puis d'Angleterre, dame des troubadours et des bardes bretons. English]
  Eleanor of Aquitaine : queen of the troubadours / Jean Markale ; translated by Jon E. Graham.
  — 1st U.S. ed.
    p. cm.
  Previously published as Aliénor d'Aquitaine in 2000 by Éditions Payot; originally published in 1979 as: La vie, la légende, l'influence d'Aliénor, comtesse de Poitou, duchesse d'Aquitaine, reine de France, puis d'Angleterre, dame des troubadours et des bardes bretons.
  Summary: "A comprehensive view of the mythical and historic significance of the great medieval queen"—Provided by publisher.
  Includes bibliographical references and index.
  ISBN-13: 978-1-59477-195-8 (pbk.)
  ISBN-10: 1-59477-195-2 (pbk.)
  1. Eleanor, of Aquitaine, Queen, consort of Henry II, King of England, 1122?–1204. 2. Great Britain—History—Henry II, 1154–1189—Biography. 3. Louis VII, King of France, ca. 1120–1180—Marriage. 4. Henry II, King of England, 1133–1189—Marriage. 5. France—History—Louis VII, 1137–1180—Biography. 6. Queens—Great Britain—Biography. 7. Queens—France—Biography. 8. Troubadours. I. Title.
  DA209.E6M35 2007
  942.03'1092—dc22
  [B]   2007024464

Printed and bound in the United States by Lake Book Manufacturing

10 9 8 7 6 5 4 3 2 1

Text design and layout by Priscilla Baker
This book was typeset in Garamond, with Charlemagne used as a display typeface

Inner Traditions wishes to express its appreciation for assistance given by the government of France through the National Book Office of the Ministère de la Culture in the preparation of this translation.

Nous tenons à exprimer nos plus vifs remerciements au government de la France et le ministère de la Culture, Centre National du Livre, pour leur concours dans le préparation de la traduction de cet ouvrage.

CONTENTS

E seu sai ren dir ni faire
Ilh n'aja. I grat, que sciensa
M'a donat, et conoissensa,
Per qu'eu suis gais e chantaire

And if I can do or say a thing or two,
let the thanks be hers, for she
gave me the understanding and the craft,
because of her I can be courtly and sing ...

TROUBADOUR PEIRE VIDAL,
1175–1205

Introduction

HISTORY AND ITS HEROES

From whatever standpoint we look at it, whether as a simple documentary narrative, as purely descriptive, or as governed by the strictest laws of structured research, history is not only a reservoir of myths—albeit the largest one, perhaps—but is also a gigantic machine for glorifying heroes. These circumstances are inherent to the historic phenomenon because its constituent events are propelled by human actions. Further, because simplification is fully in play when we recount a bygone past, our memory retains only history's privileged players to the exclusion of the other actors in this vast dramatic fresco.

In most cases, the privileged person we recall is obviously the leader, the one believed to hold real responsibilities for contemporary events, the one who stands on center stage. This is rather unjust in the sense that a leader is nothing without his followers, but history can retain only the basic outline of events, which is easily embodied in the person that assures its coordination. In fact, because human memory tends to integrate facts into a symbolic whole, the leader-as-hero takes on the value of a symbol, and his image remains graven, which eliminates the details that might scatter attention and damage the consistency of this image. This is telling of the importance of the hero in the historical narrative: he forms the pivot around which the history of a people or social group is articulated.

From this perspective, it could be said that history is quite close to the epic. Light has often been focused on their common origin—the desire to preserve the feats of an ancient time within a structured story—which also extends from exacerbated nationalism if not outright racism. It is true that the epic was an archaic form of history during a time when all that mattered was the desire to ensure the permanence of a collective mentality. With their purposes being the same, it is hard to see how primitive history can be distinguished from the epic, except that the epic is spontaneous, popular, and instinctive, whereas history, even in primitive times, claimed it was objective and, despite what some might say, still presents itself as an intellectual achievement. In fact, the epic forms part of folk culture and history belongs to scholarly culture, but identical procedures are employed by both and the hero of both is often the same person.

It is this existence of the hero in history as well as in the epic that poses problems. While the epic is the narrative of assumed events that are nevertheless considered to be real—events that have marked the genesis and evolution of a given social group—we cannot doubt for a moment that the hero it glorifies is the emanation of this group, its pure embodiment rather than merely its symbol. It little matters whether he actually existed or not; his position in the epic alone is his birth certificate, and his existence is doubted by no one. The epic may be true or false, but it is enough simply to be.

This absence of doubt characterizes an immediate assumption of the collective consciousness, because each person listening to an epic is, to a small extent, its hero and, like the hero, embodies the traditional values of the group of which he or she is a member. In fact, the epic falls into the domain of experience, but a perpetually reactualized one, thereby permitting the attainment of a veritable permanence. The epic is a challenge against death, a continuous progression toward the realization of collective desires, an ideal stabilization in the process of events that follow in a rhythm defying the most elementary laws of chronology so as to constitute only the eternal present. The hero is then immutable in his transformations, eternal in his metamorphoses, and transcendent in his ephemeral nature.

The hero of history, however, makes up only a privileged moment in the succession of events we remember. He does not possess the timeless nature of the epic hero because he has a completely defined civil status. He may enter history on a precise date, by surprise, and exit at a precise time—but during the brief lapse of time in which he acts, he consumes everything, eclipses his contemporaries, plays the demiurge, and lifts himself to the same extreme level as the epic hero. It would seem that the historical hero borrows the permanent nature of the epic hero, or rather that people have sought to make him the equivalent of the epic hero when it was no longer possible to believe in the epic and it became necessary to replace it with an objective and dated narrative. Does this mean that the epic speaks the language of the people better than does history, with its scientific classification, doubts and reservations, claims of objectivity, and lack of human warmth?

The answer can only be yes. It is easy to draw up a list of historic heroes who have become epic not only through oral tradition, such as Charlemagne (the character bearing his name in the chansons de geste is but a pale reflection of the man) but also through crystallization and idealization, such as Napoleon, whose legend maintains a false image but one that is far more compatible with that seen by the collective unconscious.

It is appropriate to ask if it is the hero who makes history by acting on events or if it is history that makes heroes. It has long been believed that uncommon individuals are capable of influencing the unfolding of history, that they have made the history of a people or a group of peoples. This is how Alexander the Great was indirectly responsible for the hatching of a neo-Greek (Hellenistic) civilization that forged a harmonious syncretism from Aristotle's philosophy and the "barbaric" inventions of the peoples of the East—but to what extent was Alexander compelled by history itself when he set off on his endless expeditions toward the lands of the rising sun?

Perhaps we should see in his adventure the result of the Greek world's strong push toward the outside in order to escape the asphyxiation that lay in wait for it ever since Mediterranean logic began ossifying around deductive syllogism. Perhaps the Greek push occurred because Alexander had no other choice but to break through the eastern borders in order to discover new markets for a Greek economy that had been faltering ever since Macedonian centralism replaced the autarkic distinctions of the former Greek city-states. Culture and economy are generally bound together so closely that it is difficult to discern the deep motivations for a political action apparently set in motion by a single man—even if this person possesses an entire people's decision-making power.

Economics, however, escape historical analysis as long as we limit ourselves to examining historical events from the angle of pure ideology, which exists and is not negligible. In fact, such ideology is necessary to guide the populace, to give the people a basis for their patriotism, and to prop up all those alienating inventions that cause people to march instead of think. Ideology is merely a means used by those in power, whoever they may be, to concentrate latent forces and direct them toward a goal that escapes common men but is quite familiar to those who hold the reality of this power—generally people waiting in the wings of the political stage who act by intermediary figures (intermediary heroes).

This is when the hero takes on his full value and meaning. He is merely the flag-bearer of a pressure group that draws its energies from him—energies from which he does not benefit personally, for he merely performs in an operation made from whole cloth that is governed with no thought of his own desires. This is why heroes are always impartial and excite the admiration of the crowd: they fight for glory or for an idea that seems generous in appearance. After all, some believe Napoleon slaughtered Europe to establish everywhere a republic of justice and human fraternity. Has anyone ever denounced the bourgeois, capitalist plot that permitted Bonaparte to become emperor and dominate a large swath of Europe for the benefit of certain economic groups? History is not paved with good intentions. In fact, it marks a permanent battle in which the strongest always crush the weak in the name of some ideology. What is important is that the strongest are never seen in their true role;

if they were, they would lose this occult power that is the heart of their strength and that makes them the beneficiaries of the heroism of others.

Of course, demystifying the hero in this way and revealing what lies behind him knocks him off his pedestal and, more seriously, reduces him to the rank of perfect cretin. This is not to say that heroism should be shown as purely unconscious or stupid—but these are values we cannot attack with impunity because they concern an entire people or social group, and their destruction could lead to the complete dissolution of social bodies.

In fact, the hero, whether epic or historical, belongs to myth. When people attack him, they are attacking myth itself, and this myth is the most important thing humanity has at its disposal for continuing or changing the course of events. It is not the hero who makes history; rather, it is history that pushes him to achievements that in turn have repercussions on the unfolding of history. Here we find the elements for a Marxist dialectic: the real prompts the intervention of thought, which then acts on the real and transforms it. The world exudes ideas, and ideas transform the world. The hero belongs to the world of ideas. He embodies myth on the occasion of this or that ordinary event, because myth, which exists on its own, would be the equivalent of nothingness if it were not integrated into matter. Thus the hero forms the juncture between the abstract and the real, between the realm of pure ideas that circulate randomly through collective thought and the realm of concrete realizations that presume a strict organization and articulation around an ideology. Despite himself and despite the analyst striving to reveal what drives him, the hero belongs to the people—who could not do without him and who, if he were taken from them, would immediately reconstruct him in another shape and under another name through unconscious transfer.

The appearance of a hero in history or in the epic is never the result of chance and is never gratuitous. The psychological mechanisms governing the creation of heroes are complex and are never clearly transmitted in the story as it is experienced or as it is repeated by tradition. Creation of the hero is primarily a projection of individual impulses that attempts to unify opposites and carry out the synthesis of heteroclite movements triggered by a given circumstance. The hero necessarily finds the solution to the problems that people face at the time of his appearance. He is the man of the moment, the providential man, so often betrayed, who remains perpetually alive in the collective mentality. By himself, the hero represents every individual in a specific social group, and each of the people in the group recognizes himself in the hero not as he actually is but as he is ideally.

This is the reason the hero appears as an uncommon individual, a fantastic figure endowed with powers that arouse envy as well as fear, a supernatural and quasi-divine figure. The hero breaks the limits of the real, he opens the doors to the lost Paradise—in other words, he attempts the impossible. Moreover, if he does not succeed, it is not his fault but instead is that of evil powers, which are always latent and that prevented him from carrying his action through to its completion.

By itself, however, myth as embodied by the hero is an absolute with no meaning. The availability of myth can be observed in the way epic tales and oral folktales are treated: they are all based on an initial mythological outline but testify to a fundamental stance adopted by the storyteller, who gives an original narrative the meaning he deems appropriate for the particular moment in which he tells it. Myth will always escape those who seek to possess it, for it is nothing but a *should be* whose reality can be discerned only in the legendary story. In the case of the historical hero, the situation is the same. He is a figure who, through a series of circumstances, is led to play a role and embody a preexisting myth whose power he does not even suspect. He achieves this embodiment of the myth for others and himself, thereby giving myth its meaning and significance.

For example, the Christian saints, who are the heroes of their realm, are all devoted to what we call *good*. They give any preexisting myths a positive direction and through their lives and examples achieve an ideal that would be incomprehensible if it was not embodied in them. According to legend, however, it is said that the devil always lurks in the shadow of the great saints in order to tempt them—but this temptation is a necessity, because good incarnate cannot be conceived without the presence of an evil incarnate. This is logical to the extent that myth is neither good nor evil, because it exists outside time and space and is automatically charged with a positive or negative sense only once it enters the material world. A historical figure such as Hitler, viewed as the embodiment of evil, the devil himself, came from the same mold: He was also the sum of an ideal of perfection, but he reversed the meaning of the myth in comparison to that of the Christian saints. In his way, Hitler expressed and crystallized certain human tendencies—the most dubious kind, perhaps, but perfectly real. In addition, the myth of the chosen race is not a nationalist socialist invention; it has existed throughout history and has been embodied by many figures, instigating here and there atrocities of all kinds that are prompted by the concept of one caste having superiority over others.

The hero is a miraculous actor on a stage that unfolds through time. Whether as a warrior, king, saint, righter of wrongs, or the devil in person, he is charged with all the potentials life has to offer, which makes him a real and often formidable figure of power—for all that's required to pull others in his wake is a word or a gesture from him. Followers do not even have to stop and consider whether they should launch into a particular adventure, for the hero thinks and acts for them—in fact they are the hero.

The hero's formidable power stems from the fact that he is necessary at a given moment in history. He is inspired by events and projected forward by a definite social group whose aspirations and interests he represents. Launched into motion, then, is a machine that no one—especially not the hero—can stop. He no longer belongs to himself; he is no longer an individual but a totality represented by one. Hence his visible isolation: the hero is not like everybody else. Recall the magnificent poem by Alfred de Vigny in which Moses, incapable of tolerating any longer being powerful and alone, asks God to grant him the sleep of the earth while Moses reviews the actions of his life that distinguish him from a "normal" individual. We learn that no one has ever truly loved him because he has inspired too much fear (though this is a form of worship). Most important, Moses is prey to an atrocious solitude—which is really the solitude of the Hebrew people, whom he represents in totality.

This is the paradoxical situation of the hero, whether historical or epic: He is both alone and an emanation of the group. He is no longer an individual, yet he is still a human being, which is how he can leave his stamp on events. He never loses his personality, and often his actions and decisions, although dictated by phenomena of the collective unconscious, are inflected by his own reaction and thought. This is why it can never be said that history would have been identical if another hero had played his part. The human factor always plays a role in such manifestations. This is another paradox, for while it is customary to say that no one is irreplaceable, we forget that there are never two absolutely identical human beings and that, consequently, the direction of history can be altered in some unforeseen way by the acting of another player. The machine that has been set in motion will revolve, but no one knows exactly how it will revolve.

We should not be duped, then, by the collective nature of the hero. Of course, he is always the incarnation of the group, but he retains the possibility of assessing, preferring, imposing, and clinging to his own views. He alters the behavior of the group, which, after his passage, can never go back to being exactly the same. It is not without reason that all societies at all latitudes have paid homage to those who have created a nation, transformed life, and changed the direction of history. The hero is important not merely by virtue of the components that move him but also by virtue of the discretionary power that places him outside the common fold and requires him to possess an individual consciousness.

It is from this angle that we must study the heroes of history or the epic to find their correspondences and the deep social impulses governing them and to identify the cultural or economic motivations to which they owe their appearance. Yet this analysis will remain incomplete if we do not take into consideration the hero's personality and its influence on people and events. The science of history, or rather that which some try to make a science, cannot neglect any factor, whatever its origin. Making history a mere series of events and benchmarks is not enough; we must also explain its causes and assess its consequences. Until the present time, myth has been neglected as a motivational value of human actions, and it must be reintegrated into all historical studies. The hero, the embodiment of myth, gives us a great opportunity for this reintegration, for through his image the true face of a particular era or civilization stands out.

This is all the more true when we are dealing with a *heroine* instead of a *hero*—which is not common in history, in which women have generally been sacrificed to the androcratic point of view. When we learn of times past, because the silence of their roles is so thick, we might ask if women even existed. Of course, a few have survived in memory, but we can quickly note that all too often these female historical figures are devalued. Often they are transformed into femmes fatales or, at the very least, into symbols of a sensuality that poses a danger to the male balance of the societies being examined. When Cleopatra is mentioned it is always in the context of her liaisons with Marc Antony and Caesar, and she herself is characterized as flirtatious and vain. When Catherine the Great of Russia is mentioned, it is obviously to condemn her nymphomania. Eventually, we come to see the famous women of history merely as sexually obsessed individuals or at least as instruments of perdition for humanity.

Here again we find myth: the theme of the great prostitute, the divine woman who bestows her power on numerous lovers of her choosing who then execute her supreme desires. The whiff of scandal given off by the lives of the great women of history is almost justification for their presence in the limelight. This characterization has been used to the advantage of those who seek to diminish the female influence and criticize women's intelligence. It is true that if women held the reins of power, they did so with secondary means that are quite feminine and thus cannot be compared to the methods used by history's "real" heroes: men. All of this is inscribed in the stories and stamped in the wax of tradition. A society built entirely on androcratic principles and additionally propped up by a masculine theocracy can accept these infringements generally only with great reservation. Yet somehow this myth of the great prostitute has survived and materializes from time to time, even if it does unleash scandal. It has its own logic, however, and if it manifests itself in this way, it is because it is necessary.

If an individual brings a myth into concrete existence, it is because circumstances demand it, and the more heroic the proportions given to the figure, the stronger the tensions exercised by circumstances. History's best-known heroes have experienced privileged moments marked by such important events as wars, cataclysms, and revolutions. During periods of peace or laxity, heroes are insignificant, and as a reaction, the old myths, which always remain intact in our memories, come back to life in epic tales, which act as a kind of compensation for the lack of real heroes. Sometimes we might even believe that the myths have vanished, but they reemerge when they are least expected. One day, when circumstances have created an intolerable impetus, tensions prompt the appearance of the hero that everyone desired without admitting this desire.

This is what happened with Eleanor of Aquitaine, the woman who was twice a queen, the female head of two different kingdoms. She was a dominant figure of the twelfth century because of her behavior, the events in which she took part, her two sons who went on to become kings, and her legend. She was born during a slack period of history at a time when the old myths (mainly Celtic ones) were being reborn in epic form—and among these myths was that of the all-powerful woman. It so happens that Eleanor was indeed a woman. At the same time that the cult of the Virgin, the perfect model of woman, was developing throughout Europe and the same time that the troubadours were beginning to spread their passionate songs to the glory of female beauty, the figure of Eleanor of Aquitaine emerged from the mists of feudal times as a symbol of a lost and found femininity. We should not be surprised, then, in the abundance of legends that circulated regarding the countess of Poitiers and duchess of Aquitaine during her lifetime—legends whose mythological foundations are obvious and which caused a sensation because of the scandal they inspired.

If we are to study the figure of Eleanor of Aquitaine and her role, it is certainly not enough to merely retell her life by accumulating its colorful episodes (however many there are). These episodes have been the joy of the authors of historical novels and even, sometimes, of historians themselves. Their only interesting aspect, however, is the context that gave birth to them or the meaning ascribed to them, for Eleanor is the heroine through whom emerged all the features of twelfth-century Western civilization at a time when transformations were so radical as to bring about a complete top-to-bottom change in society.

On the religious plane, in addition to the blossoming of the Marial cult, we can note at this time the beginnings of an original scholastic philosophy that distinguished itself from the Aristotelian model, the creation of new religious orders that would literally inundate the Christian world, the strengthening of the pope's temporal authority, and the pursuit of the Crusades, whose consequences were beyond calculation in every arena. On the economic plane, the twelfth century witnessed the renewal of agriculture and, more important, the prodigious blossoming of commerce that eventually toppled feudal society as Europe had known it. The old Continental commercial current represented by the Rhône-Seine River axis—so jealously supervised by the Capets—was now countered by a new maritime current in the Atlantic Ocean and English Channel, a preserve guarded by the Anglo-Normans with the support of the Aquitanians and the Bretons and a modern commercial current on which the Anglo-Angevin dynasty soon built an empire. On the political plane (which is only the consequence of economic growth), the rupture was complete between the kingdoms of France and England and between the western third of France and the rest of the country of France. Moreover, this was only a prelude to the great quarrel between the two kingdoms that erupted a century and a half later.*

On the social plane, the emancipation of the cities sparked the birth of a new economically rich and politically strong caste: the bourgeoisie.

---

*[As the Hundred Years War. —*Trans.*]

At the same time, the feudal hierarchy was tottering to the benefit of the powerful knight caste. In these social transformations we can see the beginnings of Western-style capitalism in the cities, with the birth of a proletariat resulting from the relaxing of the fate of serfs and, in many cases, even from their emancipation. On the cultural plane, the twelfth century was a blessed age: we can note the flowering of the Romanesque style; the appearance of the improperly named Gothic style; the rebirth of Latin letters, which had fallen victim to the previous centuries' strong tendency to overlook them; the creation of numerous schools due to the strong influence of the Church; the considerable reduction in the number of illiterate nobles; and, most important, the creation of a new literature through the merger of the Occitan spirit, Celtic tradition, Norman solidity, and the availability of the countries speaking the *langue d'oïl.**

These changes, however, took place in successive stages, in a way that was scarcely visible and without any flashy upheaval. As a result, mores softened considerably, sometimes going from the darkest barbarism to the most precious refinement, and the art of living became the art of living well. Summing up all these transformations admirably was Eleanor of Aquitaine, for she dwelled at the very center of the crucible where this fusion occurred. Indeed, she crystallized everything the twelfth century offered in the way of innovations and metamorphoses of Western civilization.

Standing at the turning point between two worlds; heiress to an Occitan philosophy that was clearly more advanced than that of the north; given enormous responsibilities at an early age; and never forgetting, no matter what the circumstance, that she was first and foremost a woman, Eleanor is one of history's figures who cannot leave us indifferent. While she is most obviously the emanation of the twelfth century in movement, while she embodied the metamorphoses of society through her intelligence and temperament, she also played an incon-

---

*[The *langue d'oïl* is the language of northern France, as opposed to the *langue d'oc*, which eventually gave its name to the southern region of France where it was spoken (Languedoc). —*Trans.*]

testable personal role in history. Through her attitude toward the Capet court, her "divorce," her marriage to Henry Plantagenet, her boundless ambition, and her passion for arts and literature she was truly a revolutionary at a time when this word did not yet exist. Not every revolution, whether consciously or not, releases its heroes. The twice-queen Eleanor is therefore the heroine of a revolution that awakened the Middle Ages from its torpor. After all, for Chrétien de Troyes and his successors, she served as model for the character Queen Guinevere, paragon of beauty and virtue and the deified image of the all-powerful woman in her rediscovered femininity.

Myth is not far away. Eleanor embodied the myth of the ideal queen that Celtic legends had preserved in memory and which was waiting only for an opportunity to resurface. Like Guinevere, Eleanor unleashed passions, both real and assumed. Like Guinevere and her Celtic archetypes, better than anyone, Eleanor embodied sovereignty, without which no man, not even the greatest king, was capable of ruling the world.

There is a long road between the frail little girl who was married to Louis of France and who was still lost in the dreams that the troubadours, her regular companions, whispered in her ears and the tireless old woman who watched over her last son, John, from her retreat in Fontevrault in order to prevent him from making his poor reign even worse. What's more, her long road is marked by many crossroads. Eleanor had to choose which face to show to others. She had to choose which direction to take. It was along this long road of eighty-two years that one of the most brilliant pages of history was written.

1

TWICE A QUEEN

*E*leanor of Aquitaine was probably born in 1122—the chroniclers vacillate between 1120 and 1122—as the daughter of William X of Aquitaine (William VIII of Poitiers) and Aenor of Châtellerault. It is claimed that the name she was given means "the other Aenor" (Alia-Aenor). In any event, her given name, Aliénor, was the Occitan form of Elléonore, and the English called her Eleanor or Ellinor. She had a brother who died at an early age and a younger sister named Petronella, and, because of this, she was the heir to the earldom of Poitiers and the duchy of Aquitaine—in other words, the entire southwest portion of what is now France.

Her grandfather, William IX (Guilhelm in Occitan), a great and colorful figure as well as a formidable combatant, was politically crafty with few scruples but was highly cultivated. He was the first of the French troubadours and one of the most original, but William IX did not enjoy a rule of complete peace: not only did he have issues with his neighbors and his vassals, but he also had a bone to pick with the Church, mainly because of the scandals in his private life (he was one of the most famous skirt chasers of his time).

In fact, William IX had a double personality that incorporated the sincerest mysticism and the most unbridled sensuality. He had a habit of calling upon St. Julian every time he embarked upon another somewhat dubious affair of the heart to ask for the saint's guarantee of success. While accompanying Godefroy de Bouillon* on the First Crusade, he found time to compose incontestably obscene poems. There is a particular story in Niort that perfectly illustrates the character of William IX: After having ordered the creation of various religious monuments, he had built a brothel in which girls were obliged to wear monastic garb. The chronicle adds that he was the brothel's first customer.

Where he exceeded the tolerance of the priesthood, however, was in openly advertising his tumultuous liaison with Dangerosa, countess of Châtellerault, who was known as the Maubergeonne and who was the mother of Aenor, whom he had married to his son William X. His son was not at all appreciative of the situation and broke off relations with the Troubadour. William IX did not hesitate simply to move his mistress into the brand-new keep named the Tour Maubergeon (hence the countess's nickname), which he recently had constructed to be the ducal palace after he had driven away his legitimate wife, Philippa of Toulouse. As a result of this deed, William IX was excommunicated, and when the bishop of Poitiers arrived to tell him officially that he had been excluded from the Church, William went into a mad rage and pulled out his sword to strike the prelate. The bishop calmly told him to go ahead, for he was in a state of grace and had no fear of appearing before the Creator. These words had the effect of calming William, so he resheathed his weapon, saying, "I don't like you well enough to send you to heaven!"

None of this, however, prevented the turbulent Troubadour from reconciling with the Church and, as old age approached, from mending his ways considerably. It is true that he never truly abandoned his faith. For him practicing a certain laxity with the rules of morality was sufficiently satisfying, and he proudly defied any who tried to bring him to heel. In fact, one day, when the bishop of Angoulême urged him to show proof of his submission, he let off a torrent of abuse while advising

---

*[Leader of the First Crusade and first to be crowned king of Jerusalem, Godefroy was considered to be one of the Nine Worthies during the Middle Ages and has also been alleged to be the founder of the Priory of Sion, the secret society behind the order of the Templars. —*Trans.*]

the bishop to "count his curls and use a comb." It so happens that the worthy prelate was completely bald.

The Troubadour's son, William X, was not cut from the same cloth. He, too, had his run-ins with the Church, however—though not for the same reasons as his father. William X recognized the authority of the antipope Anaclet instead of that of the legitimately elected Innocent II, which unleashed protests from the clergy of his lands. When St. Bernard of Clairvaux visited William X to urge his return to the orthodox fold, William overturned the altar where the monk had said Mass. Yet even this did not calm his rage. He then tried to leap on St. Bernard, who owed his salvation to his rapid retreat. This story and others reveal the violent nature of this family. It did not matter how cultivated they were or how mindful of propriety or that they were great enthusiasts of fine art and architecture—they were still easily angered and ready to do whatever they had a mind to do. It was in this kind of atmosphere that Eleanor of Aquitaine was raised.

It should be said that her relatives overlooked nothing to give her a thorough education worthy of her rank and of the claims of the house of Aquitaine to be among the most evolved and refined of the time. She and her sister, Petronella, were provided with skilled tutors, and Eleanor learned Latin and the language of the north and, most likely, other languages as well. Young Eleanor became accustomed to spending time with troubadours and listening to their songs and stories. The court of Poitiers, which she later made famous with her courts of love, had long been the meeting spot of intellectuals gathered from different countries. Here in this border land between the langue d'oc and the langue d'oïl it was also common to see troubadours and trouvères,* bards from Brittany and the British Isles, and even Muslims from Spain. The cultural milieu in which Eleanor spent her youth and adolescence explains both her brilliant intellect and all the interest she later showed in arts and letters.

Meanwhile, her father, William X, lost Aenor and soon remarried.

---

*[*Trouvére* is the northern French term for "troubadour." —*Trans.*]

Married life, however, did not suit him, and his wife casually betrayed him. Disgusted and also eaten away by a mystical crisis, he decided to go to Santiago de Compostella, entrusting the care of his two daughters to his young brother, Raymond de Poitiers, who was hardly any older than his niece Eleanor. By all evidence, the two young people who had known each other all their lives fell in love, for during the time Eleanor was placed under the guardianship of Raymond, they never left each other's side. It is even told that after a long boat ride on the Garonne near La Réole, Eleanor and Raymond had to ask for lodging at a Benedictine priory, and the priest in charge of rooms, who had poorly grasped his guests' names, offered them a chamber with a single bed. Raymond accepted it laughingly, saying that Satan had disguised himself as a monk in order to lead an uncle and niece into committing incest.

Whatever the actual case may be, the relations between the two young people lent itself to much comment. With this, the legend of Duchess Eleanor as the new Messalina was only beginning. It is also claimed, however, that once Eleanor and Raymond confessed their mutual love, it was Eleanor who did not wish to take it further. She likely would have availed herself of the simplest argument: unable to become the wife of her uncle, she could not therefore become his mistress. Yet would she recall this decision later, when, as a young queen of France, she met Raymond again in the Holy Land?

It was around this time, April 1137, that the death of William X was announced as having taken place in Compostella. There is still much that remains unclear about this event. It is claimed that William, having resolved to flee the world, had staged the entire affair. It is said that his false funeral services were performed on Good Friday, then he left for Jerusalem to obtain forgiveness of his sins before retiring to a forest near the town of Castillon.[1] All of this smacks too much of fiction—but how is anyone to know what really happened?

Regardless of the circumstances, William was gone, leaving a will that likewise gave rise to numerous discussions concerning its authenticity. This will notably says: "I place my daughters under the protection of his lordship the king, to whom I give Eleanor in marriage if my barons deem it good, and I leave to this dear girl Aquitaine and the Poitou." The king of France at the time was Louis VI, known as Louis the Fat, and his son and heir was not yet married. It is quite likely that the possibility of the Louis-Eleanor union had been envisioned long before and that negotiations had even taken place. This arrangement worked out splendidly for the Capetians, for it allowed them to directly attach to the crown a territory that today covers nineteen of France's current departments.* We should also note that this will, authentic or not, did not alter the situation much, for in accordance with feudal custom, on the death of one of his vassals who had no male heir, the king was obliged to become guardian of the deceased's eldest daughter. In any event, the power to determine the destiny of Eleanor of Aquitaine fell into the hands of Louis the Fat.

He spent no time deciding. The king knew he was ill and wished to arrange his son's affairs without further delay. He had already seen to his son's coronation and binding to the throne in 1131, in accordance with the custom of the first Capets.[2] The king's counselor, Suger, realizing that the king should not jeopardize such a golden opportunity, urged the marriage, and, after several discussions and firm promises to the Aquitaine bishops, the marriage of Eleanor and Louis, attended by Suger and the highest officials in the kingdom, was celebrated on July 25, 1137, at St. Andrew's Cathedral in Bordeaux.

There is no need to specify that this was the first time Eleanor and Louis laid eyes upon each other. Louis was sixteen and Eleanor fifteen, which did not prevent her from being "ardent," to use the words of the contemporary historian Guillaume de Neubourg. Eleanor's charm and beauty made a deep impression upon Louis, and he fell so in love with her that he subsequently became quite consumed by jealousy. Conversely, the fact that Eleanor repeatedly said later that her husband was "almost a monk" shows that she did not find in this marriage at least what she had a right to expect from it. It is known that the marriages of

---

*[The department is the regional administrative unit in France, similar to a state or county. — *Trans.*]

princes are rarely dictated by sentiment, and this one was no exception. It was perfectly political and quite advantageous for the crown, which inevitably caused some stir among the vassals of the duchess of Aquitaine. Moreover, in order to avoid any incidents, Suger had the newlyweds leave Bordeaux immediately after the wedding.

Several days later, the couple learned of the death of Louis VI. Eleanor and the young Louis were crowned duke and duchess of Aquitaine on August 8 in Poitiers, as was customary, and next entered Paris as king and queen.

We can easily imagine the impressions of young Eleanor under the sky of the Ile de France region, in the midst of a populace speaking a coarse language and in an austere court that was so different from what she had known in her childhood. For an Occitan, Paris was still a primitive, almost barbaric state. Later, however, she put everything there in good order. She immediately invited knights from Aquitaine and Poitou as well as troubadours, who ultimately had a great influence on French thought, and then imposed on the court a new lifestyle, particularly in dress and amusement, with new modes inspired by those of the south.

According to contemporary testimonies, we know that Eleanor encouraged luxury and a more overt sensuality during the twelve years she resided at the French court. There appeared bold displays of cleavage, with low-cut bodices that hugged the shape of their wearers. Shoulders and the upper part of the breasts were uncovered. Fabrics were carefully chosen, and colors sparkled in all their subtleties from marigold yellow to peach by way of herbal green. Men shaved off their flowery beards. After much reticence, Louis VI eventually got rid of his, but it is said that Eleanor had a hearty laugh when she first saw him clean-shaven.

Eleanor organized new games. Noteworthy among these were Confession to the Priest, accompanied by bizarre forms of penitence and jovial atonements; the King Who Doesn't Lie, consisting of several indiscreet and ambiguous questions; the Pilgrim Game, in which comic offerings were given to St. Coisne while players made faces that were intended to make whoever played the saint laugh. This last game was later forbidden in 1240 by the Worcester Synod because in their attempts to make someone laugh by any and all means, the players' hands often tended to stray.

All these games made the players hungry. Eleanor enjoyed eating elegant light meals consisting of waffles, warm dishes, dried fruits from the banks of the Garonne, and sweets such as the very expensive candied ginger sold by Venetian merchants. Eleanor's preferences were at first a surprise to her guests, who eventually developed a taste for these new styles and spread them in their own circles. We cannot overestimate the personal influence Eleanor had on the evolution of northern mores during this twelfth-century era when France was a kingdom only in theory and was still in search of its personality.

Further, because Eleanor was refined in every area, she did not overlook the pleasures of the mind. To the men of the north, whose chief concerns were war and hunting, the troubadours boasted of the pleasures of *fine amor* or, in other words, courtly love, which was a slow initiation to the crowning of repressed desires. They also listened to the trouvères recounting the adventures of heroes of bygone times, but these heroes were no longer the insipid and brutal figures from the chansons de geste of Charlemagne. Now they were more or less like the fairy-tale heroes from Breton tradition. King Arthur began making an appearance in the tales that were not always understood but that fed the dreams of an audience eager for novelty, bravado, and strange loves. Of course, though these tales were serious, fortunately there were also a few trouvères who told *fabliaux* and *sornettes**—for example, the facetious adventures of Renard and his enemy Ysengrin—and made listeners laugh at the expense of women and clerks. There was always a whiff of anticlericalism around Eleanor. In fact, it might be said that this was an Aquitaine family tradition!

In addition, Eleanor was not at all reluctant to take part in popular festivals. The queen grew bored easily, so she frequented the fair of Lendit and any occasion that offered her a good opportunity to mingle

---

*[*Sornette* means something trivial and hardly worthy of notice; *fabliaux* are ribald stories, such as those found in Chaucer's *Canterbury Tales.* —*Trans.*]

with the noisy, colorful crowd that lived more in the streets than in houses. After all, as in Occitan, it was in the streets where everything happened. Furthermore, because this was the time when the caste of the knights was at its height, there were many tournaments where these new heroes earned glory, riches, and reputations. Eleanor presided over these tourneys and took great pleasure from them, according to her contemporaries. In fact, her liking for jousts gave birth to many unverifiable anecdotes that are fraught with meaning concerning Eleanor's influence and the symbol of sensuality and even depravity that she embodied for some.

It is said that all the young men in these tourneys clamored for the honor of fighting for the beautiful young queen, who gradually became the paragon of all virtue and all desires for absolute happiness. It is said that one day she proclaimed: "He alone will be my knight who consents to fight entirely naked beneath one of my shirts against an adversary armored in iron." Of course, one knight, a certain Saldebreuil, did accept the challenge and allegedly responded: "If death should befall me, I will find consolation dying in your garment." It is obvious that this fetishism goes far beyond simple sexual excitation. This anecdote, whether true or false, reveals an entire amorous system. Saldebreuil was supposedly defeated and wounded. Eleanor then allegedly had him transported to her apartments, where she tenderly cared for him. As a result, she was quite late for dinner and allegedly made her appearance in the dining hall dressed in strange fashion: she was wearing her champion's torn and bloody shirt beneath her evening robe. Noted in this chronicle is that the king found it extremely shocking.[3]

In fact, although the king was deeply in love with Eleanor, her attitude and that of her retinue were a terrible shock to the northern French. As Reto Bezzola says,

> The south opposed the scholarly and clerical civilization of the north and, outside of the world of the Church, was limited to very restricted areas. With its completely profane civilization and laxity and extravagance, the south was a constant source of shock to the

north from the time of Louis the Pious, whose astronomer boasted his aversion to the detestable mores of Aquitaine, until the time of the contemporaries of Robert the Pious, who were similarly scandalized by the outfit of Queen Constance.[4]

There is a fundamental difference between sensibilities here, a rift between two civilizations. But we should not think that Eleanor's influence was felt only in the domains of style, mores, literature, and amusements. Although the contemporary texts are quite discreet in this regard, it can be rightly claimed that Eleanor had a great hold over her husband. Louis VII was not cut from the same cloth as his father; despite appearances, he was extremely malleable, and the policies he followed during the early years of his marriage to Eleanor bear her unmistakable mark.

First, Louis VII removed from his affairs Suger, the monk who had been the counselor and wellspring of the activities of Louis VI. In addition, the queen mother was sent away. Finally, the Church of the north, which had pretensions of reform, was urged to put a brake on its desires. Because of her personal anticlericalism and the long tradition of hostility against the Church that had characterized the first family of Aquitaine, there was no shortage of accusations against Eleanor for being responsible for this action against the Church. She did, however, have her supporters among the clergy, which can be seen with respect to the marriage of her sister, Petronella. This sister had accompanied the elder Eleanor to the French court and sowed discord between the king's brothers, who quarreled bitterly over her. Despite her age, Petronella was singularly precocious, and turning her back to youth, she preferred to succumb to the experience of a man in his fifties, the seneschal Raoul de Vermandois, who (what's more) was one-eyed and already married. Their liaison was the cause of a fine scandal, and because Petronella, most likely supported by her sister, did not wish to abandon her lover, the solution of marriage was conceived. Eleanor arranged matters with several officials of the Church, which has always displayed a keen sensitivity to material rewards. Raoul's marriage was annulled, making him free to marry the king's sister-in-law.

As early as 1141, Eleanor, who sought to revive the claims of the counts of Poitou over the domains of the counts of Toulouse, had convinced her husband to undertake an expedition against this part of Occitania, which remained independent. The expedition came to nothing—yet Louis VII had not been an unwilling partner in the scheme, for it gave him hopes of extending the boundaries of the holdings of the crown. Petronella's marriage with Raoul de Vermandois, however, triggered another war—this one with Champagne, for the count of Champagne, the uncle of Raoul's first wife, considered the first wife's repudiation a personal insult. Louis VII was forced to send in his troops, and during the campaign of 1143, the king of France invaded Vitry-le-François and burned down the town and slaughtered a number of its inhabitants.

This event, which weighed heavily on the mood of a remorseful Louis VII, did not sit well with Pope Innocent II or with St. Bernard, the pope's main counselor and muse. In fact, Louis VII had some difficulty extricating himself from this predicament; he was not truly out of trouble until he publicly abandoned the cause of Raoul de Vermandois, and he was not absolutely free of it until after the death of Innocent II in 1144. The king's attitude, nevertheless, did not suit Eleanor. At the conclusion of the affair, Raoul de Vermandois was still under a sentence of excommunication that Eleanor tried to have lifted, and she strove to prevent any reconciliation between her husband and Thibaud, count of Champagne.

That same year, in 1144, the solemn feasts of St. Denis took place during the inauguration and the consecration of the new choir of the abbey of Saint-Denis (of which Suger, interestingly, was the abbot). Eleanor attended these feasts and there met Bernard of Clairvaux, the pope's man for all seasons, a veritable ecclesiastical Machiavelli, a brilliant snoop and schemer ready to do anything to assure the greatness of the Kingdom of Christ (whose underlying purpose was the temporal power of the papacy). There is no doubt that this meeting between Bernard and Eleanor, as recounted in the *Vita Bernardi*, is of capital importance. His realization that the behavior of Louis VII was largely due to the influence of the king's alarming wife led the abbot of Clair-vaux, who had a gift for psychoanalysis (in this age, the psychiatrist was known as the "director of conscience"), to convince the duchess of Aquitaine to take him into her confidence.

As a result, he learned a very useful fact: Eleanor secretly lamented that her union with the king of France remained sterile. In almost seven years of marriage, she had experienced only one hope of mater-nity, which ended in miscarriage. She anxiously asked Bernard if some curse might not be weighing upon her. He adroitly turned her state of mind to his advantage: He urged the queen to stop encouraging her husband's rebellious tendencies. In exchange, he would make a plea to heaven to grant Eleanor's desire to give birth to an heir. Eleanor prom-ised, and, as a result, an accord was soon concluded between the king and the count of Champagne. Here is the clincher: Bernard's prayers seem to have borne fruit. In 1145, Eleanor of Aquitaine brought a child into the world. This child, however, was a daughter, Marie, who, by coincidence or calculation, later became the countess of Champagne.

Nevertheless, with the child's birth, Eleanor had shown proof she was not sterile. This was not merely politically satisfying; according to the words of witnesses, it was a source of true happiness. Eleanor took less note of the business of the kingdom and devoted herself to the joys of motherhood. Louis VII began ruling from his own desires and he listened more willingly to Suger's advice.

In 1146 the tireless Bernard of Clairvaux gave an enthusiastic ser-mon in Vézelay, where the social elite of the kingdom had gathered to celebrate Easter, which was actually an appeal to mount a second Crusade. Undoubtedly, this subtle monk had little trouble persuading the pious Louis VII that traveling to slaughter Muslim infidels would guarantee forgiveness for the grave sin the king had committed by mas-sacring the residents of Vitry-le-François. Louis was thereby persuaded to launch and attend the Second Crusade, and, in the atmosphere of general enthusiasm, a number of barons aped his example. The nobil-ity of this time was beginning to see a vexing plunge in its revenues; in addition to the assurance of remitting sins, a Crusade offered the hope of winning if not rich domains, then an ample amount of booty.

To the surprise of all, Queen Eleanor decided to accompany her husband to the Holy Land. She and the king solemnly renewed their vows at Saint-Denis in June 1147, on the eve of the army's departure. This decision by Eleanor has prompted much question. People have even gone so far as to claim that after having seduced all the knights of the kingdom, she wished to test those of Outre-Mer.* It has also been claimed that because she was so deeply in love with Louis, she could not stand the thought of leaving him. As testimony to her love, she would share all the dangers to which he was exposed. These touching interpretations of Eleanor's gesture would be of greater interest were it not for a text by the contemporary chronicler Guillaume de Neubourg, who is generally trustworthy and well informed:

> At the time when this famous expedition was starting off, the king, animated by his intense jealousy, decided that at no price should he leave behind his young wife, but she should accompany him to battle. This example was followed by many other nobles who brought their wives with them. And because they could not travel without their chamber maids, a large number of women were living in the Christian camp that should have been chaste;[5] hence the scandal our army presented.[6]

Now, if the king of France was so jealous, it was because he had suspicions about Eleanor's fickleness—which is not the same as proof positive that she was guilty. At about this time, rumors first began flying that the queen had intimate relations with numerous favorites, but there wasn't a shred of proof of her infidelity. Rather, these rumors show that Eleanor was not greatly liked by a certain part of the clerical establishment—or, at the very least, her attitude offended the right-minded, who are always predisposed to feel proper. In fact, there is no reason to suspect that Eleanor was fickle or untrue to the king *before*

---

*[Outre-Mer is the French appellation for the Western holdings in the Holy Land. —*Trans.*]

the expedition to the East. During this journey and after the expedition, however, was a completely different matter.

There was certainly no lack of political motives for the decision to have the queen join the king—a choice that was the king's, not Eleanor's. Michelet suggests that Eleanor's presence may have been necessary to ensure the loyalty and obedience of the Poitevins and Gascons, who had not consistently supported their lands' entry into the French sphere of influence and who regarded themselves solely as vassals of their duchess-countess. Similarly, the participation of the nobles' wives would be added encouragement for these men to accompany their king.

In any event, despite all that has been said about the joining, it was certainly not a pleasure party for the women of the expedition. First they had to cross central Europe—and it was a long road from Metz, where the army had been assembled, to Constantinople by way of Ratisbonne, Belgrade, and Andrianopolis. It was not until the troops reached Byzantium that they could finally take a break from their travels and indulge in the invitation extended by the emperor Manuel Commenius, who was an attentive if obsequious host with some unsettling personality traits. Commenius was nevertheless a refined man and a great enthusiast of war and tournaments. In addition, he had a passion for theater, medicine, and theology. His wealth was considerable and his mores were not beyond reproach—although his drunkenness paled in comparison to the refined, Regency-style parties he organized—and even his entourage was scandalized by the open display of his liaison with his niece Theodora.

This was Eleanor's first contact with the East. Though it was a part of the world that was but a remnant of a once-great empire, it nevertheless remained bathed in the aura of a peerless prestige. When we think of the strange descriptions that appear in the *Pilgrimage of Charlemagne,* the chanson de geste whose wonders and adventures make the song seem more an Arthurian romance, as they might be seen by dazzled eyes, we find the spectacle of the Celtic Otherworld, with its wealth and fairy-tale attributes. In the eyes of Eleanor and the anonymous trouvères, Byzantium was undoubtedly cloaked in an unreal aspect so that it became the materialization of all the dreams and desires of a humanity beset by quotidian realities.

Here we do not make a gratuitous reference to the *Pilgrimage of Charlemagne.* The chansons de geste are known to have often been based on a historical fact on which was grafted an adventure incorporating ancient myths. According to the *Pilgrimage of Charlemagne,* one day in Saint-Denis, King Charles considers his crown and asks his wife if she knows of anyone whose head is more deserving of the sphere. The queen answers, somewhat foolishly, that she actually can think of one deserving man. After Charles goes into a violent rage and threatens to behead his wife if she does not reveal the name of his rival, she tells him it is King Hugh the Strong, who rules in Constantinople. Charles decides to judge this man's worthiness for himself by going there and also decides to take advantage of this journey in order to make a pilgrimage to Jerusalem.

It could be simple coincidence, but it is certain that the rift between the king and queen began at the time of the Second Crusade. What, however, were the exact causes for the misunderstanding that only grew worse over the following months? No one knows, or at least no witness of the time has left any valid account. It is plausible that Louis VII brought Eleanor to the East both out of jealousy and to let her see for herself that he was worthy of wearing the crown. It is also said that at the Council of Sens, which judged Abelard's doctrines, an old man named Jean d'Estampes alluded to the prophecies of Merlin, stating that Eleanor was, as Merlin put it, the great eagle and that she extended her large wings over both France and England. If this anecdote has any basis in fact, Eleanor could only have been flattered by such words. She nevertheless had to face up to the fact that it would not be Louis VII, a fine but rather vapid man of no ambition, who would enable her to add another crown to his. What's more, it was during this time that she began spreading the rumor that she had married a monk, not a man. All together, there are many elements that argue in favor of a growing rift between Eleanor and the king of France at this time, and it is likely that their stay in Constantinople did not help smooth matters.

In Byzantium, Eleanor found herself in a refined atmosphere that was closer to her heart than the world of the French court. Further, she must have recognized the Orient, so often described by the troubadours, as the ideal land in which her own ambitions and sensuality could find expression. Manuel Commenius was spellbinding, and, while there was no question of the two of them having any kind of illicit affair, we must be aware that he probably gave the beautiful duchess of Aquitaine food for thought and, most important, provided an object of comparison to her "monk of a husband."

Yet Manuel Commenius was no king of the Golden Age. His feet were firmly planted on the ground, and he owed the survival of his empire to the more or less secret arrangements he had recently concluded with the Turks. The advisors of Louis VII warned the king that Manuel was plotting something and it was thus urgent to leave. As he took leave of his host, Louis VII heard that Emperor Conrad of Germany, Manuel's brother-in-law who was already involved militarily in the Crusade, had recently won a huge victory over the Turks—but this was false. Shortly afterward, the army of the king of France encountered survivors of Conrad's army, who explained that the army had been led astray and abandoned by its Byzantine guides in the Anatolian wilderness. The Turks then had little difficulty in harassing a weakened army that was short on food and unaccustomed to this harsh climate. This was proof that Manuel Commenius had betrayed the Westerners in deference to the modus vivendi that protected his empire. In order to keep the French army from suffering a similar fate, Louis VII opted to take a longer but safer road. We know nothing of Eleanor's activity during this long march—which is why numerous chroniclers tried to fill the gap by embroidering on the theme of the Amazon queen, who was described as wearing solid armor and riding at the head of a troop of women that took part in battle. In fact, if Eleanor was on horseback, it was surely at a distance from the military troops and in the company of the other women of the expedition, and this band of women was likely completely surrounded and protected by Crusaders.

The long route brought the French army to Paphlagonia, not far from Mount Cadmos. Here an engagement took place against the Turks that fell just short of a full-scale disaster: the army suffered heavy losses and the king himself barely avoided being slain or captured. The leader, Geoffroy de Rancon, was a knight of Saint-Onge and a vassal of Eleanor. Some said she had personally given the order to Geoffrey to pull back. Others even claimed that Geoffrey was the inseparable favorite of the queen and was entirely devoted to her. This was all malicious tongues needed to start wagging: people said that the failure of French troops was the fault of the queen. According to eyewitnesses to the event, however, in reality no one knew precisely what happened. These interpretations of the battle can be seen as the effect of their authors' ill will toward Eleanor—as efforts to depict her as the lowest kind of Messalina and a woman incapable of making sound decisions.

The Mount Cadmos disaster caused Louis VII to think that the Byzantines could not be trusted; treachery was second nature to them. Furthermore, the land route had proved to be dangerous. The king therefore decided that the army would take the maritime route to Antioch. It was March 19, 1148, when Eleanor and Louis VII made land at the small port of Saint Simeon. There they were welcomed by an old acquaintance of Eleanor, her uncle Raymond de Poitiers, who, after many rather incredible adventures and a marriage of circumstance, had become the all-powerful master of the principality of Antioch.

Louis VII and Eleanor spent only ten days in Antioch, but it seems clear that these ten days constituted a major moment in their lives that had unexpected repercussions on European political life. It was also in Antioch that the queen's reputation became permanently stained, but the circumstances of this are cloaked in complete mystery. We have little save allusions, a few recorded phrases, and many legends that, though they developed at a later date, are no less revealing of certain historical realities.

The stated purpose for Louis VII to go on the Crusade was to make a pilgrimage to Jerusalem. Raymond, however, had other interests. Even in his initial discussions with the French king, as he sought to profit from the troop reinforcements offered by the French army, he tried to convince Louis to forget Jerusalem for the moment and concentrate military efforts against Aleppo and Hama. Passed through the filter of historical criticism, his argument did not lack wisdom: Aleppo and Hama, Turkish fortresses placed at strategic points in the Holy Land, constituted real dangers not only for the principality of Antioch but also for all the Christian kingdoms. Capturing Aleppo and Hama would have considerably strengthened Frankish power in the Middle East and would certainly have allowed for a longer period of peace. Louis VII and his advisors, however, would hear none of it. He wished to go to Jerusalem as soon as possible. It is likely that the Vitry massacre weighed heavily on the conscience of the French king.

Unable to make Louis VII see reason, Raymond turned to Eleanor, whom he was certain he could convince of the rightness of his plan. Obviously, this was the moment when tongues started wagging about an affair between the uncle and his niece. For her part, Eleanor tried to convince her husband to accept what Raymond suggested, but Louis VII stubbornly refused and even grew angry. It should be noted that he especially paid great heed to the counsel of his advisor Thierry Galéran, who had also been a counselor to his father, Louis VI. Yet it so happened that Eleanor detested Thierry Galéran and often fired off wicked and somewhat indelicate remarks about him because he was a eunuch. But Galéran gave back as good as he got, and all Eleanor had to do was suggest something for Thierry immediately to say the opposite. The rupture between Louis VII and Eleanor truly dates from this moment, whatever their personal motives may have been.

This is the reason why Eleanor, furious about her views being ignored, declared before Raymond's plan had been realized that she would remain in Antioch with her own vassals instead of following her husband to Jerusalem. The tenor of the situation only grew worse. Louis declared to Eleanor that her wifely duty was to follow him wherever he went. The king of France then received from Eleanor the sharp retort that when it came to spousal rights, he should stop and think a moment: she and Louis could no longer live together because they were relatives within a degree prohibited by canonical law, and their marriage was thus invalid.

This was perfectly correct, at least according to literal canonical law, which was generally recalled only when a party sought to annul a marriage. In cases of such relation, the Church was always quite accommodating and dispensations were easy to obtain. In addition, Eleanor and Louis were related nine times removed, which was not an insurmountable obstacle. Yet why did a furious Eleanor who had run out of arguments hurl this threat against the king at this time? Why hadn't it occurred to her earlier? Most important, had she really given any thought to what she said to the king?

Regarding this last question, it seems clear that the answer should be yes. Of course, various authors added legends about the love she allegedly held for the sultan Saladin—whom she had never seen— because of his valor and qualities of greatness. Recognizable here, however, is one of the most frequent themes of troubadour poetry so skillfully sung by Jaufré Rudel and several others: the idea of distant love. It was even said that Eleanor had planned a rendezvous with Saladin so that he could carry her off and that Louis VII, warned in time, beat his rival to the meeting place and carried his wife off himself.

All of this is completely ridiculous, for at this time Saladin was only ten years old. Any foreign love on the part of the queen could involve only Sultan Nur-ed Din, and this was highly improbable and completely contradictory to the alleged liaison Eleanor had with Raymond de Poitiers. It was a fact, however, that attempts were made to sully the name of the queen of France as much as possible at this time. Yet because there is never smoke without fire, it should be admitted that the question of "divorce" came up in precise and clear terms in Antioch during the royal couple's stay there. *Something necessarily took place.* Louis's jealousy and haste to leave Antioch are evidence of this. Moreover, the legends concerning Eleanor are not due to chance. It should be concluded that the rift between Louis and Eleanor (the king had momentarily contemplated separating from his wife and it was Thierry Galéran who prevented it, describing the scandal that would ensue) took place in Antioch in June 1148, because of the king and queen's divergence in military and political views and because of illicit relations the queen might have been having—with whom no one knows for certain, but probably with her uncle, Raymond de Poitiers, prince of Antioch.[7]

A page in history had turned, although scandal did not break out, as may have been feared. Louis of France brought his wife to Jerusalem. The Franco-Occitan army, poorly led, poorly advised, and, most important, beginning to lose confidence, wore itself out in pointless battles with the Damascans, who could have become allies of the Latin kingdoms. The sequence of events that followed proved Raymond de Poitiers was right; the Muslim threat grew only more formidable. Conrad, the emperor of Germany, sailed away again on September 8, 1148, without accomplishing anything. Louis persisted, not wishing to accept the fact that he was pursuing an incoherent strategy. Unable to find support from the Byzantines (who, instead of providing the Crusaders with the rest of their fleet, simply handed it over to the Turks), he formed an alliance with the king of Sicily, Roger, who, incidentally, was a bitter enemy of Raymond de Poitiers. The results of this alliance were quite meager: the Second Crusade ended in defeat, although the expedition had cost a great many human lives.

The king of France set off from the East on Easter 1149, but he did not sail in the same ship as Eleanor, which might indicate a breach that was quite significant. The crossing was not completely without incident, for the French fleet found itself caught in the middle of a conflict that pit Roger of Sicily against Manuel Commenius. The queen's vessel was captured by the Byzantines, who, enchanted with their capture and wishing to use Eleanor as a hostage, directly set sail for Constantinople. The Normans of Sicily, however, freed the queen, and she landed at Palermo. Meanwhile, the king had landed in Calabria, and the queen and king found themselves together in Sicily, where they were received with great honor by the Norman king. It was here that they learned of the death of Raymond de Poitiers: he was killed the previous June 29 in Maaratha during a battle against Nur-ed Din.

After this, the royal couple began making their way through Italy and in mid-October were received by Pope Eugenius III, who was then holding court in Tusculum. Suger had fully informed the pope of the conjugal differences between Louis and Eleanor, and the pope did all in his power to reconcile the couple, making it clear that their consanguinity was quite remote and that the Church would regard it tolerantly. It seems that the pope succeeded at least temporarily in restoring peace between Louis and his hot-tempered wife.[8] Here again, a chanson de geste, *Girart de Roussillon,* transposes this reconciliation scene. The anonymous author of this chanson was a native of the Angoumois and lived in Eleanor's entourage. It is almost certain that he took the queen-duchess as the model for Charlemagne's wife, whom the emperor was thinking of repudiating, but Charlemagne was turned from this path by the pope. The similarity is too striking to be coincidental.[9] Regardless, shortly after their return to France in 1150, Eleanor gave birth to a second daughter named Alix.[10]

Now, however, circumstances were quite different for Eleanor. She was no longer the triumphant and active young queen, and it is likely Louis no longer involved her in the kingdom's affairs. Furthermore, the king was once again entirely under the thumb of Abbot Suger, thereby justifying his wife's comment: "I have married a monk!" The trauma this caused was quite serious. Though the royal couple was apparently united, the wounds that had been opened had not healed for either side. Eleanor had plenty of time for contemplation: The banks of the Seine were not the banks of the Otronte and the austerity of the French court could not withstand comparison to the luxuries of the East, whether Constantinople or Antioch. In addition, Raymond de Poitiers was dead. In all, the queen's dreams did not correspond with the realities of the moment. What exactly was going through Eleanor's mind? It is quite difficult to assert the answer for certain, but we may be sure that by this time, the queen was a woman quite disappointed by life.

In January 1151, Louis VII lost his counselor, Abbot Suger. History has recognized the importance of this man and his eminent role in the rule of both Louis VI and Louis VII. He did all he could for the greatness of the Capets to whom he had dedicated his life at the same time that he devoted his service to God. A man of integrity and intelligence,

Suger was always able to perceive what was in the kingdom's best interests and to follow his perception without any compromise. With Suger dead, Louis VII was left to his own devices. In reality, the king of France was nothing without the abbot of Saint-Denis, and subsequent events proved this.

During the summer of 1151, a trial took place at the French court in which the accused was Geoffrey Plantagenet, count of Anjou, who had gained the ducal crown of Normandy in 1141. While the king was still on the Second Crusade, the count had imprisoned a royal officer, Giraud Berlay, and refused to free him although this count of Anjou was under a sentence of excommunication for committing a serious transgression against his sovereign, the king of France. Geoffrey came to the king's court accompanied by his son Henry, then eighteen years of age, and he impressed all there with his beauty—his nickname was Geoffrey the Handsome—tenacity, and violent behavior.

Bernard of Clairvaux stepped in at the right moment and succeeded in making peace between Louis VII and his quarrelsome vassal. Giraud Berlay was freed, and Henry swore homage for the duchy of Normandy. Eleanor took part in this exceptional court, where for the first time she saw the future king of England. She already knew Geoffrey, having met him during the Crusade, and malicious tongues maintained that she knew him only too well. It is true that Geoffrey the Handsome corresponded quite opportunely to Eleanor's ideal man. He was an intransigent adventurer and social climber who, while still an adolescent, had married Matilda, the daughter of the king of England. This woman was always called the empress because she was the widow of the German emperor, Henry V. Matilda was fifteen years older than Geoffrey, and she had an exceptional personality and maintained her claim to the throne of England, which had been taken instead by her cousin Etienne, count of Blois and grandson of William the Conqueror. This created problems in England and the partisans of both sides waged a veritable civil war, somewhat egged on by the king of France, who, after respecting a strict neutrality, eventually sided with Etienne de Blois, whom he deemed more docile.

The visit by the two Plantagenets to the trial in Paris is important politically because it settled a difficult situation: by capitulating to the king of France, the count of Anjou henceforth had his hands free in England, for the existing alliance between Louis VII and Etienne de Blois no longer had any moral authority because Louis VII could no longer find grounds to criticize his repentant vassal. Yet this episode undoubtedly played an even more important role in the life of Eleanor, and consequently in the history of both France and England. There is evidence that testifies to Eleanor's premeditation concerning her future marriage to Henry Plantagenet. These same testimonies allow us to see that Eleanor's meeting with the young Henry made a strong impression on her.[11] This meeting, however, did not prevent Eleanor and the king from going on a long progress through their lands. Nevertheless, the chroniclers stress the strained atmosphere that existed between the couple and speak again of the king's jealousy with respect to his wife.[12]

It was at the beginning of autumn that the two learned of the death of Geoffrey the Handsome, who passed away prematurely from an illness contracted after bathing in the Loir on an extremely hot day. It was Henry who inherited the Angevin legacy at the same time that he received the duchy of Normandy and a claim to the English throne. Continuing their journey, Louis VII and Eleanor spent Christmas of 1151 at Limoges and Candlemass in 1152 at Saint-Jean-d'Angély, in the lands of the duchess of Aquitaine. The testimonies from this time seem to present a liquidation of their union in good and proper form. In fact, the king called back the troops he had placed in Aquitaine as if to provide a clean space for those of the duchess, and one month following Eleanor and Louis's return to Paris, the news traveled throughout the kingdom that a council had hastily been assembled in Beaugency, in the Orleans region, in order to declare null and void the marriage of the king and queen of France.

By all evidence, Eleanor and Louis VII had long since decided to separate. It is even quite likely that Eleanor took the initiative for this separation. Suger was no longer around to plead for reconciliation and make the king see all the problematic consequences that might be caused by a separation. What's more, the king's entourage hated Eleanor and openly accused her of leading a dissolute life. This could not help but influence the weak Louis VII, who was already deeply mortified by what had taken place during the Crusade and was superstitiously alarmed by the fact that Eleanor had not provided him with a male heir. Despite the interdiction of Pope Eugenius III against using consanguinity as reason for separation and because the fear of scandal was a constant given Eleanor's character, it seems the king allowed himself to be easily swayed. It was necessary to obtain an annulment because no other legal means of separation existed.

The council assembled on March 21, 1152. Numerous prelates took part, and not merely lesser luminaries; those in attendance included the archbishops of Rouen, Sens, and Bourdeaux along with their supporters and an equally large number of barons. It is interesting to note that the archbishop of Bordeaux, Geoffrey du Lauroux, who had blessed this union fifteen years earlier, was now one of those meeting to annul it.[13] The trial followed standard procedures, but, of course, all the witnesses obligingly swore on oath to the king and queen's consanguinity. Even if this were true, such frankness is surprising given how late in the marriage this question of consanguinity was raised.[14] No one paid any attention to the statements delivered by Pope Eugenius III in 1149. Moreover, it was said that Bernard of Clairvaux, who had great influence over the Cistercian pope, washed his hands of the matter and actually authorized the king to request this annulment.[15] The debates were short and the annulment of the marriage was proclaimed, with the caveat that the two daughters Eleanor had borne were officially recognized as legitimate.[16]

Eleanor wasted no time. As soon as the official writ was drafted and signed, she abandoned her seven-year-old and eighteen-month-old daughters (quite casually, it seems) and left the court for the Aquitaine domains, which she recovered in their entirety because her marriage had been declared null. She was finally free, as she had wished to be—but for how long?

Indeed, the journey she took from Beaugency to Poitiers was not totally without incident. She had brought only a small escort and had decided to stop in Blois to rest. It was the eve of Palm Sunday. During the middle of the night, however, she gave a discreet but hurried order to leave, for she had just learned that the count of Blois, Thibaud V, better known as Thibaud the Cheat, had formed a plan to kidnap her and marry her by force.[17] There is no need to specify that his plan was inspired not by the love he bore for the duchess of Aquitaine but by his ambition to take possession of her vast domains. Eleanor had become a profitable match.

The return to Poitiers turned into a flight. Cautious now because of Thibaud's plot in Blois, Eleanor sent out scouts to dig up information. This was an inspired idea on her part, for she learned that a veritable ambush had been laid for her at Port-de-Piles, the very spot where she planned to cross the Creuse River. This time, the instigator was Geoffrey d'Anjou, second son of Geoffrey the Handsome and brother of Henry Plantagenet, a boy of sixteen who was ambitious and violent and who, disappointed because he had not received paternal legacy, sought to become the count of Poitiers and the duke of Aquitaine. Eleanor thwarted his plan by fording the Vienne River upstream from where it met the Creuse, then by racing at top speed for Poitiers. There, surrounded by her loyal followers, she was no longer threatened by any of her potential suitors.

We might think Eleanor would have taken advantage of her freedom and governed her vast territories as she intended, using all the experience she had gained as queen—and in truth, this is what she did, taking an interest in all that occurred in Aquitaine and Poitou and entrusting certain well-defined tasks to some of her vassals. At the same time, however, she was sending messengers to an unknown destination and receiving emissaries from who knows where. The secret behind all these maneuvers was highly guarded, and the veil was not lifted until May 18, 1152, less than two months after the annulment of her marriage to the king of France: in Poitiers, Eleanor, countess of Poitiers and duchess of Aquitaine, solemnly wed Henry, count of Anjou and duke of Normandy, her junior by eleven years.

Eleanor had certainly refrained from requesting from her sovereign authorization for this marriage, as the laws indicated she must, though it is likely that her ex-husband would have been fiercely opposed. Indeed, when Louis VII learned the news, he grasped the reasons for Eleanor's newfound love and at the same time realized the immensity of the error he had made by giving his wife her freedom. Aquitaine and Poitou, once united to the French crown, now escaped the Capet sphere of influence once and for all, which no doubt caused the ghost of Suger to roll over in his grave.

The rapidity of Eleanor's remarriage can seem as surprising now as it did to her contemporaries. In fact, as we now know because of strong evidence, it was for this purpose that Eleanor requested the annulment of her previous marriage. It is more than likely that she had contact with Henry Plantagenet when he visited Paris the year before with his father, Geoffrey the Handsome. She had likely arranged all circumstances to achieve this end.[18] Eleanor was certainly in love with Henry, who was a very handsome man who corresponded exactly to the masculine ideal she had imagined. It was incontestably a marriage of love on her part at the same time that it was a shrewd scheme. She clearly hoped to play the top role with this younger man, and her personal ambition matched that of Henry, whom she knew was ready to win new domains. For Henry's part, even if his union with Eleanor could not properly be labeled a love match, it should be said that he must have been quite aware of the charm of the duchess, whose beauty had been lauded by all his contemporaries. Instead of a love marriage, Henry Plantagenet had a very beautiful wife who brought with her the entire southwest part of the kingdom, which, when added to his own domains, equaled roughly a quarter of modern France.

We should not overlook the fact that despite his young age, Henry Plantagenet was a remarkable man. Physically hale and virile, tireless, skilled at hunting and warfare, he was the complete opposite of the more fragile Louis VII, who was better prepared for a monastic life than that of a temporal leader. This did not prevent Henry from being "a clerk [cleric] to his teeth": He was a highly cultivated man who knew

Latin and several languages, including Occitan. He was a protector of arts and letters and was surrounded by great poets and writers his entire life—indeed, he very much liked the poetry of the troubadours. There is no doubt that Eleanor felt more at home with him in a society that was more refined and intellectual than that of the court of France. Furthermore, upon her marriage to Henry, Europe witnessed Occitan literature invading Anjou, Normandy, and England, where it eventually had the most fortunate effects on the literature of these lands. In fact, in all these arenas, the two newlyweds were in perfect accord. As for character, both Henry and Eleanor were ambitious, intelligent, politically deft, and endowed with formidable tenacity. In addition, Henry had an authoritarian nature that could become violent and he was given to thoughtless outbreaks of anger, which was apparent later in their marriage on numerous occasions. In short, in Henry Plantagenet, Eleanor found a partner that was her equal. Consequently, their life as a couple came to be periodically shaken by crises that matched their personalities in size.

After remarrying, Eleanor distributed favors to all those who had been her faithful servants during her reign as queen of France, such as her uncle Raoul de Faye, brother of the viscount of Châtellerault, and Saldebreuil de Sanxay, the constable of Aquitaine, whom she named seneschal[19] (and whom gossips added to the list of her former lovers). She also took time to confirm to the abbeys all the donations she had made as queen of France. Eight days after her marriage, she visited the abbey of Montierneuf, and the next day she stopped at the abbey of Saint-Maxent, where she began the writ of donation with these words: "I, Eleanor, by the grace of God, duchess of Aquitaine and Normandy, united to the duke of Normandy, Henry, count of Anjou."[20] Several days later, she stopped at the abbey of Fontevrault, which was always her favorite sanctuary and where she was eventually buried.

Fontevrault Abbey, founded by the Breton hermit Robert d'Arbrissel, was a monastery and convent that housed both men and women, following the model of those Irish monasteries such as Kildare that had made the greatness of Celtic monasticism. In addition, Fontevrault was under the authority of an abbess who governed the men as well as the women—which was an arrangement that Eleanor, who had always been something of a feminist, would not have found displeasing. At the time of the duchess's visit to Fontevrault, the abbess, traditionally a widow,[21] was Matilda of Anjou, whose husband, William Adelin, son and heir to Henry Beauclerc, king of England, had died tragically in the sinking of the *White Ship* in 1120.[22] Matilda gave a warm welcome to the new wife of the duke of Normandy, who confirmed by charter all the gifts that her father, Duke William X, and his first wife had granted the abbey.[23]

After this visit to various abbeys, Eleanor rejoined Henry Plantagenet and spent several weeks in Aquitaine with him. At this time, based on the documents we have, it seems that Eleanor was forced to face reality: though she had thought it would be easy to dominate her young husband, he followed his own will—meaning he behaved like a duke of Aquitaine who was fully determined to show his own authority over his wife's domains and not play the role of prince consort. Because Eleanor was in love, however, everything went smoothly and without incident. After all, she had married a *man,* which was what she wanted, and she could not help but be content.

Meanwhile, at this same time Louis VII hastily convened a council that declared that Eleanor had committed a serious transgression: she had married without asking authorization from her sovereign. She and Henry were summoned to appear before the court of the French king, but as we might expect, this citation went unheeded. Louis VII then began scheming until his plots drew into the game Henry's brother, the young Geoffrey the Cheat, who claimed Anjou as his birthright and hated his elder brother for inheriting all the Plantagenet domains. The French king's troops invaded Normandy while Geoffrey incited revolt in Anjou.

Henry wasted no time. With the Norman barons who remained loyal to him he answered these troops' every move, and in the summer of 1152 he succeeded in recapturing the principal strongholds of the duchy before turning against his brother and defeating him at Montsoreau, despite the diversionary moves carried out in Verneuil-sur-Avre by the count of Dreux, brother of the king and presumptive heir to the throne of France. Louis VII eventually gave in and made peace with his vassal. Henry's hands were now free to recover the throne in England that was vainly claimed by his father.

He set sail for England in January 1153, leaving Eleanor pregnant in Normandy. It seems that by now he sought to separate his wife from her Aquitaine territories and oblige her to live in the Plantagenet domains—certainly a calculated move to show Eleanor that, first and foremost, she was duchess of Normandy and countess of Anjou. It was also a display of Henry's growing authority over her.

In England, civil war continued raging. The two factions were the partisans of an aging Etienne de Blois and the nobles whom he was no longer capable of ruling and who had rallied to Empress Matilda and thus to Henry. The situation dragged on, however, and Henry was still there when he learned that Eleanor had given birth to a son on August 17, 1153. At age twenty, the duke of Normandy already had a male heir. No doubt Louis VII heard this news with some melancholy, for he had only two daughters from fifteen years of marriage to Eleanor.

The duchess named her son William in order to carry on the Poitevin tradition and as a sign of her desire to continue the work of William X and William the Troubadour. The name was not at all displeasing to Henry Plantagenet, for it was also the name of the conqueror of England. As it turned out, the naming of baby William was a kind of fortunate omen, for in the next year, at the end of October 1154, Etienne de Blois died after designating Henry Plantagenet as his successor.[24]

Henry and Eleanor made haste to Barfleur to set sail for England, but dreadful weather kept them from crossing the sea. They had to wait for a month before they could reach the island so coveted by Henry. At the beginning of December 1154, after having discovered the East during the Second Crusade, Eleanor was introduced to the misty isle of which she would be queen. On December 19, 1154, she and Henry were solemnly crowned beneath the Romanesque arches of Westminster Abbey, built by Edward the Confessor a century earlier. If the anecdote is true regarding the Sens Council attended by Eleanor, the prophecy uttered by Jean d'Estampes[25] proved to be correct: Eleanor extended her wings over the Continent and the island of England at the same time.

Henry Plantagenet and Eleanor then began to make a series of journeys both in England and on the Continent. Henry restored order to the island nation that had long been devastated by civil war and whose barons too often behaved like local tyrants, and he restored to honor the Norman justice and administration that made this land a much more centralized state than France was at this same time. He rewarded his loyal subjects by entrusting them with important missions and new duties, and he verified the way in which the sheriffs he had assigned to each shire meted out justice. Most important, Henry knew how to compel the barons' obedience. In addition to their island holdings, all of these barons had lands on the Continent—in Normandy, in particular, where they were under the jealous eye of Empress Matilda, who kept watch to ensure that things did not get out of hand and who always acted promptly to confiscate the lands of those barons who acted too independently.

Yet the task of monitoring was too great for one individual, so Henry took the step of sending Eleanor into various domains when he could not visit them personally. For example, when he was in England, Eleanor supervised Normandy and Anjou as well as her own Aquitaine lands. When the king was on the Continent, Eleanor was in England, in the midst of its political turmoil, making decisions in the name of Henry II. We might not imagine a better-matched couple, for each rivaled the other in the arenas of political wisdom and ambition. Undoubtedly, however, Eleanor missed the peace and refinement of the court she had begun forming in Poitiers, which included some of the finest minds of the time.

On February 28, 1155, another boy was born to the royal couple. In homage to his father, he was named Henry, and he was baptized at Westminster Abbey and given the title count of Anjou. Soon he was called the young king. Yet the birth did not stop Eleanor from continuing her journeys across the entire Plantagenet empire—and fifteen months later, she gave birth to a daughter who was named Matilda in honor of the queen mother. With the births of these children, Eleanor and Henry's union appeared to have been blessed by heaven. In June 1156, the eldest son, young William, whom Eleanor wished to see made count of Poitiers, died. He was scarcely three years old. Nevertheless, in the following year, on September 8, 1157, a third son, Richard, was born at Oxford, and a year later, on September 23, 1158, the couple had a fourth son, Geoffrey. At this time Henry was still racing over hill and dale on both sides of the Channel.[26]

Toward the end of 1158, Eleanor accompanied her husband to the siege of Thouars, which was intended to bring reason to Guy de Thouars, who had rebelled against Plantagenet authority. Eleanor's presence as Thouars's lawful suzerain was necessary. After this, Henry and Eleanor held a plenary court at Cherbourg, and immediately on its heels they again crossed through their southern domains to Blaye, where, in the beginning of 1159, Henry II and Raymond, count of Barcelona, had significant discussions. The couple then returned north to Poitiers, where a large army was assembled to conquer the earldom of Toulouse. We know Eleanor had never renounced her rights to this territory, and eighteen years earlier, she had cast the king of France against Toulouse in an expedition that had failed dreadfully. Through the irony of fate, in 1159 Louis VII found himself defending Toulouse against the claims of the duchess of Aquitaine. Nevertheless, the results of this Anglo-Aquitaine expedition were no better than the earlier attempt so many years before.

At Christmas 1159, Henry and Eleanor held plenary court at Falaise. From there, because Henry was still at odds with some of his rebellious vassals, the king sent the queen to represent him in England, where she was given full authority to act as she saw fit. The following autumn the situation in England was of greater concern, and Eleanor was unable to restore order. As a result, Henry summoned her back to Rouen with the heir prince, who was five years old, and set sail for England himself, where he succeeded in quelling his vassals. Eleanor remained in Mans and in Domfront, where, in September 1161, she gave birth to another daughter, Eleanor, who was baptized in the presence of Robert de Thorigny, abbot of Mont-Saint-Michel and a valuable chronicler of this era. The queen-duchess was now thirty-nine years old, and witnesses said she had lost nothing of the beauty that had cast its spell on so many.

Soon after, she asked her husband to order the construction of a magnificent cathedral in Poitiers, and work on the church began immediately. Even after all this time, we can sense that Eleanor had a preference for Poitiers, her own capital, and she wished to embellish the city and make it a place of prestige where she could gather all the elite of her time in arts and letters. Yet hostage to her duties as queen and subject as well to the demanding desires of Henry Plantagenet, she could never stay there long. She spent Christmas 1162 in Cherbourg before embarking for England. In 1163 and 1164 she stayed in Hampshire, Wiltshire, Marborough, Winchester, on the Isle of Wight, and in Dorset. She was accompanied by her five children but rarely saw her husband.

Indeed, Eleanor could see it clearly now with a good deal of bitterness: Henry had never been in love with her and had married her only for her domains. While he did respect her, he considered her as primarily the mother of his children. In fact, Henry had numerous liaisons, which were all quite fleeting and generally very discreet. Eleanor knew this and suffered from it deeply, for she still loved this refined and brutal prince to whom she had given all she had. Furthermore, with a few rare exceptions, the gossips who attributed to her an entire collection of lovers when she was queen of France never mentioned these paramours again after she became queen of England. The only one mentioned specifically was the troubadour Bernart de Ventadorn, whom Henry II sent away from his court.[27]

Meanwhile, in October 1165, Eleanor gave birth to another daughter, Jeanne. She spent the winter in Angers, where Henry joined her in the Easter season, but six months later she set sail for England. There, at Oxford on December 27, 1166, she gave birth to her tenth child, John, the eighth of those Henry had fathered and the seventh of those who still lived. By this time, Eleanor no longer ruled over the court or the heart of the Plantagenet king, and it seems that now her husband took all possible steps to remove her from any position of responsibility. The queen had already witnessed the rise in power of an intelligent man whom Henry II had chosen to be his chancellor, Thomas Becket. In fact, she had butted heads with Becket several times, just as she had opposed Abbot Suger when she was queen of France—and like Suger, Thomas Becket, another man of the cloth, would not back down when confronted.

In 1168, however, after having quelled numerous revolts on the Continent and having razed the castle of Lusignan, Henry had to turn to Eleanor to calm her Aquitaine subjects. Forced to go to England, he left his wife with a free hand to deal with her vassals and undoubtedly hoped that they would show her more obedience than they had shown him.

So Eleanor set off for Aquitaine, but during this journey the count of Salisbury, who escorted the queen, fell mortally wounded in an ambush set by the Lusignans, who had no desire to lay down their arms. Despite everything, however, Eleanor managed to restore some order to this tumultuous country where each vassal acted in his own self-interest and wanted no part of the king of England. It was a fragile peace, certainly, but it was Eleanor's personal achievement, because no one questioned her legitimacy in Aquitaine; there her strong personality, her perfect understanding of the Occitan world, and even her legend allowed her to impose through persuasion what her husband could achieve only through force.

Henry Plantagenet realized all this, and he decided to reach an understanding with the king of France. He first sent Thomas Becket to negotiate a nonaggression pact, then he himself met with Louis VII to sign the Treaty of Montmirail. Once it was achieved, he could concentrate his efforts on achieving the structural reforms necessary to maintain the Plantagenet dynasty's immense empire, which was wealthy but was scattered across a vast territory. Richard, the king and queen's second son and without question Eleanor's favorite, was proclaimed duke of Aquitaine at the age of twelve and was placed under his mother's direct authority. Eleanor and Richard then settled in

Poitou, where they held a sumptuous court at Niort on Easter 1170, in the stronghold that Henry had heavily armed to supervise the Lower Poitou region. At the same time, the eldest son, Henry, age fifteen, was crowned and bound to the throne, in accordance with the Capet method, which was accomplished on Eleanor's counsel to make the Plantagenet dynasty equal to that of the French. The ceremony took place on June 14, 1170, but Eleanor did not attend, for she was guarding the young Marguerite of France, daughter of Louis VII and his second wife, who had been engaged almost at birth to the young Henry. It was claimed that Eleanor was not at all upset about playing the role of jailer to a French princess, although attending the coronation of her eldest would have been an occasion of great joy.

These were dark times for Henry II. He was embroiled in a conflict with his old friend, Thomas Becket, now archbishop of Canterbury, and had him murdered on the very steps of Becket's altar. This action aroused great hatred among the English against the Plantagenet king, and the Saxons rose up against the one they called the usurper. Neither could the Church accept such a crime, and it pulled back its support. Henry was excommunicated and was forced to battle alone against everyone, abandoned by some and scorned by others.

At this time, however, it seems that Eleanor benefited from complete freedom. She gloriously traveled through Aquitaine with her son Richard, and she introduced him to the troubadours, who had already left such a deep imprint on her life. Richard, in turn, came to be a poet, a fervent disciple of those amazing men who turned upside-down the culture of the medieval West—after all, Richard was the great-grandson of William IX! At this time, Eleanor conducted herself as a queen and saw to the construction of magnificent buildings—religious sanctuaries, of course, such as the Augustine Monastery in Limoges, but also residences. In Poitiers, which, even more than before, became the queen's personal capital, Eleanor gathered a court full of poets, artists, and musicians from every horizon, all of whom went on to have an exceptional influence on European literature.

Eleanor was now almost fifty, but she retained a charm that her contemporaries praised enthusiastically. Her daughter Matilda had left to marry the stormy Henry the Lion, who was twenty-seven years her elder. Her second daughter, Eleanor, had become queen of Castile, and her daughter Blanche later married the heir to the throne of France, thus making Eleanor, the repudiated wife of Louis VII, great-grandmother of Louis IX. In addition, combining her intrigues with Henry's own aims, Eleanor saw to the engagement of Geoffrey and Constance, the heiress of the duchy of Brittany and the daughter of Conan IV, who wished to retire to his English earldom of Richmond.[28] Because she was as ambitious for her children as she had been for herself, the queen worked tirelessly to ensure their prosperity.

As for her relations with her husband, the least that can be said is that these were distant and episodic. While the king had temporary mistresses, Eleanor seemed to display great understanding. Around 1166, however, Henry II had fallen in love with a young girl, the beautiful Rosamond, of whom legend eventually took possession much in the same way as it owned Eleanor. Initially, this love was a kind of fantasy for the king, but later, when his passion for Rosamond took over, instead of remaining secret, his liaison was openly trumpeted. Eleanor took offense at this, and at this point relations between the king and queen became strained.

History knows little about Rosamond. She was the daughter of a Norman knight, Gautier de Clifford, whose domain was Bredelais on the Gallic frontier, and, according to the chroniclers, she was extremely beautiful.[29] Of course, legend has embellished this considerably, making Henry II an extremely cautious and jealous lover. To stave off his rivals and also to thwart Eleanor's anger, he allegedly built a veritable labyrinth in Woodstock Castle and imprisoned Rosamond in a magnificent chamber to which he alone had access. It is said that this did not prevent Eleanor from bribing Rosamond's guardians, entering the castle, and killing her rival in cold blood. In reality, we know that the Plantagenet king eventually grew weary of his mistress, and Rosamond died quite piously in 1177 at Godstow in a nun's convent, like the majority of royal favorites throughout history.

While the affair was going on, however, it is absolutely certain that Eleanor was jealous of Rosamond. She never forgave Henry II this liaison and did all in her power to get revenge. Yet while legend shows her exacting her revenge on Rosamond personally, history shows us something entirely different: she actually attacked Henry II with a Machiavellian plan of turning the sons against their father. Here, after all, was an area in which Eleanor's intelligence and skill were given free rein, because it was a task requiring great patience and was an effort that she assumed in the shadows with complete hypocrisy and not a single scruple.

It is true that the sons of Henry II themselves had no scruples (this was an Angevin family tradition) and felt constrained by a sense of family ties only when such bonds concerned inheritances. Eleanor alone had influence over her sons, and she took advantage of it, telling the eldest that he did not need to wait for his father's death to take power (was he not crowned and bound to the throne?) and telling Richard that the time had come to prove that—under her direction—he was the true duke of Aquitaine, officially recognized by the barons. She also whispered to Geoffrey that as future duke of Brittany, he owed nothing to his father. Because he was too young, only John was left out of her plotting. Based on the knowledge we have of his character and later behavior, however, we can be sure that if he had been made part of these plans, he would not have failed to distinguish himself. Most important, Eleanor demonstrated the fragility of the Plantagenet empire, with one leg on the Continent and one on England (and even Ireland, for Henry II recently saw to his own "election" as high king of Ireland) and divided between two legal statuses (the kingdom of England in principle recognized no temporal suzerain[30] and the holdings on the Continent were all fiefs of the Capet monarchy). Eleanor then advised her sons to take counsel with her former husband, Louis VII.

Meanwhile, Henry II finally reconciled with the Church. After the scandal following the death of the archbishop of Canterbury, an interdict of some duration had been placed on the kingdom of England and Henry was refused entrance to all holy sanctuaries. Pilgrims had been flooding nonstop to the cathedral in Canterbury, where no services had been held for a year, and specifically to the tomb of Thomas Becket, for it was said that miracles had been occurring at this tomb. In fact, the unfortunate archbishop was soon canonized. Sincerely affected by this drama, Henry II, who perhaps did not mean for events to go as far as they had, protested his innocence, but no one believed him. As a result, on May 21, 1172, in the presence of his eldest son in Avranches and before an assembly of prelates and barons, he swore on the Gospels that he had neither ordered nor desired the death of Thomas Becket, and then he offered his naked back to be whipped by monks. This penitence of Avranches, as its known, erased one of the most dramatic moments in the life of Henry Plantagenet.

So it was a new man who held his court in Chinon on Christmas that same year. He asked the queen to take part, but it was not really her presence that mattered; he wished to learn if the government of Aquitaine and Poitou, which she'd managed for three years, had been well led. Eleanor provided him a precise report of her mission, which fully reassured Henry. Two months later, he held another assembly in Limoges in which Henry the young king and Richard took part. It was at this time that spies paid by the English king—he had a highly organized intelligence service, which enabled him to quickly parry the strikes of his adversaries—revealed to him that odd things were taking place in the shadows and that suspicious comings and goings had been observed between the court of France and the entourage of his sons.

The ever-distrustful Henry II sought more information, but no proof could be provided, so the king decided to act as if he had heard nothing. He had prepared the assembly in Limoges with meticulous attention to detail and for the purpose of winning. After all, he had set the stage for the marriage of his youngest son, John, to the heiress of Maurienne and was planning to announce to his barons a series of gifts to John, who by all evidence was his favorite but, poorly placed in the line of succession, was still known as Lackland. He was also going to receive the solemn homage of Raymond V, count of Toulouse, against whom he had warred several years earlier on Eleanor's instigation and who, having recently betrayed the king of France, wished to move into the Plantagenet sphere of influence. He was also going to announce the marriage plans of his last daughter, Jeanne, to the king of Sicily. Henry Plantagenet believed himself to be at the height of his career. He had come to Limoges in triumph to declare aloud that he was the most powerful sovereign in the West.

The Limoges assembly marked a turning point in the history of Eleanor and Henry. After receiving the homage of Raymond V, the king shared his plans concerning John Lackland, but Henry the young king rose up to energetically protest these arrangements favoring his younger brother. Most important, he reminded his father that he had been crowned and bore the title of king; he claimed full sovereignty, without which his coronation could have been considered merely a comedy.

The assembly ended in confusion. Henry had seen his moment of triumph compromised by this lightning strike. He thought it was his son's bad mood that had led him to adopt such an attitude, but the count of Toulouse requested a private interview with him and revealed all he knew about the plot of the king's three sons and accused Eleanor of being its originator. Henry II did not know what to think. He did not trust Raymond V, whom he knew to be capable of all forms of lies and betrayals.

Meanwhile, on March 8, 1173, Henry the young king reached the court of King Louis VII, and several days later, on their mother's orders, Richard and Geoffrey joined him there. It is easy to imagine how pleased the king of France was upon welcoming the three sons of his rival. What a fine revenge! Yet it is also easy to imagine the disappointment and rage of Henry Plantagenet, especially because his problems continued: he had recently learned that his Aquitaine vassals—particularly Eleanor's relatives, Raoul de Faye, the Lusignans, the Saint Maures, and the Rancons—supported the cause of his three fugitive sons and openly rebelled. This time, Henry II could no longer doubt Raymond V's accusations: Eleanor was clearly at the heart of the plot hatched against him.

As he had done in similar cases, Henry prepared to riposte. So they wanted to take Aquitaine away from him? He would win it back by force. He knew he could rely on the Norman barons and some English lords. He brought them together and, in November 1173, went on the offensive after repelling a French attack against Normandy. He recruited mercenaries, which was not customary at the time, and because he had no means to pay them, he placed all he owned as security to cover the cost. With disconcerting speed and the skill of a great general, he led his army from Normandy into Poitou and set siege to the castle of Raoul de Faye, whom he suspected—correctly—of being the queen's most faithful supporter. The fortress soon fell, but Raoul had already fled to Paris. Henry next made arrangements to retake Poitiers, where Eleanor remained.

For her part, Eleanor realized that the wager had been lost. Given that she had no desire to fall under her husband's power, she sought to flee. Perhaps she was resigned to asking asylum from the king of France, which would be fate's final stroke of revenge in the arrangement. North of Poitiers, in the direction of Chartres (or in the direction of the Capet domains), a band of Brabançons paid by the Plantagenet king blundered into a small group of knights. The mercenaries slaughtered some of the knights and imprisoned the rest. Among these prisoners they found, dressed as a man, the queen-duchess Eleanor.

Henry's war of reconquest was over. The Poitevins and Aquitaines submitted, at least in appearance and only for the moment. Meanwhile, Henry brought Eleanor to Chinon as a prisoner and incarcerated her in the fortress there. Until the death of Henry II in 1189, the queen-duchess remained a prisoner, shunted from one castle to another with all the regard due to her rank but closely watched by men her husband could trust. For close to sixteen years she remained in the shadows, stripped of all authority and abandoned by her sons, who made no attempts to free her.

When the king embarked at Barfleur on July 8, 1174, after apparently settling matters in Poitou and alarmed at what was afoot on the Scottish border, he brought Eleanor with him as his prisoner. She was not alone; she was one among other prisoners securely guarded by Henry II, including Marguerite, the young wife of his eldest son, whom Henry wished to use to make his rebellious son see reason. Accompanying these two were also several vassals, including the counts of Leicester and Chester, who were paying for their revolt. In England, Henry Plantagenet imprisoned his wife in a tower at Salisbury.

It was here that she learned that her sons, beaten on the field despite the assistance given them by Louis VII, had come to make their submission to their father. She could see that no chance remained to become the queen she once was. Henry II had theoretically pardoned his sons but refrained from doing anything on his wife's behalf. Instead, what we know indicates that he wanted to be rid of her, either because she was no longer of any use to him politically or because he wanted to be free to live the debauched life that he had begun pursuing some time before.

In fact, in October 1175, the pope sent to England a legate, Uguccione, cardinal of Saint-Ange. Henry welcomed him with much honor and friendship and, according to the chroniclers,[31] studied with him the possibility of annulling his marriage to Eleanor. Again, the reason invoked was consanguinity.[32] Nonetheless, whether because the papal legate refused to contemplate this solution or because Henry had considered the problems posed by the dissolution of the marriage—mainly in the Aquitaine domains that Eleanor could take back[33]—nothing came of the matter.

The queen's captivity continued from fortress to fortress under the guard of Ralph Fitz-Stephen and Raoul de Glanville, both of whom were of good Norman stock and were the henchmen of Henry II. Being imprisoned, however, did not prevent her from remaining abreast of what was happening in the Plantagenet empire, of receiving messages carrying the greetings of various vassals, and of communicating with various people. Though she had lost all hope of regaining her royal authority and though she was on chilly terms with Richard, whom she accused of cowardly abandoning her, she knew she could count on the sympathy of a large number of her Poitevin and Aquitaine subjects. We have an almost lyrical testimony of this in the chronicle of Richard the Poitevin, whose author, addressing Eleanor directly, reminds her that she is the eagle of Merlin's prophecies and announces that the day will come when she will be freed and returned to her country, Aquitaine.[34] The times for this freedom and return were not yet propitious, although the three eldest sons of Henry II continued to wage an underhanded struggle against their father as well as against each other.[35]

In 1177, Eleanor learned of the death of her rival, Rosamond, but because she was now completely detached from the man she had once loved so passionately, the news likely left her rather indifferent. Henry II continued to lead an eventful love life: we know now that his mistress at this time was the young Alys of France, daughter of Louis VII, who had been engaged to Richard, a situation that later provided him with solid arguments for not marrying her. At the same time, Eleanor's youngest daughter, Jeanne, left for Sicily at age eleven to marry William, king of Sicily, a highly cultivated and very courteous knight. In 1179, the queen learned that her former husband, Louis VII, in the company of Henry II, had made a pilgrimage to Canterbury to visit the tomb of Thomas Becket in order to fulfill a pledge Louis made after an accident befell his heir, Dieudonné, whom we know as Philip Augustus. On this occasion the king of France and the king of England laid the groundwork for an apparent reconciliation. Furthermore, when Louis VII crowned his son the following November 1, it was Henry the young king, sent to the French court on his father's orders, who had the honor of carrying the crown during the procession. On September 18 of the following year, Louis VII died at the Cistercian abbey of Saint-Port. In him Henry Plantagenet had found an honest adversary with little skill for politics, but the situation would be quite different with Louis's successor, Philip.

Meanwhile, Eleanor's captivity endured, as did Henry's surprising activity. Followed by a motley band of jugglers, mountebanks, and prostitutes, the king went everywhere by forced march, taking care of finances, delivering justice, fighting rebel barons (and hanging several as an example), and tearing down rebel fortresses. After the death of Louis, under the influence of Philip Augustus, his sons once again picked up their arms against him.

It was under these circumstances that during a campaign in Quercy in June 1183, his eldest son, Henry the young king, died of an illness that his doctors could not cure. Before dying, though, he begged his father's forgiveness through a messenger, who returned with a ring, a symbol of the pardon Henry II granted his rebellious son and heir. Henry the young king died piously, asking that his father agree to restore his mother's freedom.

Because of this tragic death of their child, starting in 1184, Henry II agreed to ease significantly the conditions of Eleanor's incarceration. We should not be led astray, however; it was not sentiment but political calculation that led the Plantagenet to act in this way. Henry the young king's death had upset the political equation, and the heir was now Richard—but Richard was already duke of Aquitaine, and Henry II distrusted him more than the others because he was Eleanor's favorite. Henry was also fully aware that Richard was homosexual and would most likely never produce an heir, even if he agreed to marry for the sake of appearances. Arrangements needed to be made, and for this Henry II needed Eleanor.

On Easter 1185, he brought his wife to the Continent, but not to free her. Rather, he wished to use her as a crude instrument of blackmail to force Richard's surrender, for the son had once again risen up against his father. If Richard did not immediately return Poitou to his mother, who, Henry declared with splendid hypocrisy, was its legitimate countess, the king declared that she would march upon this province at the head of an army and ravage it. Not wishing for matters to fester, Richard gave in, but once the rebel had apparently submitted, Henry II saw to it that Eleanor was conducted back to England and imprisoned again, perhaps even more heavily supervised than before. In 1186, she was housed in Winchester, where, in August, she learned of the accidental death of her son Geoffrey at a tournament at the court of the king of France. Geoffrey, duke of Brittany, left his wife, Constance, pregnant, and she gave birth the following year to a son whom Henry II, for various reasons, had named Arthur, probably hoping that one day, like the legendary King Arthur whose mythical adventures he strove to develop, the child would be able to unify England and Brittany in the vast Plantagenet empire.[36]

Nevertheless, Henry II was increasingly scorned by his vassals.

During August 1188, he met with the king of France at Gisors to try to work out a definitive peace. Yet not only did he not find an accord with Philip but also he had the unpleasant surprise of seeing his own son and heir, Richard, at the side of the French king, whose support he received, demanding his birthright. Henry, who interpreted this as a replay of the Limoges assembly, when Henry the young king had demanded authority, was not disposed to give in. In truth, we can wonder if he hated Richard, for at this time his son paid him back quite well: During this meeting, Richard went down on his knees before the king of France and swore homage for all his Continental domains, asking the French king for aid and protection because he was Richard's legitimate sovereign. When everyone departed to go their various ways, Richard departed with Philip, and at this Henry II was mortified and full of rage. He had no one to count on now for his revenge but his youngest son, John, in whom he subsequently placed all his hopes.[37]

Henry's time of greatness was now over. He was undermined by illness, aged before his time, and ulcerated by family betrayals. He held his Christmas 1188 court in Saumur in the presence of John Lackland, but the majority of his vassals abstained from coming. They all abandoned him, one after the other—even those who had once been his warmest supporters. Henry then considered disinheriting Richard officially and leaving all his domains to John, but he hesitated: he had great affection for John, in whom he saw himself, and John was courageous, active, unscrupulous, hypocritical, and ambitious, qualities common to all the Plantagenets and dear to Henry's heart, but unfortunately his son was also often thoughtless, capable of the worst stupidities on a whim, and gratuitously cruel in a way that could focus much hatred upon him. Henry's paternal love was not blind, and Richard remained the designated heir.

This, however, did not prevent war from resuming between Henry and Richard, who was actively supported by the French king. In July 1189, at Azay-le-Rideau, the two kings attempted a truce. At this time the king of England was in such terrible condition that the French king took pity upon him, and a truce was declared. At its completion, Henry returned to Chinon to sleep a sleep that would never end. He was fifty-six years old, and several loyal followers, such as William Marshal, remained by his side. Before dying, Henry gave Marshal a list of the lords who had betrayed him, and heading the list was John Lackland.[38]

The king is dead, long live the king! When Eleanor learned the news, although saddened by another bereavement (her daughter Matilda had died on July 13), she could not help but rejoice. For a long while she had ceased to love Henry, and she knew she was going to recover her freedom and some of her authority. In fact, Richard had hardly been acknowledged as king when he sent messengers to England with orders to free Eleanor immediately. It was as if no time had been lost; the emotional and political combination of Eleanor and Richard was reborn as if no time had passed. Eleanor recovered all her energy and will to act despite her sixty-seven years. She went on a campaign to strengthen the throne of her favorite son, hoping that she could thereby hold the strings of a power she had always coveted but had never truly obtained. She traveled from town to town and castle to castle through all the English counties, freeing all the captives that Henry II had accumulated in his prisons, overseeing the swearing of oaths to King Richard, and recruiting men she knew were loyal or whom she determined to be endowed with great political abilities for preparing her son's future government.

For one year she was the true mistress of England. Richard made only a short appearance on the island on the occasion of his coronation, September 3, 1189. He took advantage of it to reconcile with the men who had faithfully served his father—William Marshal in particular—and greatly rewarded those who had been his own supporters. Neither did he overlook his younger brother, John, whom he made the count of Mortain in Normandy and to whom he gave the castles of Marlborough, Nottingham, Lancaster, and Wallingford and the hand of Havise of Gloucester,* heiress to one of the richest duchies of the island. He named as archbishop of York one of his father's two bastard sons,

---

*[Also known as Isabel. —*Trans.*]

Geoffrey,* who was a priest, and the other was made count of Salisbury through marriage. It is easy to see that Richard I of England tried to erase a past full of trouble, revolt, and hatred. He had deeply generous tendencies that were equally matched by his audacity and courage. It was for good reason that he was nicknamed the Lion Heart. He was also very much an Aquitanian, as refined, cultivated, and generous as his great-grandfather William IX, his grandfather William X, and his mother, who was now more than ever queen mother and duchess.

Because of this same Aquitain-Poitevin heritage, however, Richard did not care for England. In fact, he never felt at his ease there, and never has an English king been so French. He left England for the Continent on December 11, 1189, in order to actively prepare something close to his heart at this time: a third Crusade to reconquer Jerusalem, which once again had fallen into the hands of the Turks. Having as few scruples as his father and because he firmly believed in his mission, he took money from wherever he could find it to equip his army and he sold castles and lands to acquire funds.[39]

Eleanor joined her son on the Continent on February 2, 1190. There was much that needed to be put into order before Richard's departure for the Holy Land. First was the neutralization of John, whom the two suspected, quite rightly, of having dark designs. This was the reason they offered a substantial prerogative to John, now the count of Mortain: the English counties of Cornwall, Devon, Dorset, and Somerset. In no case, however, did they contemplate giving him any governmental responsibility; they distrusted him too greatly. In Richard's absence, the kingdom's affairs would be handled by William Longchamp, former chancellor of Henry II, who was so adroit that he had become an indispensable figure in the Plantagenet empire. In fact, though, it was Eleanor who, without bearing the title of regent, would be the true mistress of Richard's domains. The young king trusted his mother completely and he knew she would deal ruthlessly with any who threatened his territory's integrity.

---

*[Not to be confused with Henry's legitimate son Geoffrey the duke of Brittany. —*Trans.*]

Richard was not making the Third Crusade by himself; he needed an alliance with the king of France. Of course, Philip and Richard had an established relationship for the moment, for Richard had officially recognized Philip as his sovereign for all his Continental holdings. Yet Richard also had a bone of contention with the French king: the fate of Alys of France,* Philip's sister and Richard's fiancée. First, the king of England had no desire to marry, and second, the princess had been the mistress of Henry II. Richard met Philip in Gisors and succeeded in having the marriage plans postponed. Then he and Eleanor made numerous donations to abbeys, mainly Fontevrault, and, on June 24, the English king took leave of his mother in Chinon to meet with the Crusader army that was assembling in Vézelay.

The Crusade, however, was delayed. Richard and Philip spent the winter of 1190–1191 in Messina, where they reached agreement on the fate of Alys. Richard refused to marry her, which, after many stormy discussions, Philip accepted. It should be said that Eleanor was entirely against this union, which she knew was doomed to failure. It was a certainty that Richard was capable of procreating; he had a bastard child from his youth, probably the result of a moment of straying, for he was staunchly homosexual. Eleanor told herself that if she could find a princess who was capable not of curing Richard of his penchants— the duchess had long since abandoned hope of that—but of accepting a physical relationship with her son for several days and nights, Eleanor would have some chance of witnessing the birth of a legitimate heir. She would ask for nothing more. Eleanor began traveling in search of such a rare jewel, which was how, one fine day, she headed for Messina accompanied by a young girl named Berengaria, daughter of King Sancho of Navarre. The chroniclers of the time described her as "a wise maiden and gentle lass, gallant and beautiful."

At the time she landed in Messina with her son's presumed fiancée, Philip was leaving, probably out of spite, his mind still full of the Alys matter. Richard was seduced by Berengaria's charm and promised his

---

*[Also known as Aylis or Adelaide. —*Trans.*]

mother to marry her. In fact, some six weeks later in Cyprus, without the presence of Eleanor (she had already begun the long journey back to England) the marriage took place. For whatever reason, however, this union remained sterile, and Eleanor never knew the joy of seeing the birth of an heir to her favorite son. Meanwhile, on several occasions, Richard performed public penance and confessed before everyone his "sins against nature" and promised not to repeat them.

Eleanor's return to England at this time is explained by her fear of leaving John by himself to hatch plots behind his elder brother's back. John was in fact traveling throughout England—his country of preference—repeating everywhere that Richard would not be returning from the Third Crusade because he preferred to gain a kingdom in the Holy Land than govern the immense legacy left him by his father. This younger son even managed to strip William Longchamp of his duties as chancellor, forcing William to flee to France. The exact circumstances, however, are far from clear. At Christmas 1191, Eleanor presided over the plenary court in Normandy, at Bonneville-sur-Touques, and six weeks later she hastily went back to England. She had heard news that was not at all pleasing or a good omen: Philip Augustus, king of France, had secretly returned from the Holy Land and had left behind the king of England, who was all alone but covering himself with glory in his battles against Saladin's Saracens. Philip's sneaky arrival in Richard's domains surely hid something, especially given that he and John had been maintaining contact. Eleanor was alarmed and prepared to counter whatever might develop.

It is quite certain, however, that the king of France did not simply abandon to Richard the honor of pursuing the Crusade. By taking John's side in his quarrel against Richard, much as he had supported Richard's quarrel against Henry II, the clever Capet hoped to win Normandy, which he regarded as essential for protecting the royal domain and which, once in his possession, would halve the Plantagenet empire.

Once back on English soil, Eleanor set about nipping in the bud her youngest son's plotting, and, with the help of the archbishop of Rouen, she succeeded in temporarily arresting the damage, using a very effective weapon in her arsenal: she threatened John with feudal resumption. In fact, in Richard's name she could confiscate all of John's domains for felony proved by an assembly. She actually set up such an assembly to frighten John, count of Mortain, who knew full well his mother would find enough loyal barons to condemn him. He himself was not yet certain of his own partisans and did not feel he yet had enough support from Philip Augustus. As a result, the rebel backed down and submitted to his mother's ultimatum, but he obviously continued plotting in the shadows. Eleanor, who foresaw a time when a test of strength between the two sons would be inevitable, sent one message after another to Richard, asking him to return at once.

Richard, however, had no desire to return to England. He enjoyed the Crusade, where his reputation as a formidable and knightly warrior kept growing. It is probable that he was even contemplating carving out a kingdom in the Holy Land. Yet he was unable to free Jerusalem,[40] so on September 29, 1192, Richard sent by boat to the West his wife, Berengaria, and his sister Jeanne, widow of the king of Sicily, and declared that he himself would be taking the sea several days later. He set sail on October 9 and made a stop in Corfu. At this time, his fleet was seen off the coast of Brindisi, looking for a harbor to shelter from the storm. Then, silence.

Eleanor grew worried. She sent messengers in search of information, but they could learn nothing. Several days after a sorrowful Christmas, she received a strange missive, the copy of a letter that the king of France had received from the emperor of Germany and which the archbishop of Rouen had somehow procured:

> We wish to inform your Highness by this present letter that at the moment the enemy of our empire and the disturber of your kingdom, Richard, king of England, was crossing the sea to return to his domains, it happened that the winds brought him to the region of Istria, his vessel having been shipwrecked. Because the roads were watched and guards were placed everywhere, our dear and beloved cousin Leopold, duke of Austria, captured the said king . . .

Thus Richard had been made a prisoner of the duke of Austria with whom he had quarreled in the Holy Land. Later, it was learned through the messengers hastily dispatched by Eleanor that after being transferred through a series of different prisons, Richard had been handed over to Henry VI, the emperor of Germany, who was holding him at Spire and let it be known that the king would be freed only for the fabulous ransom of fifty thousand silver marks.

We have no documents on what really transpired between the time of Richard's capture by Leopold and the decision of the emperor to hold him, but it is easy to imagine that Philip Augustus played some role in this manipulation. With a promise of we know not what to the emperor of Germany, the king of France arranged the English king's temporary removal. Indeed, the emperor was undoubtedly personally delighted to have this opportunity to avenge himself in this way for the rebellions of his brother-in-law, Henry the Lion, the duke of Saxony. The situation was now clear: it was Philip, the king of France, and his ally John Plantagenet against Eleanor, the septuagenarian queen-duchess. John was completely untroubled; he dealt directly with the king of France and even conceded to him by treaty a good portion of Normandy.

Eleanor, however, was not weakened by age and had lost none of her tenacity. She knew she represented the legitimate king and used this to her advantage. She also knew she had the backing of her Aquitaine and Poitevin barons as well and that, out of respect for King Richard, numerous Angevin, Norman, and English knights were ready to march under her command. She used all the weight of her political experience and knowledge of the European courts. Seconded by the archbishop of Canterbury, Hubert Walker, who was also the high justice of the realm, she was able if not to restore the situation to its original state, then at least to keep it in balance. John Lackland was obliged to hole up in Windsor with his supporters and was besieged by the majority of English barons under the leadership of William Marshal, who, after the death of Henry II, was now on the side of Richard and Eleanor, for Richard was the legitimate ruler. The French king threatened to land his troops on English soil, but Eleanor summoned all her vassals and once again asked them to swear their loyalty to Richard.

All of Europe's eyes were fixed on this strange situation, but no one dared say or do anything. In one sense, Richard was put on auction by Henry VI of Germany. Who would be the highest bidder—Eleanor or John (meaning Philip Augustus)? Furthermore, Richard was a crusading prince who was theoretically under the protection of the Church, and he was being detained by a Christian prince in contravention of all civil and religious laws—but the Church did nothing. It is likely that after supporting the endeavors of Henry II, particularly in Ireland,[41] and because Philip Augustus and Capetian power upheld order, the papacy, which was always more skilled in political *combinazione* than in matters of dogma, wagered everything on the French king.[42] Whatever the reason, Pope Celestine III definitely refrained from intervening in this conflict. He also sought to handle the emperor of Germany with kid gloves, for the emperor was also the titular king of Sicily and had been looking for an opportunity to invade Italy.

Eleanor saw to the writing of three letters addressed to the pope and probably actually written by her secretary, Peter of Blois,[43] which began with these words: "I, Eleanor, by the wrath of God, queen of England, duchess of Normandy, countess of Anjou, and unhappy mother." These letters were not gentle to the pope (but judge for yourself):

> I had resolved to keep silent. My spontaneity, the violence of my pain, could in fact allow some word beyond control of reason to spring forth, because grief, when it is in full rise, easily comes close to dementia and knows no master. You cannot pretend to know nothing of our misfortunes, which are many and endless, for you would be labeled criminal and infamous, you who are the vicar of the Crucified One, Peter's successor, priest of Christ, and anointed by the Lord!

Then Peter of Blois really had to buckle down to his task and take it a step further: "I, Eleanor, by the wrath of God, queen of the English, my flesh is wasted with grief and my bones cleave to my skin. Please be to God that all the blood in my body, my brain, and the marrow of my bones has dissolved into tears. My very bowels have been torn away. I have lost the staff of my old age and the light of my eyes." This letter then provided a golden opportunity for some acerbic criticisms of the Roman Curia:

> Often for matters of little importance your cardinals have been sent to remote lands with sovereign powers, but in this desperate and deplorable affair, you have not sent so much as a single subdeacon or even an acolyte. Today, it is the quest for profit that moves your legates to travel, and not consideration of Christ, the honor of the Church, and establishing peace between kingdoms. Yet, what more beneficial thing could there be than the liberation of this king?

Resorting to threats, Eleanor even turned to reminding the pope that her late husband had put an end to a schism by rallying to Alexander at a time when the emperor of Germany was supporting an antipope.[44]

> The kings and princes of the earth have conspired against my son, the anointed of the Lord. One keeps him in chains while another ravages his lands; one holds him by the heels while the other flays him. And while this goes on, the sword of St. Peter reposes in its scabbard. But I declare to you that the day foreseen by the Apostle is near when the seamless tunic of Christ shall be rent again, when the net of Peter shall be torn, when the unity of the Catholic Church dissolved.

She continues, using a play on the Latin words and her acerbic wit: "Three times you have promised to send legates and they have not been sent. In fact, they have rather been leashed than sent."[45]

The pope, however, remained deaf to these pleas that displayed the full measure of Eleanor's impassioned rage. Certainly, he had excommunicated the duke of Austria and threatened the king of France with interdiction if he took possession of his rival's lands, but these were just words in the air. The queen-duchess was therefore forced to manage these problems by herself, without the support of the Church. Through the intermediary William Longchamp, sent on a mission to Germany, she received a letter from her son asking that the money for the ransom be gathered and given to Eleanor. This was an enormous task to which Eleanor had to devote all her efforts. She began campaigning for this money both in England and on the Continent, reminding her vassals that the feudal oath demanded they contribute to the ransom for their sovereign.

All those loyal to King Richard gave what they could, but because of the enormous size of the ransom, Eleanor had to tax the monasteries, especially those that were swollen with wealth. Nevertheless, putting together a sum of this size, which amounted to almost thirty-four tons of pure silver, was an operation requiring time, especially given that John Lackland's supporters often managed to divert the sums accrued, occasionally by force and especially in England.[46] During this time, Richard the Lion Heart moped in his German prison, wondering if his friends had abandoned him.[47]

Finally, during the winter of 1193–1194, Eleanor left for Germany, accompanied by many loyal supporters, not wishing to entrust to anyone the money for the ransom. She arrived in Cologne for the Christmas holidays and was in Mainz for the days of Candlemass. On February 4, 1194, her son was finally delivered into her hands after having sworn homage to the emperor of Germany for the kingdom of England (probably on his mother's counsel). This homage was of little importance, however, and was purely formal. Important in Eleanor's eyes was that her son had been freed from prison and could now restore order to his immense domain.

Five weeks later, Eleanor and Richard landed on the shores of England, in Sandwich. Welcomed in triumph by his subjects, Richard was crowned a second time at Winchester Cathedral in April. Amazingly, Eleanor had answered the challenge set by the king of France and her youngest son—and she had won. At seventy-two years of age, this woman who had been queen of two different countries still astounded the world. Would she finally now find tranquillity? Could she now follow through on her plan to retire to Fontevrault and spend her final years in peace and prayer?

She knew Richard still needed protection, though, and she could not abandon her beloved son; in her eyes, he was a good king who had to be given every chance to successfully maintain the Plantagenet legacy. Eleanor now employed her energies in this task. She followed Richard, who received the homage of his vassals, one after the other, as well as the submission of those who had been tempted by John Lackland in the king's absence.

This was not at all to the liking of Philip Augustus and John, who viewed with alarm Richard's rebuilding of his empire over the ensuing days. Philip decided to launch a large strike; he began an invasion of Normandy, which had always been the target of his aims. John had ceded to him the Vexin region of Normandy, but Philip wished to have the entire Norman realm, so vital to French stability. He knew that if he succeeded, the rest of the Plantagenet domains would fall like ripe fruit. When news of the resumed hostilities reached them, Eleanor and Richard returned to the Continent. Like his father, Richard hired mercenaries, and, with their support and the employment of the tactics of Henry II, who always moved with disconcerting speed, they managed to stave off the threat with a series of small victories that forced the French king to retreat.

Eleanor, however, still had one more plan close to her heart: she wished to reconcile her two sons. Unbeknownst to Richard, who at this time had thoughts only of avenging himself on his brother, Eleanor sent messages to John. Finally, in the spring of 1194, when Richard and Eleanor were in Lisieux, the queen mother took advantage of the situation and brought in John, who threw himself on Richard's knees and asked his pardon. Ever generous but no dupe, the Lion Heart forgave his rebel brother and solemnly reconciled with him. Of course neither the king nor his mother trusted John, for they knew that his about-face had been dictated by his immediate self-interest, but John's request for forgiveness was important in that as long as he saw advantage in his alliance with Richard, he would not be tempted to encourage the elaborate politics of Philip Augustus. As a result, Eleanor, satisfied as both a queen and a mother, could enter semimonastic retirement at Fontevrault, a haven from the tumult of this troubled world whose foundations she herself had long contributed to shaking.

Yet it should not be thought that Eleanor had reached the end of her active life. Worries continued to assail her with as much force as ever, and she could not really hold herself apart from what was going on. For instance, she was worried by the sterility of Richard and Berengaria's union. Richard had resumed his debauched habits, and Berengaria did not live with him. She was also alarmed by the attitude of John, who continued his obsession with shadowy plotting. She was worried about the fate of her daughter Jeanne, the widow of the king of Sicily and remarried by Richard to the count of Toulouse, Raymond VI, for purely political reasons. Raymond was a libertine of the worst sort and this was his fourth marriage: he was the widower of one of his former wives; had placed another inside a Cathar convent; and had cynically repudiated the third, Bourguigne of Lusignan. Jeanne gave him a son, the future Raymond VII, then later, again pregnant and ill, she sought refuge in Fontevrault, where she died in her mother's arms.

Meanwhile, Richard conducted himself like a great king, and he was even offered the imperial crown of Germany. This idea momentarily tempted him—it would obviously mean the triumph of the Plantagenets and the definitive crushing of the Capets—but he had little liking for Germany, which held only bad memories for him. Instead, he made sure the country elected one of his nephews, the son of Matilda and Henry the Lion, who would become the famous emperor Otto. He also secured the alliance of Baldwin IX, count of Flanders and Hainaut, and of Renaud de Dammartin, count of Boulogne. Richard was thereby able to surround the Capet domain with a skillfully woven web that could serve his interests in his perpetual struggle with Philip Augustus. The king of France clearly sensed the trap closing in on him. On the Seine, beneath the fortress of Château Gaillard, he held a meeting with Richard the Lion Heart to negotiate peace.

The two kings eventually found agreement and signed a treaty that pledged a truce of five years. Of course, once this time had passed, the war would resume. The French king tried to bribe some of Richard's vassals, in particular the count of Limoges, while John was crafting dark plans in Brittany, which was then under Plantagenet rule. In Paris, Philip Augustus raised the young Arthur, son of Geoffrey and Constance of Brittany, and, of course, the French king arranged to provide the boy with a very Francophile education and reasons to one day hope for the crown of England and the ducal crown of Brittany. After all, wasn't he the closest heir to his uncle Richard in the order of succession?

To bring the count of Limoges to reason, Richard set siege to his castle at Châlus. During the course of an inspection of the battlefield on the evening of March 25, 1199, the king was struck in the shoulder by an arrow. The wound became infected. Richard had no illusions about his fate and summoned his mother.

Eleanor received the message at Fontevrault. Without losing a moment and terribly stricken both as a queen and a mother, she raced to Châlus, arriving there on the morning of April 6. Richard had made his last confession and had forgiven his slayer, the king of France, and all his enemies. He gave his mother his last counsels and last wishes and then expired in the arms of the person who had given him life. He asked that his heart be laid to rest in the cathedral of Rouen and that his body be laid to rest in the abbey of Fontevrault. Thus Eleanor saw her beloved son die when he was forty-one years old and still at the height of his strength and glory.

A mystery remains surrounding the final moments of Richard the Lion Heart: Did he dictate a will? Whom did he name as his successor? The answers to these questions remain lost; we know absolutely nothing. Whether he took a position for or against John Lackland does not change the fact that the ultimate decision of succession belonged to Eleanor herself and the principal barons of the kingdom, for Richard had two heirs between which Anglo-Angevin custom could not choose. Normally, as Richard had replaced Henry the young king on the throne, it would be Geoffrey who came next in the order of succession. Because Geoffrey had died in 1186, however, it was his son Arthur who should receive the crown.[48] The claim could be made, however, that the right to the crown should go to the surviving son of Henry II.

The situation was unsolvable, especially because it seems that Richard considered Arthur to be his successor and had his vassals swear an oath of loyalty to his nephew.[49]

Richard's funeral took place at Fontevrault on April 11, 1199. The Mass for the Dead was said by the bishop of Lincoln, assisted by the bishops of Poitiers and Angers, and on this very day Eleanor made a new donation to the abbey for the soul of her very dear lord, King Richard.[50] Over subsequent days, she made similar donations to various other monasteries. Meanwhile, at Fontevrault an endless procession of high figures appeared to give their condolences to the queen-duchess, and others came to discuss the succession.

In fact, the problem of succession had extremely serious ramifications. To choose John, the count of Mortain, was to choose for exposure to all manner of potentially unpleasant events. John was violent, cynical, and unscrupulous; he was a man who often acted with unconscious motives and who was, in fact, almost a lunatic. The principal authorities of the kingdom knew he did not have the makings of a king. Even Eleanor did not trust her son. What, then, was to be done? Selecting the duke of Brittany was tantamount to giving the Plantagenet empire to a minion of Philip Augustus, to surrendering the kingdom to Capetian lust. If Arthur succeeded, because he was still too young to govern, the regency would go to his mother, Constance of Brittany, an enemy of Eleanor who hated the Plantagenets. It seems clear, however, that Henry II and Richard had chosen Arthur. Eleanor and the nobles of the kingdom chose John—albeit reluctantly—because in order to maintain the unity of the Plantagenet empire they needed a man to rule and not a child influenced by the king of France. This is the sole plausible explanation for the decision that made John Lackland the most catastrophic king in the history of England.[51]

We can rightfully wonder if here Eleanor made her greatest political misstep. By all evidence, John was an incompetent. By supporting him during King Richard's lifetime, Philip Augustus knew full well what he was doing: He was seeking to eliminate the intelligent and adroit Lion Heart for the benefit of the sinister John Lackland. This would give him the opportunity to intervene constantly in English affairs to his own great advantage. In addition, he was placing his bets on two different scenarios, for at this same time, with remarkable hypocrisy, he had convinced Arthur of Brittany that he was the legitimate heir. On analysis of these facts and with no pretension of rewriting history, we can be certain that Arthur of Brittany, liegeman of the king of France that he was, would certainly not have lost the Plantagenet domains as stupidly as his uncle. Nevertheless, it could be said that Eleanor thought to make full use of her power and prestige as well as her maternal authority to make John if not a great king, then at least a solid defender of the Plantagenet empire.

She demonstrated this immediately. She followed the troops that had formed Richard's elite horseback corps, she marched against Anjou, which had chosen Arthur, and she crisscrossed Aquitaine, seeking the same oath of loyalty to John that she had asked for Richard on his ascent to the throne. During this time, John concerned himself with Normandy and England, where reservations were equally keen. The result: at the end of the month of May, he was crowned in London.

This was only a symbolic gesture, however; the match was far from being won on either the Continent or in England. Eleanor, pursuing the task with a kind of fury, continued traveling through Aquitaine in what was both a show of intimidation and a propaganda campaign. In actuality, she felt that Philip Augustus was spying on his prey and that this prey was close to falling into her adversary's hands. Would she have taken back Aquitaine and Poitou from Louis VII only to see them fall again into the possession of that king's heir? Hers was the kind of energy that can be generated only by despair. She threatened her barons; thwarted the perfidious maneuvers of the Lusignans, who were always ready to betray the Plantagenets (at the end of 1199 she fell into an ambush set by Hugh of Lusignan, who released her only after extorting a ransom from the count of the Marche); and, foremost, she came to terms with the cities by granting them charters of franchise and more.

Yet these charters were obviously decoys. By granting them Eleanor was not only showing proof of liberalism but also was catching in her trap the bourgeoisie of these towns. She knew that the bourgeois class was on the rise and held the financial means essential for any undertaking. The nobles, meanwhile, had been ruined by ceaseless wars and were unable to supply a sufficient number of soldiers. This could not stand! In these communal charters it was arranged that the bourgeois of the cities would be considered the equals of the greatest vassals. Flattered at seeing themselves placed on even footing with the kingdom's nobles, the bourgeois class did not read further: as vassals they owed *service d'ost*—in other words, in the event of war, they were obliged to pay for military equipment and to guarantee the formation of sufficient troops for their sovereign. Because vanity is always what sells best, however, Eleanor pulled off a master stroke by attaching to the crown cities that in reality passionately scorned the Plantagenet-Capet rivalry.

This was how Eleanor brought to heel Aquitaine and Poitou, but she had less luck with the viscount of Thouars. He remained an unwavering supporter of Arthur, and his brother Guy was about to become the third husband of Constance, Arthur's mother. Incidentally, the marriage of Guy and Constance gave birth to Alix, who was heiress of the duchy upon Arthur's death and was later married by Philip Augustus to Pierre de Dreux, a union that inaugurated the Montfort dynasty.

Eleanor then tried something that would have been impossible for anyone else: she met Philip Augustus at Tours between July 15 and 20, 1199, and swore feudal homage to him for all the Continental territories of the Plantagenets. It is likely that though the king of France was not duped by this imaginative and shrewd move by his father's first wife, he accepted it, telling himself that Eleanor would not live forever.

In fact, with this gesture, Eleanor wished to protect her youngest son—and thereby the legacy of Henry II—one last time. By personally swearing homage, she *personally* acknowledged herself vassal to the king of France but also acknowledged herself ruler of Normandy, Anjou, Poitou, and Aquitaine. John was thus no more than her vassal, rather than the direct vassal of Philip. The Continental domains of the Plantagenets would form a fief only once removed from the crown. If any difficulty emerged, it was Eleanor and not John with whom the king of France would have to grapple. In fact, she assumed the responsibilities of her son and served as a buffer between John and Philip. This is telling regarding the little faith she placed in John's political abilities, for in acting in this way, she moved him out of the loop, preferring to solve any problems personally before the titled English king could commit any irreparable blunders.

Shortly after the Tours meeting, Eleanor reached Rouen, where she joined John. She explained the situation to him and gave him directives, and it seems that he followed them, at least for a while.

Somewhat reassured, the old queen-duchess undertook a long journey during the winter of 1199–1200: she went to Spain to visit her daughter Eleanor, who had been the queen of Castile for thirty years and who had given her husband, Alfonso VIII, a large number of children. It was during the course of her stay at the court of Castile that Eleanor designated who among her granddaughters would be engaged to the heir to the French throne. Though she was no longer queen of France, it is ironic that, through her granddaughter Blanche of Castile, Eleanor would become the great-grandmother of one of the greatest Capet kings.*[52] She then returned to France, accompanied by her granddaughter Blanche, and spent the Easter holiday in Bordeaux before handing Blanche over to the archbishop of the city, who solemnly turned her over to the envoys of the king of France.

After this and, as described by the chronicler Roger of Hoveden, "worn out by age and by the fatigues of the long journey, the queen went to Fontevrault abbey to stay." Yet this was not a true retirement; she continued to lend her son all the diplomatic aid at her disposal. It is no exaggeration to say that during the final years of Eleanor's life, the thinking capital of the Plantagenet empire was Fontevrault.

As was foreseen, John piled stupidity upon stupidity, committing his most serious blunder at the end of August 1200, when he kidnapped Isabel of Angoulême, official fiancée of the count of the Marche, Hugh

---

*[Louis the IX, or St. Louis. —*Trans.*]

de Lusignan, and married her soon after. As a result, the old hatred the Lusignans held for the Plantagenets was revived, and they appealed directly to the sovereign (meaning they went over Eleanor's head)[53] by asking Philip Augustus to intervene directly. He did not let this opportunity slip by and put John on notice that if he did not return Isabel, whom he had already wed, he must at least pay compensation to Hugh de Lusignan. The balance that the old queen-duchess sought to maintain in the Plantagenet domains was broken.

John crowned his young wife at Westminster on October 8, 1200, and shortly thereafter (which was not at all surprising), Philip Augustus cordially received the king and queen of England on the Ile de la Cité. It should be said that Philip was grappling with great difficulties and was unable to make any moves against his vassal: He had been excommunicated for repudiating his wife, Ingeborg, and for marrying Agnes of Meranie. His kingdom was even under a Church sentence of interdiction. During this time, Eleanor was not inactive; eventually, she even reconciled with Aimery de Thouars, the uncle by marriage of young Arthur and one who had always resisted Plantagenet authority. Aimery visited Eleanor at Fontevrault and left promising to work at maintaining harmony among the Poitevin barons.

On September 4, 1201, Constance, the mother of Arthur of Brittany, died. This was followed soon after by the death of Agnes of Meranie, the subject of the litigation and scandal in which the French king was embroiled. With her death there was no longer any reason for the interdiction to remain in force, and Philip Augustus regained his ability to act on his territorial ambitions, using the marriage of John and Isabel as a pretext for taking whatever actions he deemed necessary.

During the spring of 1202, a delegation of Poitevin barons, headed by the Lusignans, filed a complaint with the king of France regarding the actions of John. It should be noted that John himself was taking no steps to reconcile with his restless vassals. To the contrary, he treated them with scorn, violence, and arrogance. Philip seized the opportunity and ran with it. Involved in the same problem was Eleanor, who, we must remember, was John's sovereign, and Philip cited the king of England to appear before his court to answer the accusations lodged against him. Of course, John turned a deaf ear to this summons, and the court, which met in Paris on April 28, declared him a felon and proclaimed that all the feudal relations between John and Philip Augustus were broken. Thus the French king now had full legal right to intervene in the Plantagenet domains. He marshaled his troops and knighted Arthur of Brittany, who solemnly swore homage to him not only for Brittany but also for Anjou, the Maine and Touraine regions, and Poitou.[54]

The war began immediately. Philip Augustus captured a number of sites on the frontier separating Normandy from his kingdom. Drunk on success, he decided to strike a massive blow: He sent Arthur at the head of a troop of elite soldiers, assisted by Hugh de Châtellerault, to capture Poitou. Thus the grandson, at fifteen years of age, set off to attack his eighty-year-old grandmother.

Eleanor learned what was happening while at Fontevrault, where Arthur's preparations at Tours were described to her. She did not feel safe at Fontevrault and did not wish to leave Poitou defenseless, so she decided to go to Poitiers, where she had many supporters and could organize the defense of her domains. Arthur, however, was quicker: his army barred the road beyond Loudun, and Eleanor's only resort was to seek refuge in the fortress of Mirebeau.

Arthur and Hugh de Châtellerault hastened to the town, which fell almost immediately. Yet Eleanor, in the keep, resisted with a handful of men. It was now mid-July, and the queen-duchess managed to send a messenger to John, who was in the Maine region. For once, the king of England wasted no time. He raced to his mother's aid, and on August 1, the very day Arthur decided to assault the fortress, John attacked Mirebeau, freed Eleanor, and gained a number of captives, one of whom was the young duke of Brittany.[55]

It was a close call, and the defeat was a heavy blow against the king of France. It was also the only great victory that could be attributed to John Lackland. The English king had gotten his hands on his rival, who was also his nephew and heir.[56] John gave the captive young

Arthur to one of his entourage, Hubert of Bourgh, ordering him to castrate the young duke and put out his eyes. Instead, Hubert of Bourgh held Arthur prisoner in the tower of Rouen and refrained from obeying his master's malevolent command. As a result, in order to have done with it once and for all, John decided to take matters into his own hands. On April 3, 1203—Holy Thursday—with a sole companion, his right-hand man, William of Briouse, he entered Rouen Tower, took the captive away on a boat, strangled him, and tossed his body into the Seine.[57]

During this time, after a short stay in Chinon, Eleanor had returned to her retirement in Fontevrault. In April of 1203 she received a message from her son in Falaise dated April 16 and containing this mysterious phrase: "Thanks to God, things will now go better for us than this man can tell you." Some might see in these few words a somewhat outrageous allusion to what had taken place in Rouen on April 3. Without a doubt, Arthur's death arranged John's affairs somewhat. First, he rid himself of a rival whose actions had been prompted by the king of France. He had also put an end to the quarrels of succession; he was now the only heir to Henry II.[58] Yet this criminal act cost him all his Continental territories. It was the opportunity of which Philip had been dreaming: after shedding a few crocodile tears on hearing of the fate of the unfortunate Arthur, the French king now engaged his murderer relentlessly and with the same blow also toppled the Plantagenet empire.

It is certain that Eleanor never knew what had happened. Of course, she suspected her son was involved in the death of her grandson—she knew John too well to nurture any illusions—but though she never displayed any sympathy for Arthur, son of Constance, whom she detested, she would never have agreed to a crime such as this. We can criticize Eleanor and Richard the Lion Heart for many actions, but crime is definitely not among them. Truth be told, for a king or a baron, crime was actually quite exceptional in this era. Eleanor died without ever learning the truth, but she heard the prophecies circulating throughout the Anglo-Angevin empire, and these heralded the worst misfortunes, proclaiming that her race was cursed and that never again would a Planta-genet rule.

Meanwhile, the war raged on. John was now in a period of apathy during which he initiated no effort, even when the enemy was at the very gates of his palace. The French flooded across Normandy. Châ-teau Gaillard, built by Richard in 1196 to bar the road to Rouen, fell into French hands on March 6, 1204, and Rouen found itself directly threatened. Eleanor, who witnessed the triumph of the Anglo-Angevin empire under Henry II and Richard, contemplated the disaster from her retirement. It is likely that the grief this caused her advanced the time of her death on March 31 (or April 1; the date is not known exactly), 1204, in the abbey of Fontevrault, where she had decided to spend her final years.

The queen-duchess rests there in eternal sleep next to her husband, Henry II, and her favorite son, Richard the Lion Heart. Dead at the age of eighty-two, this odd woman was queen of France, then queen of England, but always duchess of Aquitaine and countess of Poitou. Two of her sons were kings, one of her grandsons was briefly duke of Brittany, and another, Otto, was emperor of Germany. She was the first wife and mother of a line of kings of England and also of a line of French kings. "The true Melusine, a blend of contradictory natures, is Eleanor of Guyennem," says Michelet. He is not wrong. Through her history, which is rather stormy, and through her singularly rich legend, who can know the true face of Eleanor?

2

ELEANOR'S STRANGE
"DIVORCE"

*O*ne of the most significant events in the life of Eleanor of Aquitaine that had repercussions over the entire political life of Europe during the twelfth century and the beginning of the thirteenth is the "divorce" of Eleanor and Louis VII, king of France. Much has been embellished upon this theme and attempts have been made to come up with different interpretations of events, but each time these efforts have collided head-on with how much is not known. What events actually led to the Council of Beaugency in 1152, in which the marriage of the king of France and the duchess of Aquitaine was annulled for reasons of canonical consanguinity?

From the start we might ask: How could the Church accept the importance and relevance of this consanguinity in 1152 when the pope had formally dismissed it in 1149? In fact, Pope Eugenius III had done all he could to reconcile these two who, even in 1149, were obviously on chilly terms with each other, and he threatened ecclesiastic sanctions against anyone who brandished the motive of kinship to attack the union of Eleanor and Louis. Yet, based on the most authentic testimonies, it seems that Bernard of Clairvaux—the same man who, several years earlier, received Eleanor's complaints about her apparent sterility and gave her consolation, promising her heaven's aid—personally encouraged the king of France to separate from his wife for this reason. What strange comedy led to Bernard's renunciation of his earlier attempt to preserve their marriage and the hasty decision—the Council of Beaugency was a race against the clock—to annul the royal marriage (whose fertility was proved by the birth of two daughters)?

The only possible answer is that there was a very serious reason and motive for dissolving the marriage—but unfortunately, we have absolutely no idea what this serious reason could have been.

Of course, there was the matter of the queen's adultery, but we should remember that we have no proof of Eleanor's assumed amorous adventures. What was said at the time smacks more of gossip than testimony. We might believe in Eleanor's betrayal, especially during her stay at Antioch, but legend has covered these events with a thick fog. Furthermore, any betrayal—including any during the time in Antioch—would have occurred long before 1152. Hadn't the couple since reconciled?

Of course, at the opening of the council, in the queen's absence, the bishop of Langres brought up Eleanor's reprehensible conduct; in his opinion, she was guilty of adultery. Yet in the speech attributed to this bishop there is mention of the relations Eleanor supposedly had with the sultan Saladin, so the *official* accusation of adultery at the Council of Beaugency cannot be taken seriously. The charge was lodged so that it could officially be put to rest; the accusation was part of the charade of this orchestrated court-mandated separation. We should not forget, however, that to declare the queen of France an adulteress would leave a singular stain upon the crown. There are some things that are never completely unveiled in a certain world, even if they are common practice.

Of course, the royal entourage may have been nursing concerns regarding Eleanor's future behavior. Perhaps they were thinking that after a temporary reconciliation the queen would commit new indiscretions that would cause an even greater scandal for the kingdom of France. In any case, what can be seen clearly in this fog is that someone in the court of Louis VII knew something, and it is our task here to determine what was known.

From the beginning, the marriage of Eleanor and Louis had been a political match, but we have proof that the king of France had fallen deeply in love with his young and beautiful wife. Louis VII loved Eleanor passionately; this is beyond question. What started as a political match had turned into a marriage of love, at least for the king. For her part, the queen was not insensitive to the tenderness and the thoughtfulness of her husband, at least up to a certain time, for if she has been recorded as saying "I married a monk, not a man," these words are perhaps not an allusion to the Church's influence over Louis VII but refer instead to his personal manner in their intimate life. Eleanor liked strong and virile men who were also refined and cultivated—and this description certainly did not fit Louis VII. Thus, if there was a cooling off in their conjugal relations, it was due to the queen and not the king.

According to the chroniclers, it was also Eleanor who was the first to bring up the notion of consanguinity when her husband sought to compel her to accompany him to Jerusalem. We might ask if she used this as a simple threat to counter marital will or if she already thought to use it as an argument for separating from the king. We simply do not know—but it is certain that she was extremely well informed on this subject and had sought out this information specifically, so we can accept that at least since the time of the stay in Antioch she had the idea of "divorcing" Louis VII, either to break a marriage that weighed her down or to contract a new union.

Following the couple's reconciliation at Tuculum and the birth of Eleanor's second daughter, the degree of misunderstanding between the king and queen doubtless only intensified. Probably less in love with his wife at this time, Louis VII had begun considering the dangers to which Eleanor exposed his house and also—this was very important at the time—the purity of his lineage.[1] We can assume that Eleanor did nothing to reassure him on this account. To the contrary, everything leads us to believe that the queen had added to her own legend and intentionally placed herself in ambiguous situations in order to supply her husband with motives. It is definitive, despite what some historians with too strong a penchant for writing novels may say, that Eleanor wanted the Council of Beaugency to annul her marriage—and it was clearly an annulment she wanted, for a simple physical separation for reason of adultery, which was one legal solution, would have prevented her from remarrying.

Once the bishop of Langres made his speech for the prosecution against the queen, which highlighted the idea of adultery, the archbishop of Bordeaux took the floor to make an eloquent plea on Eleanor's behalf. He rejected these accusations, which he claimed had no foundation, and put forth the notion of consanguinity. Should this lead us to conclude that the duchess of Aquitaine had prepared the way for her vassal, and all of this was merely a carefully planned mission? It is yet another question that is difficult to answer, but we can determine only that it is highly probable.

We also come to problems when we look at the position adopted by the king of France. Why did he allow his wife to leave without hindrance, and why were no attempts made to retain her Aquitaine and Poitevin domains? We know that until his death, Abbot Suger strongly supported the reconciliation of the king and queen. While Eleanor and he did not always see eye to eye, the queen respected him and the abbot of Saint-Denis permitted no criticism of Eleanor. After all, it was he who instigated their marriage, pulling off the tour de force of bringing all of southwest France into the royal domain. He was prepared to make any compromise with the duchess to ensure that Aquitaine became part of the birthright of the heir to the throne. The trouble was that there was no heir. The two daughters that had been born of this union proved that the queen was not sterile,[2] but in fourteen years of marriage the couple had no sons. It is likely that this situation was a source of concern for the king.

So Louis VII, left without Suger's counsel, pathologically jealous and certainly having good reason to believe in Eleanor's past acts of infidelity, and alarmed at seeing her—infrequently—giving birth to only daughters and no longer able to live with the thought that Eleanor might give birth to someone else's child, gave in to the queen's insistent demands as well as to the urgings of his entourage.

The king's entourage detested Eleanor. To the regulars of the court, the duchess of Aquitaine was a foreigner who possessed poor breeding and a poor reputation. She introduced a soft and sensual note into a land whose mores were reputedly austere, and she was not forgiven for having invited minstrels and singers who preferred instead of virile Crusade songs and exalting chansons de geste, love songs and stories about the fabulous exploits of knights of another world. She was not forgiven her preference for the Occitan tongue and for surrounding herself with those who spoke it, and she sparked indignation for drinking wine and enjoying it.[3] Among the attacks made on Eleanor was the attempted drowning of her dog, under the pretext that the animal had rabies. What's more, rumors ran wild: there can be little doubt that it was partially the French king's entourage that gave birth to all the legends portraying Eleanor as an unscrupulous Messalina adorned with all the vices the East had to give.

This reputation of the queen and the feeling against Eleanor was what gave the king the resolve to separate from her. When, just before the council, he undertook a large royal progress of the southwestern portion of their domain, accompanied by his wife, the couple's personal demeanor revealed nothing. There are a few clues, however, that allow us to state that they had already made their decision. It is significant that the French garrisons and administrators throughout the region were replaced with Aquitanian troops and officials. The king had likely decided to avoid an abrupt rift that would have emphasized the scandal and further complicated matters. By the same token, he had resigned himself to the loss of Aquitaine and its eventual return to Eleanor.

Here we touch on a point of feudal law: Women could easily inherit the succession in the majority of states—including Aquitaine; the situation was not the same in the kingdom of France, however, where women were customarily removed from the line of succession. This barring of women from succession was known as the Salic Law (though incorrectly, for it was not a law, only a widely observed custom).[4] Thus, as the eldest daughter of William X, Eleanor was truly William's legitimate heir (her brother, who died young, would normally have been the successor) and became the titleholder of the duchy. In the same way, later on, Henry Plantagenet legitimately inherited England through his mother, Empress Matilda, daughter of the king of England, who held the throne on the death of Etienne of Blois.

But one difficult question remains: Was the male or female holder of a state such as Aquitaine or Poitou the actual owner of the domains? The answer is complicated by the fact that not all the states dependent on the French crown were originally lands subject to the king of France. For example, Lorraine was a dependency of the Holy Roman Germanic Empire, and Armoricain Brittany, which was never occupied by the Franks, was not a territory ceded by the French king to one of his vassals. In fact, there is a fundamental law in feudal society built upon the basis of the recommendation system established by Charlemagne that says that all land basically belongs to the king or emperor, and he then disposes of it as he sees fit, by entrusting it, temporarily or perpetually, to a baron. In a way, then, the duke or baron was only the renter of a property—at least at the beginning of feudalism. A domain was given as a fief to a trustworthy individual, who exchanged an oath of loyalty—a kind of lease or contract—with its owner. The vassal was only the servant[5] of the lord, the true owner of the holding.

It was only later that the territories ceded by the king or emperor could be automatically transmitted to the heir of the titleholder. Fiefs subsequently became hereditary, whereas the monarchy, theoretically, was not. How did this development occur? By virtue of entrusting his territories to vassals, the king saw his personal domain shrink while the fiefs, especially in the case of various marriages and successions, became immense and much wealthier. The vassals clung to their lands not legally but by force, and if the king wished his moral authority (indeed, the only authority he had left) to be respected, he was forced to accept the situation. This is how the large fiefs of Burgundy, Normandy, Anjou, Poitou, Aquitaine, the earldom of Toulouse, the Languedoc, Auvergne, and Champagne arose in France. The king, the theoretical owner of these states, now possessed as a last resort only the authority of the lord who was responsible, but the situation constrained the king largely to submit to the desires of his vassals.

Louis VII has been criticized for acting foolishly by giving back to Eleanor her domains—but the truth is that he had no other choice according to the customs and circumstances of the time. If, when freeing Eleanor of the chains of marriage, Louis VII had confiscated her states, he would have caused the uprising of all his lesser vassals, meaning the lords of Poitou and Aquitaine, who were already quite unmanageable and undisciplined by nature. Furthermore, doing so would have earned Louis VII the disapproval of most of his other vassals, who would become incensed at the idea that the king could take back fiefs they considered to be their personal property.

The king of France had to take all of this into consideration before making his decision. Meanwhile, Eleanor certainly must have been long aware of the possibility of a confiscation, but for the same reasons that ultimately kept Louis from seizing the domains, she remained unworried. Though he was king of France and prince of Aquitaine (a purely honorific title he received at Poitiers in 1137), Louis VII could not take away her rights. This is why she took the risk of suggesting the annulment of her marriage.

Once both the king and queen were resolved, all that remained was to make the annulment a reality. For the reasons already mentioned, there was no question of admitting adultery. Annulment for reason of consanguinity was a much simpler and much more radical means available and was used by many medieval kings and princes. It was obviously the most hypocritical kind of strategy, for it called for actually perceiving after the fact of marriage the bonds of kinship existing between a husband and wife. Yet this was a time when genealogical trees were always examined carefully before any marriage was formalized.

Nonetheless, it was time to be done with this matter, and the *impedimentum cognationis* was the ideal method because it left no room for discussion: The Church, omnipotent in civil matters, strictly prohibited marriage between individuals united by blood ties. In fact, canon law, of all legislation, conceived the harshest and most extensive ban on marriages contracted in defiance of consanguinity. Barring marriage for reasons of consanguinity is also a sign of a society seeking to be completely exogamic. Of course, dispensations were available, but at the beginning of the Middle Ages, the Church was prone to absolutely forbid such unions. After numerous proposals, the prohibition was finally set as the seventh degree of separation, as figured canonically.

We can obviously raise questions concerning the reasons the Church displayed such firmness in this regard. In the first place, as in all organized societies, the predominant fear was of incest. In addition, it was necessary to react against the widespread Germanic custom that tolerated close marriages. Finally, there was a eugenic motive: it was necessary to safeguard the purity of the human race by eliminating all risk for defects and, in the medieval context, to rein in the disastrous effects that could be observed in the small, rural communities whose people lived in great promiscuity.

It was only later that this prohibition was justified by a higher theoretical principle. Support for the ban was found in the ideas of St. Augustine, which had been widely aired by Pierre Damine during the eleventh century in his treatise *De Gradibus Parentelae*. In addition, Pope Alexander II published a decree promulgating the 1059 decisions of the Council of Rome on degrees of kinship. Marriage was conceived not only to ensure the perpetuation of the human race and as an outlet for sexual instincts (the reason why St. Paul tolerated marriage) but also to develop sentiments of charity and Christian love between human beings through kinship and affinity. According to theologians, such a marriage could produce its full effects only between two individuals who were strangers to each other. Marriage, then, was no longer a private act that involved two people; it had become an institution that was essential to the proper functioning of a civilized, Christian society.

But how were these degrees of kinship to be calculated? They were determined in a way that was different from Roman Law and was inspired by Mosaic Law. The principle was this: The number of degrees was equivalent to the number of generations. When the two individuals were at different degrees from their common root, the farthest degree served as a reference. Therefore, in the simple example of an uncle and his niece, the first is in direct line with one degree of separation, but the second is two degrees from their common ancestor. Canon law thus considered them as kin twice removed.[6] Yet this only increased the possibility for debate concerning the couple's degree of separation.

In the case of Eleanor and Louis VII, it is probable that the prelates and barons of Beaugency did not have a clear-cut view of the degree of kinship between them that constituted the supposed obstacle. They had known for a long time only that one existed: in an 1143 letter to Bishop Etienne de Préneste, Bernard of Clairvaux wrote that the royal couple were kin *tertio consanguinatis gradu,* "almost at the third degree"—Eleanor and Louis VII descended from the French king Robert the Pious at the fifth canonical degree[7] and also, by another branch, from William the Towhead at the sixth degree.[8] In any event, because the consanguinity was confirmed on the faith of oaths sworn by carefully selected witnesses, the nullity of the marriage could only be obvious to everyone.

The procedure was thus set in motion for a common accord between the two parties. Prior to the Council of Latran in 1215, which changed the procedures for annulment—considerably limiting the obstacles and restricting the use of degrees of kinship for proscribing marriages—a marriage that had lasted twenty years or more could not be annulled. The prescribed time had not yet lapsed for Louis and Eleanor. To prove consanguinity before an ecclesiastical tribunal (the one body with the authority to decide such matters), the Council of Troy in Apulia in 1093 determined that all that was required was an examination by witnesses. It was therefore sufficient for relatives, allies, and friends of the couple to simply testify under oath in order for their declarations to be taken as proof. It was not necessary to make any further investigation, which was a great advantage.

The Council of Beaugency met on March 18, 1152. After the accusation of adultery against the queen made by the bishop of Langres and its rejection by the assembly, the theme of consanguinity was presented and witnesses were called to make their declarations. There was not even any discussion. The archbishop of Sens, who presided over the council, declared the marriage null, but because the couple had married in good faith, their two daughters could be considered legitimate. This was all that Eleanor requested.

We might ask another question regarding Eleanor's strange "divorce": Had she and Henry Plantagenet already arranged to marry once she was free? The answer to this would reveal what motivated the personal actions of the duchess of Aquitaine and her personal political views and would shed some light on European politics of the twelfth century, which remains fairly obscure to the twentieth-century observer who might be accustomed to the notion of the modern state and is not familiar with the subtle games of feudal society.

Taking into account the facts (but without being able to come up with proof), it seems that Eleanor and Henry Plantagenet, the duke of Normandy, had arranged to marry. The timing of the celebration of this marriage—less than two months after the Council of Beaugency— was much too rapid to have been decided by the duchess of Aquitaine, who had barely returned to her lands and was the object of the schemes of various covetous lords. After all, Eleanor was much too cautious and shrewd to pledge her fate on a simple whim. Based on what we know of her, she would not have made the decision to remarry without serious motives and deep reasons, both emotionally and politically.

It is surprising, however—if we take the contemporary testimonies at their word—that she had met Henry Plantagenet only once before she married him: when he visited the French court in the company of his father, Geoffrey. In addition, at the time of their meeting, Geoffrey, who in fact died several months later, did not appear to be on the verge of transferring his power to his son. To the contrary, he had many plans for the future, and Henry was merely the faithful subordinate who carried out his father's orders. What, then, are we to think about the discussion he might have had with Eleanor? And what should we think about the rumors that circulated later about an affair Eleanor allegedly had with Geoffrey the Handsome?

We know that during the summer of 1151, Eleanor decided to leave the king of France. In autumn, the attitude of Louis VII toward his spouse became openly disagreeable, and the king increasingly displayed pronounced jealousy.[9] It so happens that Geoffrey and Henry's visit took place this same summer, and the visit of the count of Anjou and his son seems to have either precipitated events or aggravated the royal couple's already shaky situation. Something must have taken place during this visit, but it is quite difficult to know exactly what happened.

We can assume there was some complicity between Geoffrey the Handsome and Eleanor. Geoffrey was an ambitious man, and it is possible that, knowing the problems affecting the royal couple, he somehow approached Eleanor with an eye to later forming a kind of federation between the Aquitaine states and his own. Though we don't know for certain, perhaps he discussed the possibility of a marriage between Eleanor and his son Henry, which would permit all of western France to fall into Plantagenet hands. Such an accord between Eleanor and the count of Anjou might have spawned the rumors of an amorous liaison between them. In addition, because Geoffrey had taken part in the Crusade, Eleanor doubtless knew him well and met him previously on several occasions.

As for Henry, the summer of 1151 was the first time that he and Eleanor met. He was young and handsome, and numerous chroniclers stress the strong impression the Plantagenet heir made on the queen of France.[10] Under these conditions, we might assume that for once politics and love could have been perfectly reconciled.

With no risk of error, we can conclude that Eleanor had made her decision after this summer discussion: she would marry Henry Plantagenet when she was free of the king of France. Everything had been settled at this time—however, this agreement between the Aquitaine heir and the Plantagenets was kept secret, even if some chroniclers make vague allusions to it.[11] In fact, it was essential that the decision take place in complete silence, for if Louis VII had gotten wind of it, he never would have authorized Eleanor's freedom from marriage to him. Testifying that this plan was secret was the stupefaction that gripped the French court at Eleanor's marriage to Henry; Louis VII knew nothing of what was being plotted during the summer of 1151.

The consequences of this marriage between Eleanor and Henry Plantagenet were in fact disastrous for the kingdom of France. It marked the defeat of Suger's centralist policy and the triumph of the feudal lords over royal authority. It would have been tolerable if Eleanor had returned to her lands and married another vassal of the king of France, but it was unacceptable for the duchess of Aquitaine to unite with a lord as powerful as Henry, who, in addition to his Continental holdings, claimed right of succession to the English throne. Such a union meant that the authority of the king of France could never be exercised over England. Louis VII had no say in England, and because English power was already a source of concern for the Capetians, it is easy to imagine that the news of Eleanor and Henry Plantagenet's marriage placed Louis VII in an awkward position. At that moment he must have keenly regretted his consent to the separation that Eleanor requested.

In fact, the "divorce" of Louis VII and Eleanor remained the cause of numerous subsequent events. First, it was a challenge to the king of France and his claimed authority. Second, it was a challenge to France's unity, for after the marriage, certain portions of the kingdom paid fealty to another kingdom rather than to the Capetian realm. Finally, to be considered are the later quarrels between the Capets and the Plantagenets. For better or worse, it was not until the rule of Philip Augustus, who profited from John Lackland's incompetence, that the monarchy succeeded at reducing the influence of the opposing dynasty and thus creating a state of relative peace that lasted throughout the thirteenth century.

The quarrel sprang back to life, however, on the death of the last direct Capet descendant. If at that time the English monarchy could then press the English king's claim to the succession of the French throne through the grandson of Philip the Fair, it was because Isabelle of France was Eleanor incarnate. The first queen brought the Aquitaine domains to the Plantagenets, while the second could bring the entire kingdom of France. Later, Isabeau of Bavaria, who has been the target of much ill will at the hands of French historians, acted consistently with Eleanor's example by carrying a large part of the kingdom of France to one whom she considered its legitimate heir.[12] Of course, Isabeau did not have the same scope as Eleanor of Aquitaine and the circumstances were different, but it could be said that both women exemplified female will using every available means to oppose a legal situation determined solely by men. This is where Eleanor's politics perhaps carried the most weight: she forced acknowledgment that a woman is not only mistress of her own fate but is also mistress of the fate of the land entrusted to her.

In this way, the Council of Beaugency marks an important date not only in twelfth-century Western history but also in the history of the medieval world. Formerly, every time a woman was repudiated or had her marriage annulled, she was compelled to submit to patriarchal law; with the council, for the first time, a woman who was queen of an important kingdom had personally requested the annulment of her marriage—and it was granted to her. This is why the dissolution of the union of Louis VII and Eleanor of Aquitaine, whatever its circumstances and motivations, will always remain a strange "divorce."

It is important to consider that the rupture made official in Beaugency in 1152 was intended and even instigated by the queen of France. Until that time, a queen—outside of a few uncommon individuals such as the Fredegondes and Brunehauts of the Merovingian era—was mainly a breeder or an object of exchange and alliance between princes. Her personality was practically of no account. In 1152, however, one of them lifted her head and claimed the right to rule as she wished. Because of this, we must consider the real power Eleanor held and what her personal politics were in a social and political context that was not favorable to this kind of behavior.

It is first necessary, however, to place the events of Eleanor's life in the social and political context that begat them, that was their common denominator. This context is obviously western European, but in no way can we consider context one of *state* or *nation* as we currently construe these words. Eleanor lived in a western Europe that emerged from the wreckage of the Roman Empire bearing the stamp of Roman Christianity.

In fact, the entire system in force during the twelfth century arose out of Carolingian organizational methods as conceived by Charlemagne and modified by the Treaty of Verdun in 843, which enshrined the definitive division of Europe into autonomous albeit interdependent spheres. At the time, the administration of a modern Europe was moving forward without anyone being able to determine what ultimate direction the political system would take. Of course, there was the Christian empire, particularly visible in the Crusades, but within this empire numerous divisions were emerging that would prompt waking from Charlemagne's great dream of a kind of union.

Charlemagne, the son of Pippin the Short and probably one of the greatest political minds of all time, had acquired through inheritance, force, or diplomacy an immense territory that was as varied as it was extensive, and which, it should be said, was ungovernable. Basically, this territory corresponded to the former Roman Empire, minus England, Brittany, and Spain but with the larger part of Germany. When Charlemagne took the title of emperor in 800, he thereby declared his will to rebuild the Western Empire for his own benefit. The Eastern Empire still survived in Byzantium, and he did not entertain any ideas of attacking what was still a considerable force; yet his failed expedition against Spain shows he had designs on the Mediterranean basin and wished to wrest the entire western Mediterranean from the Muslims. Having suffered defeat against Spain, at least militarily, Charlemagne worked constantly to consolidate the domain he had carved out, and, in its broad lines, the organization he conceived was absolutely brilliant.

Aware that the Church was the large, permanent force that permitted the cohesion of the empire, he formed a close alliance with it—one that his father, Pippin, had already begun. Because the Church was installed according to the administrative criteria of the Roman Empire, it was loath to change this organization. In Rome's former territories, then, the basic cells were the dioceses, which were grouped in provinces or metropolises. The system was all the more convenient because it encompassed, *grosso modo,* the former borders of the barbarian peoples, Gallic and otherwise, who had been integrated into the Empire.[13] So this structure was built upon diocesan configuration, and Charlemagne delegated his powers to a *companion,* a count, whom he named and who was responsible to him for the sound administration of his assigned territory.

To prevent this count from conducting his affairs as an absolute master, however, the emperor made certain he was supervised by the regional bishop. In the same way, the bishop, who was theoretically dependent upon the papacy, was under the count's eyes to avoid any encroachment on temporal power by spiritual authority. Because Charlemagne distrusted both authorities, he had them watched by itinerant ambassadors, the famous lord's envoys *(missi dominici)*. In his opinion, this was the sole means to correctly govern regions that were both far from each other and far from the central authority. Furthermore, to establish justice among his subjects, Charlemagne established bonds of interdependence between the different leaders and property owners of domains, hence the system of recommendation that consisted of establishing a veritable hierarchy inside the empire. In this system, a small landowner was automatically protected by a larger landowner, but in return the small landowner owed clearly defined aid to his protector. The rich landowner was bound in the same manner to one richer than he, then to the count, and so on throughout the hierarchy from bottom to top, where the emperor sat.

There were certain advantages to this system. On the one hand, no one was isolated and true solidarity was established among the members of a single social body. It also allowed for a more objective form of justice, for counts and bishops were closely supervised. On the other hand, this arrangement formed a powerful governmental system that allowed orders from the central authority to flow down the hierarchy without any difficulty in a relatively short time as each level took responsibility for understanding and applying these directives until they reached the bottom of the chain. Theoretically, the administrative problems that excessive centralization could render insoluble were settled in the best interests of regions and men.

Moreover, theoretically, a system like this, which is perfect on paper, could not function unless strict criteria were met: it first required that the counts be individually named by the emperor and that they not be landowners who might be tempted to consider their own interests before those of the community of which they had charge. It so happens that on Charlemagne's death, the counts did become landowners, for in order to ensure their devotion and loyalty, the sovereign found himself obliged to give them lands, as the Merovingians had done until they had completely divested themselves of their domains. Complicating matters further was that the counts considered their charge as hereditary, which led to the establishment of an aristocracy based on land ownership, the sole proof of wealth and power during that era.

The system also required perfect accord between the pope and the emperor. We know that this was far from a reality, however, and that divisions only intensified as the Church became a temporal power that rivaled imperial power. The quarrels between the priesthood and the empire were in large part responsible for the crumbling of Carolingian unity into multiple entities whose purposes and sizes were quite different.

The system finally required that there be only one emperor. Nevertheless, this was not the case during the reign of Louis the Pious, when all three of the sons of Louis claimed the succession, thus necessitating three empires. It was this rivalry among Charlemagne's three grandsons that finally brought down the structure so skillfully built by their grandfather. The 843 Treaty of Verdun enshrined the break-up of Europe, creating in one stroke a Germany and a France, as well as a hybrid territory that would become the coveted prey of its two neighbors. The Germanic Louis held Germany, Charles the Bald took the western part of the Empire, and Lothar took the rest, from the mouth of the Rhine to Italy, with the title of emperor as consolation. This region, Lotharingia, soon fell into the hands of Louis, and his territory then formed the theoretically powerful Holy Roman German Empire.

This dismantling broke the pyramid: each member of this hierarchy started pursuing his own ends. The structures remained, but they functioned in a vacuum rather than on a scale consisting of the whole of Europe. This led to the birth of feudalism, which enshrined the influence of the richest and most powerful counts who could do perfectly

well without a king or emperor and who busied themselves with repro-
ducing this hierarchy in their own domains, making sure they themselves were at the top.[14]

The Holy Empire was definitely the most divided of all the Carolingian domains, because it contained the most ill-matched elements.
The kingdom of Francie (it was not yet France, with all due respect to
history textbooks) retained a semblance of unity for a certain time, but
in fairly short order, with the Carolingian king losing his personal holdings to his vassals, the situation soon became like that which existed
during the time of those called the lazy kings.* This loss of strength
was caused by the fact that the king had become no more than a moral
suzerain, or sovereign or feudal lord. He received sacred anointment at
Reims, inherited from Clovis, which conferred divine status upon him,
but he no longer bore the title of emperor or the rank attached to that
office. If he managed to cling to his authority to some extent, it was by
virtue of his divine nature: he was God's representative, and it was in
this respect that the powerful vassals deigned to give him their respect.
Nevertheless, in this truly paradoxical situation, the king was the least
powerful of all the lords of his realm, and his personal domains barely
extended from Senlis to Orleans. We should also note that he was not
necessarily the master within these domains. This situation could easily be seen with the lord of Montlhéry, who openly defied the king
until Louis VII managed to wrest from the lord the clump of land that
defended the Paris road to the south.[15]

In addition, this monarchy of divine right was quite fragile in the
sense that it was not hereditary but elective. The king was chosen by his
peers as the one most capable and most worthy of representing them.
Certainly, this quickly transformed into the hereditary transmission of
authority, but the status quo was respected until the time of Louis VII
in that the current king until that time always took the precaution of

---

*[From 637–750 the palace mayors took over the true power, and the Merovingian kings of this
time were labeled as the *rois fainéant* (do-nothing, lazy, or sluggard kings). Pippin III, who had
become the sole mayor by this time, declared himself king in 751 and began the Carolingian
dynasty. — *Trans.*]

having his eldest son elected by the barons of the kingdom before holding the coronation at Reims. It was by virtue of this custom that the Capet monarchy, the legal successor of the Carolingian monarchy as a result of the election of Hugh Capet, became a dynasty officially recognized by all.

As the holder of the Holy Empire during the twelfth century, however, the French king could act only if his vassals agreed to follow and assist him. He needed them to wage war, for they provided him with arms and troops, without which he would be able to rely on only his own guard. It was thus important for the king to avoid angering his vassals, largely by recognizing and maintaining the privileges they had acquired over the course of the centuries. The king's position was thus fairly uncomfortable, especially because frequently his vassals might also be vassals of another lord, sometimes even of the emperor, as a result of a lord owning a remote fief. Yet Capetian politics was centered on restoring lost unity by weakening whenever possible the authority of the great lords through manipulation of the clauses of succession and the arranging of advantageous marriages.

This consciousness toward unity is evident in the first Capetian kings and became a rule of conduct under Louis VI, whose chief advisor, Abbot Suger of Saint-Denis, grasped that the royal institution could maintain itself only through a policy of expansion based on the middle class. This is why the kings of France were always at pains to see justice served to the most unfortunate; they were not motivated so much by honesty as by the knowledge that such serving would build a body of constituents that was loyal to them. In fact, the majority of commoners often suffered extortion from their lords, and their final recourse was the king as sovereign judge and keeper of the balance of the kingdom. This policy continued throughout the Middle Ages, when the kings used the bourgeois class to support their attempts to crush the claims of the highest vassals and finally bring them to their will.

In England, the situation was slightly different by virtue of the fact that this island escaped Carolingian domination. First administered in accordance with Saxon methods, England since William the Conqueror

had known Norman law, which had been slowly recast by Saxon legislation. The traditional division on the island was not one of Roman
dioceses but of shires or counties at the head of which could be found
sheriffs. Moreover, these shires were much more Celtic than Saxon in
origin (they can be found in the notion of the *cantrev*, or one hundred
inhabitants, in Wales), and it is not unlikely that the Germanic invad-
ers borrowed certain island customs from the Briton era and used them
for their own benefit. In this merger of Norman and Saxon laws, however, the masters were Normans and thus natives of the Continent, and
their predominance grew over the years until by the twelfth century
England had almost the same feudal system as the Capetian kingdom,
taking into consideration local features and the legacy of the ancient
Saxon heptarchy.[16]

Be that as it may, the Holy Empire, the Capetian kingdom, and
the Anglo-Norman domain were ruled one way or another by an even
more tenacious and arbitrary authority: the papacy. We cannot begin to
understand the external and internal politics of twelfth-century European countries unless we have taken into account the preponderant
influence of the Church. In truth, it was more than preponderance;
it was an absolute supremacy at all times. Europe must be Christian
or nothing. Either directly, through the channel of the ecclesiastical
organization—the only body that was truly permanent and stable—or
indirectly, through diplomatic endeavors, the pope was the sole master
of the game. What's more, he had two formidable means at his disposal
to compel the obedience of the kings and princes: excommunication
and interdict. While certain kings such as Philip Augustus scoffed at
excommunication (certainly because it concerned only the king personally), interdiction was a terribly effective means for compelling a country to follow the papal will. In fact, a kingdom or a county under the
sentence of interdict was stripped of all religious ceremony and sacrament, and the lord responsible for this status could not long hold out
when confronted by a population that banded together against him in
order to obtain a normal religious life.

Charlemagne believed that spiritual authority and temporal power had everything to gain by joining together, each taking care of its own sphere. The possessions of the Church, however, grew unceasingly, and the Church became a veritable state endowed with an incontestable advantage. When it extended its power within the other states, it could take action both internally and externally. Church politics during the Middle Ages therefore comprised a perpetual double game that did not fail to cause quarrels, revolts, and war. Yet instead of devoting itself to the glory of God, the ecclesiastical institution placed more effort on establishing its earthly courts, which enabled it to withdraw huge taxes from its holdings everywhere.

The kings and princes spent their time striving to control this sometimes secret, sometimes declared power, but they were powerless to do anything without it. Furthermore, through a subtle exploitation of circumstances, the Church succeeded in channeling the bellicose energies of the nobility and codifying them. This was the origin of the knighthood that first served as a powerful unit of the Church and then of the princes, who soon formed a formidable caste. In the name of the noblest princes, they appropriated exorbitant rights and practiced a kind of blackmail among the kings whom they served as the core army.

Within the feudal system, this knighthood was often used by the Church to sow alarm by instigating outbreaks among rebellious fiefs— but because the knights were armed and could be formidable, they were used warily. At the time when the Church felt no longer capable of containing the knighthood, it invented the Crusades against the Muslims in order to send away the most quarrelsome knights and empty their lands of these warriors' lively forces. Likewise, the princes, enthralled by such a windfall, were also playing the Crusades card without realizing that they were thereby weakening the domains they were supposed to protect. The knight caste then returned from the Crusades stronger and richer than before, better organized—and increasingly marginalized. When we study the unfolding of the twelfth century, we must take into consideration the presence of these knights, for they formed the pivot around which the society revolved. Consecrated by the Church, used by the princes, earning their pay through right of pillage and conquest, the knight caste was the true master of power during the twelfth century—and Eleanor of Aquitaine knew this, for she contributed to coupling the oath of feudal fealty the knight took with the oath of loyalty to his lady. She realized that she could accomplish nothing unless she attached herself to this social caste.

We have learned that Eleanor seemed perfectly at ease in this political and social context. Ever since her youth she had the feeling of belonging to a privileged class to which all was permitted, she was heiress to an earldom and a duchy, and there was no Salic Law that could prevent her from assuming the responsibilities that birth and rank conferred upon her. She was the veritable embodiment of Aquitaine and Poitou, which at this time were the richest regions of the Continent. We can safely say that during her marriage to Louis VII, Eleanor carried consequential weight, which explains why she has always been regarded differently and why the political role that she could play was so significant.

It can also be cause for surprise that the royal authority—not only the king, who was undoubtedly in love with her, but the entire council—always displayed deep respect for the queen, although, as we know from numerous testimonies, she was considered to be a troublemaker. In fact, they needed her because she alone represented legitimacy in her states. It was necessary to go through her to earn the loyalty of the vassals and any of those once removed of Aquitaine and Poitou. If Eleanor had not been heeded, there is no doubt that her vassals, who were traditionally restless and looked with little favor on centralized authority, would simply have taken back their freedom to act. As it was, some of them who were fairly appalled at seeing themselves so definitively attached to the French crown did indeed revolt, and Eleanor asked Louis to intervene militarily to bring them back to the proper feudal path. From the beginning, the young duchess was not liberal, nor did she wish to sacrifice her prerogatives—and in so doing she was simply following the example set by her father and her grandfather William the Troubadour.

It is quite certain that during the marriage and subsequent "divorce" of Eleanor and Louis VII, the heiress of Aquitaine was never considered merely the bride of a king but rather as a queen, a completely separate sovereign. In acquiring her as queen, it was as if the kingdom of France had married the duchy of Aquitaine.[17] When a higher (thus ecclesiastical) decision annulled her union with the king, it was expected that Eleanor should go back to what she was before.

Thus it was not only her person and her domain that Eleanor brought to the court of France but also her considerable weight first because of the prosperity of the immense territory that covers almost one-fourth of modern France. This prosperity included agricultural riches (both wines and grains), wealth from all kinds of crafts, commercial riches, and especially maritime riches that stemmed from the ports of Bordeaux and La Rochelle. Her weight also consisted of men—the great lords of Chateauroux and Issoudun, in the Limousin, those whom the Capet king needed most. In Poitou were Eleanor's direct vassals: the viscount of Thouars and the lords of Lusignan and Châtellerault were all important figures themselves with numerous vassals. Likewise, the lords of Chateauroux and Issoudun hailed from the Berry region; in the Limousin there were those of Turenne and Ventadorn; in Gascony there were those of Fézensac and Armagnac; and there were the counts of Limoges, Perigord, Angoulême, the Marche, and Auvergne, all of whom were important to have in the king's or anyone's camp against any potential enemy.

There is no surprise, then, that at the beginning of their marriage, Eleanor had a profound influence on the politics of the young king. His childhood had not prepared him at all for these high duties, and his tastes were instead those of a contemplative and a clerk. Confronted with the hard realities of power, Louis VII never displayed himself as his father's equal. Of course, he was full of good will and aware of his mission. Of course, he still had Suger, his father's wise counselor, the one who had somehow instigated the Aquitaine marriage and arranged its tiniest details. Nevertheless, it seems clear that Eleanor instinctively distrusted the abbot of Saint-Denis, whom she considered overly representative of the northern French spirit, which was the opposite of the system of Occitan thought that she incarnated so magnificently.

Suger soon had little influence over Louis VII after his accession to the throne, for the young king was in love with the beautiful Eleanor, and under her spell he sought to satisfy her every whim. Similarly, there was a rift between Eleanor and the queen mother Adelaide of Savoy. The widow of Louis VI, who had scarcely been heeded by her husband, had decided to start a new life after the death of the king. She had wed a member of the minor nobility, the lord of Montmorency, and lived far from the court and took little interest in what was decided there.

Thus stripped of the advice of both his mother and Suger, Louis VII was left to his own inspiration and all the charms of Eleanor. As we know, she instigated quite a revolution in the palace as far as everyday lifestyles are concerned. These, however, were obviously not serious matters, and it is likely that the king took little offense to his wife's influence on them, at least as long as he entertained no doubts as to Eleanor's fidelity.

As king, one of the first decisions he was forced to make regarded leading an expedition against the inhabitants of Poitiers, who intended to form their own local authority. Eleanor was outraged at this intention. She considered Poitiers her capital and personal domain, and thus she could not tolerate the thought of its city escaping her authority. She begged her husband to bring the straying sheep back to the fold. Consequently, Louis organized his expedition, which took place in the best possible conditions, and, without spilling a drop of blood, he captured Poitiers and demanded the immediate dissolution of the local government and the delivery of hostages that were the young sons and daughters of the most important bourgeois residents of the city. The people of Poitiers resented this, but, oddly enough, they did not vent their spleen on Eleanor. After all, wasn't the king responsible?

This event demonstrates that at the beginning of her career, Eleanor was not very open to the innovations of the century. In most regions, the tendency of rulers was to grant communal charters, but she revealed herself to be resolutely reactionary. As we will see, however, that changed over the course of time. At the time of the Poitiers incident, though, she was not yet aware of the real power represented by the bourgeoisie. In this era, wealth was beginning to change hands;

the large landed domains earned less and less for their owners, and commerce and craft, the prerogative of the bourgeoisie in the cities, were forming what would later be called the beginnings of capitalism. In addition, Eleanor was reared in the strictest aristocratic principles and convinced there was nothing of worth outside the nobility—she assumed the principles of the knights as they appeared in the courtly literature of the era.

Though Poitiers ended well for the king, Eleanor also dragged her husband into expeditions with less happy endings. He managed as best he could to bring back to reason Guillaume de Lezay, who was guilty of refusing to pay homage and, more important, of having stolen gyrfalcons from the dukes of Aquitaine in their hunting reserve of Talmoud. Most significant, however, was the Toulouse affair.

The new queen of France, who never lost sight of the fact that she was first and foremost the duchess of Aquitaine, had claims on the earldom of Toulouse, one of the richest domains in all Occitania. She claimed the succession by virtue of her grandmother Phillipa, wife of William the Troubadour, whom he had repudiated. In his expedition in Toulouse, however, the king ran into stiff resistance put up by the nobility and bourgeoisie, and the incident was a complete failure for him. Eleanor was somewhat mortified, but as a thank-you gift to her royal spouse upon his return, she was said to have given him a gift: a magnificent carved crystal vessel mounted on a gold foot and adorned with a carved band set with pearls and precious stones.[18]

It was Eleanor's influence that also triggered the war of Champagne. In supporting it, Eleanor was in fact supporting the marriage of her younger sister, Petronella, and Raoul de Vermandois, who was already married to the niece of the count of Champagne. As we know, this war ended tragically with the burning of a church in Vitry-le-François and the loss of many innocent lives. This loss inspired great remorse on the king's part and contributed to his departure for the Crusades, and the events of the end of the war marked the end of Eleanor's influence on French political life.

In fact, Louis VII was deeply scarred by the tragedy of Vitry and was at odds with the papacy on several matters. As a result, threatened with excommunication, he began reflecting on the consequences of the actions he took to please his wife. Taking advantage of the celebrations on June 11, 1144, to inaugurate the choir in the abbey of Saint-Denis, he turned to Suger for help. Suger immediately took charge of concluding a peace between Thibaud, count of Champagne, and the king and subsequently, it appears, reassumed for the king all the importance he once held.

As Suger ascended, Eleanor found herself removed from any real power—and it is probable this inspired some resentment. It was at this time, upon seeing Louis placing more stock in the counsel of Suger and Bernard of Clairvaux, that she allegedly declared, "I married a monk." Certainly, it was quite painful to her to see herself relegated to the simple rank of wife—which was one of the motivating factors that likely led her to ask for a "divorce." The authoritarian temperament of the duchess of Aquitaine was ill suited for participating in politics solely as an official in ceremonies.

In truth, she had grander designs, and Eleanor sincerely believed that Henry Plantagenet could allow her to achieve them. In fact, for eighteen years, from the time of her remarriage in 1152 until she retired to Poitiers in 1170, Eleanor worked closely with Henry in the governing of the Plantagenet empire. Not satisfied with merely appearing at the king's side, she replaced him whenever needed, and she had the opportunity to publicly display her intentions and desires. These eighteen years were as much Eleanor's reign as Henry's, and there can be no doubt that the deepest hopes of the former queen of France were realized when she found that her personality was recognized and her voice was heard.

If Eleanor was therefore a true sovereign almost equal to her royal spouse, she certainly paid for this perception in the physical toll it demanded. In this era, a person could be a king or prince only if he was capable of riding for days and nights on horseback through his domains to render justice, to settle quarrels, and to lead troops into combat. In fact, because people felt this work was hardly feminine, a king was preferred to a queen. As Henry's equal, Eleanor was always on the move—even more than would be usual because of the immensity of Plantagenet territory, which stretched from the Pyrenees to the Scottish frontier. It is certain that she did not take part in any battles, but it is incontestable that she was always present wherever the higher authority she represented needed to be. This only added to her legend: not only was she beautiful and intelligent, but she was also as quick and active as a man and as tireless as the formidable King Henry.

The boundless ambition that consumed her and that fit so well with Henry's own desire for power formed a powerful engine for her tireless activity. For example, she had not given up her idea of ruling the earldom of Toulouse. She insisted on it so long and so tirelessly that Henry made an appeal to all barons to send troops to Toulouse and compel Count Raymond V to acknowledge the duchess of Aquitaine as sovereign. It was also in Toulouse, in 1159, that the king of England began resorting to the systematic use of mercenaries. He could thus meet any eventuality without relying on his vassals, who were bound to provide only forty days of armed service per year and could well leave him in the middle of a campaign.

In the Toulouse affair, Henry received the support of the count of Barcelona, who was on chilly terms with the count of Toulouse. Henry surrounded the city and set siege to it, but shortly thereafter he abandoned pursuit of his plan, dispersed his army, and returned to his domains. What happened? The question has been fuel for debate. Militarily, Henry could have prevailed quite easily. The obstacle was inside the city of Toulouse itself in the person of the king of France, Louis VII. The French king had little liking for Raymond V, who was capable of committing many violent acts, but he nevertheless decided to protect his vassal. Doing so would prevent Plantagenet encroachment on the Mediterranean route (which was evidently Eleanor's plan) and would solemnly assert the feudal law that every vassal deserved his sovereign's protection, and it was a felony to launch such an attack against a vassal (for even if the vassal owned his fief this was still an attack against the king himself).

Henry realized that this situation would grow only worse if he persisted to push his plan forward. Certainly, the sight of the duke of Normandy capturing and holding prisoner his own suzerain could have only a poor effect. By flouting the most elementary feudal laws, Henry risked turning not only all of Europe against him but also his own vassals, who would be alarmed at the sight of their lord's treatment of their sacred rights. The Toulouse campaign was thus a failure, especially for Eleanor, who once more saw reduced to nothing her hopes of ruling the earldom.

Yet Eleanor and Henry had a long-range plan that could be achieved more easily and would thus fill the former French queen with joy: the unification of the kingdom of France and the kingdom of England, to the benefit of the Plantagenets, of course. The plan was simple, at least in appearance. Louis VII had only one child—Marguerite—from his marriage with Constance of Castile, and Thomas Becket, Henry's chancellor, had obtained the French king's consent for Marguerite to marry Henry the young king, the Plantagenet heir. A dowry had even been provided: the Norman Vexin region, a source of constant strife between France and Normandy. Now if Louis VII had no male heir, which looked increasingly likely, what would become of the French crown? Eleanor had given the matter some thought, and her most cherished dream was seeing her eldest son recover a throne that she had voluntarily abandoned. In fact, there were two major obstacles to Eleanor's plan: the so-called Salic Law and the presence of the two elder daughters of Louis VII and Eleanor, Marie and Alix. Yet Eleanor still had enough influence over her daughters to convince them to renounce their potential rights.

It is very likely that if Henry Plantagenet had abandoned the siege of Toulouse, he did so to avoid upsetting Louis VII and thus Louis's refusal to permit the planned marriage, whose consequences were much more important than sovereignty over the earldom of Toulouse. France, however, was not yet without an heir. Louis VII lost his second wife during the birth of their second daughter, and several weeks later he married a third time, this time to Adele of Champagne. This marriage was a blow to Henry and Eleanor, who thus saw the increased influence of the House of Blois-Champagne around the king of France and the possibility for Louis VII to have a son. Nevertheless, they celebrated the marriage of Henry the young king and Marguerite of France in Rouen in 1160. The new groom was five years old and his bride was only two—and Henry recovered the Vexin without Louis VII being able to put up the slightest resistance. We know, however, that these gains were made fruitless by ensuing events: in 1165, a male heir, the future Philip Augustus, was born to Louis VII, while Henry the young king died prematurely. Eleanor's dream vanished once and for all.

These were obviously failures. But Eleanor's political strategy was varied—which we can see in 1165, when she began detaching herself from her husband. Once she realized Henry II was betraying her after she had supported all his claims (because he supported hers), she started playing her own game. It first looked like a kind of retreat, a kind of turning inward: Instead of concerning herself with the kingdom's major affairs, she was content to restrict her focus to the internal organization of her own states. She went from queen of England to a completely independent duchess of Aquitaine and countess of Poitou and personally handled the various problems of Aquitaine economic life. In fact, at this time Aquitaine became richer and increasingly modern, and commerce with England flourished. Everything now needed to be codified, primarily to satisfy the needs of those who were the true keepers of the money and its power—the bourgeoisie.

It was during this time that Eleanor made her liberal "conversion" and granted charters and franchises to those she had considered as mere submissive subjects just a few years earlier. This conversion earned her more popularity, and all the people of Aquitaine and Poitou were prepared to serve her loyally. This is why, at least initially, Henry II displayed such tolerance toward his wife, whom he knew for a fact to be responsible for several rebellions of his vassals and even the rebellion of his own sons. He knew that to strike Eleanor too directly was to attack a formidable force, and in deciding later to imprison the queen, he did so with great pains never to strip her of her domains.

Because maritime commerce was the most important, Eleanor

became increasingly interested in all matters affecting sailors, and it is claimed that she had frequent contact with them in order to learn their needs and desires. Under her direct inspiration, there was written a maritime code of forty-seven articles, Rôles d'Oléron. Together they reveal that she wished to foresee the most difficult as well as the most common situations affecting the lives of sailors and that she very clearly intended to strike a balance between overly authoritarian customs and protecting the individual from abuses of arbitrary authority.

Several articles in the code regulate the food of sailors, the captain, and the fleet owners. There are even specifications we might find surprising: "Sailors of the Breton coast should have but one cuisine (meaning a meal) a day by reason of the fact they have wine on both legs of the journey. Those of Normandy should have two, because they drink naught but water on the outward journey. When they are in a wine region, the master should provide it to them." Other articles anticipate the treatment sailors should receive in the event of injury or illness and the conditions under which every patient should be taken to shore and entrusted to the people who will care for him. There is also emphasis on the freedom that must be observed with respect to the conclusion of contracts, with an assertion that any proof of fraud is just cause for the cancellation of a contract. The captain of a ship was expected to behave like a father: his colleagues were his companions, and he shared their responsibilities. Not a man among the sailors could be struck by the captain more than once: "If the master strikes him twice, the sailor can defend himself." Also noted, though, is the respect due the ship's master, for if a sailor strikes the captain, "he will pay 100 sous or lose his fist, at his choice." While this punishment may appear harsh, it was customary at a time when an inferior could not defy the authority of those above him. The captain, however, was not absolute master inasmuch as he was forbidden to scorn the advice of his men. In several circumstances, namely going to sea in bad weather, he was obliged to ask his crew's advice before deciding to set sail.

Pilots also had special rights and duties. In the case of proven abuse of authority or incompetence, the sailors could even behead them with impunity, and it is certain that this clause gave candidates for pilot cause for serious reflection and inspired them to act quite cautiously. It should be said that it was not unheard of for pilots to have ties to shipwreck pillagers; indeed, they would often arrange to wreck their boats off shores that had been agreed on beforehand. The Rôles d'Oléron also set the conditions for the recovery of flotsam from wrecks and also addressed the thorny issues of sailor salaries, fishing rights, the inscription of names on anchors (which would become the ship's registration), and the repayment for damage incurred by vessels. The last article of the code specified that none of these arrangements would apply to any pirate vessel. This code illustrates how strongly Eleanor tried to ensure that everything went well in her kingdoms.

In addition, as she became more understanding of the bourgeoisie, she granted charters. One of these, which clearly bears her imprint, is known as the Établissements de Rouen, but it is likely that a charter was first granted to the inhabitants of La Rochelle, a city her father had created from nothing and which in several years, due to the activity of its port, had become the most important commercial center serving Poitou.[19]

We can see in the text of this charter—first written in Latin, then translated into the common tongue—that the word *commune,* which Eleanor formerly reviled and detested, has obtained, if we may put it this way, the right to be cited. According to this text, the commune is simultaneously the association of the bourgeoisie, the armed militia, and the entire city. The citizens elected one hundred peers, who in turn elected twenty-four jurors—twelve deputy mayors and twelve counselors.

The deputies were supposed to meet twice a week and could not leave—mainly, they could not go to England—without the express permission of their colleagues. This assembly of deputy mayors was thus both the administrative council and the court of first hearing of the city, and in public session it was required to sit in judgment on possible rebellions, insults, and civil affairs. The jurors swore an oath to judge in accordance with their conscience and to keep their deliberations secret. They also swore to refuse to receive all litigants, or to accept any gifts or goods, failure of which would exclude them from all public office and would result in their houses being razed. Any accused who tried to solicit a judge would have his punishment doubled. It is easy to see that the Établissements de Rouen were highly advanced for their time and showed a sincere desire for objective and equal justice for all.

At the time, more serious matters, particularly crimes, were reserved for the usual royal tribunals (bailiffs, viscounts, provosts), but all matters that infringed upon the sacraments—for example, adultery—were a matter for ecclesiastical tribunals. Nevertheless, all municipal justice was suspended during the time that the king or his son was present in the city. Each year the peers would choose three candidates from whom the king would name the *major,* or "mayor." He could be reelected but he had to swear to refrain from any scheming in order to remain in office. The mayor represented the city before the royal tribunals, presided over municipal administration and justice, collected revenues from the cities in the commune, ordered seizures, led the commune to war and could exempt individuals from military service for serious reasons, and held the power to summon before him on the day and time of his choosing any citizen he wished to question. His power was thus extensive, but if he violated communal regulations his fine was twice as high as that of the other magistrates.

It can be seen that based on this system, the bourgeoisie were protected from any arbitrary abuse of authority, even that of knights and men of the Church, who, when they did not pay their due, were specifically placed in quarantine, even if they were members of the privileged classes. The commune personally defended the interests of its members before the provosts and bailiffs who showed a constant tendency to exceed their rights. Eleanor's charter was therefore an extremely liberal document for the era, and we cannot find its equivalent in either the charters granted in France by Louis VII or those granted in England by Henry II.

It must be assumed, then, that Eleanor—who, we must remember, was surrounded by clerks, scholars, and men of law as well as artists and poets—took great pains in her maturity to reconcile with the bourgeois class of the cities under her dominion. This was obviously a political calculation. Colliding ever more frequently with problems generated by her quarrels with her husband, the queen felt the need to procure allies. She knew she could not place too much reliance on her unruly vassals, whom she had seen at work constantly tearing each other to pieces. She realized that the new power belonged to a class that had only recently emerged from the people, and she decided to benefit from it. This reconciliation, however, did not prevent her from being the most aristocratic of the ladies of her era.

Yet if she granted these charters, even in King Henry's name, it is because it was possible for her to do so. During her marriage, then, Eleanor held real power with the king of England that was fairly extensive and could not be compared to the power she had enjoyed at the French court. She was not only the woman who used pillow talk to fill the king's ears with her inspirations but also the woman who made decisions herself and let her husband deal with them as accomplished facts. This, in any case, is what emerges from the chronicles of the time.

In encouraging her sons to rebel against their father, she clearly showed that she was not a woman to let things slide. The political game at the time may have been dictated by feminine vengeance: as a lover deceived by Henry, as a wife scorned by a king with no great scruples, she decided to take her revenge where it would most hurt Henry the Plantagenet—in his bonds with his own children. In doing so she also hoped to recover all her prestige.

In these years she truly became the countess of Poitou. She made Poitiers the rendezvous of the intelligentsia of the time, and, despite her advancing age, she was still beautiful. Aware of the weight she represented, she first arranged the placement of all her pawns on the chessboard. If her sons were impatient to share their father's power, she would profit from it, for truthfully, the only one she loved with a mother's deep love was the son whose sensibility most agreed with her own, Richard, the poet knight. Because Henry was the eldest, however, it was his job to collect his birthright. Eleanor urged him to demand more and more of his powers because she knew that she would stand in the background and inspire her son's actions.

We know what happened. Henry II did not allow himself to be easily deposed and reacted vigorously. Thus began the long period of Eleanor's imprisonment in various castles and fortresses. At this time, she was nothing politically, but she did remain the ruling queen and the lady in the eyes of all her subjects in Aquitaine, Poitou, and also Normandy (for, oddly enough, this duchy over which she had no right in principle nevertheless always remained loyal to her). We could even say that her legend grew stronger during this period, as did her moral authority. She was seen as a victim of the tyranny of Henry II, for whom his Continental subjects had little liking but supported because they could not do otherwise.

With Henry's death and Richard's rise to the throne, Eleanor had her revenge, and it was a true triumph. On hearing the news of her husband's death, she made an incredible progress throughout the Plantagenet empire, stopping at every castle and city where she was welcomed, like the true holder of the crown. She labored everywhere with an eye to assuring Richard the greatest consensus. She abolished the dictatorial measures Henry II had enacted everywhere, for during his waning years he maintained his kingdom's unity only by brute force. She freed prisoners and lightened the regulations in force: Henceforth, a person would not risk hanging for simple poaching, as was the case right before Henry's death. She even found the means to resolve an economic difficulty that was specific to England by unifying the measures used to weigh grains and liquids. Without exaggeration we might say that for this period preceding the coronation of Richard—from July to September 1189—Eleanor was a veritable sovereign in her own right. And she was sixty-seven years old.

When Richard left for the Crusades, she played this role yet again, and did so again when he was held prisoner in Germany, when it was she who organized the collection of the king's ransom, and it was she who foiled the attempts of John Lackland who, with the help of the king of France, sought to steal the throne. Again, it was she who, during this span of time, displayed her skills as a diplomat by seeking alliances wherever she could and concluding advantageous marriages for family members. We cannot help but acknowledge the extraordinary activity and intelligence of this septuagenarian woman to whom all Europe paid heed and who won the respect of all her vassals.

We know that the death of Richard, her son *carissimus,* as she referred to him in official writs, dealt her a dreadful blow—but she did not use it as an excuse to give up. Quite the contrary, deeming her grandson Arthur too closely allied to Philip Augustus, she put all her talents to work to ensure that John kept the Plantagenet domains intact. Yes, she knew her son was violent and half mad, but necessity required that unity of the kingdom be preserved. It was necessary for all the vassals to recognize John Lackland as the official heir of Henry II. During this time, she undertook another progress throughout the entire country to gain the trust of some and allay the reservations of others. To retain the loyalty of the bourgeoisie in John's name, she increased the number of charters granted the towns and cities. Further, when John was crowned—that is, when he was accepted by all, for better or for worse—she did not interrupt her supervision, rather maintaining it until her death.

The amount of work she performed as queen of England, especially during the second half of her life, is thus immense, which raises an interesting question: If she had remained queen of France, would she have accomplished so much?

Of course, we cannot rewrite history, but the answer is no. In the French Capetian context—one that was patriarchal and, some may say, paternalistic—never would so much power and moral authority have been allowed to fall into the hands of a woman, especially for such a long period of time. The king of France, Charlemagne's heir and thus heir of the Roman emperors, was the father of the people, both a protector and a guide. His role was truly that of an *imperator*, and his military aspect was more important than his civil aspect in a feudal climate in which power resided wherever it found strength. In this culture, women were not eligible to inherit, which automatically kept them out of the royal succession and in a state of almost total dependency.

This rule, however, was not in effect in the grand fiefs or in England.

Eleanor was in full right the titular heir of Aquitaine and Poitou—and no one dared gainsay it. Meanwhile, Henry II was king of England because the title came to him through his mother, Empress Matilda.[20] Therefore, a woman could embody sovereignty and exercise it when no direct male heir was available. The context was completely different from that of France.

In the final analysis, this difference comes not only from established and respected custom but also from opposing philosophical judgments. In the Capetian system, in which the king is viewed as the representative of God charged with leading a people, we find the integral concept of the Latin *rex,* which evolved into imperator. He is a leader who may not have been chosen necessarily but who is obeyed unreservedly, because what is most needed is a leader capable of defending his people and of attacking others. This leader is an individual apart: he is not part of the community, because his strength resides primarily in his specificity. This quickly leads to the notion of absolute monarchy as it occurred under Louis XIV, the notion that the king who makes and unmakes laws is not required to observe them himself, for in the final analysis, he is answerable only to God. In fact, this is the definition for *despot* that Montesquieu later provides.

The Anglo-Angevin concept, however, is completely different. It was inherited from Norman law, Celtic law, Saxon law, and Occitan customs. Of course, in practice, Plantagenets often behaved like veritable despots, but the forms were maintained and royal power was ever subject to the evaluation of its vassals, as is seen during the reign of John Lackland, whose throne was taken from him by his barons and was returned only when he agreed to the rules of the Magna Carta in 1212. There is a very significant article in the Magna Carta, the ancestor of modern constitutions, which reads: "There are laws of the state, laws belonging to the community. The king should respect them. If he violates them, loyalty ceases to be a duty and his subjects have the right to rebel."

The principle here is that sovereignty belongs solely to the community, which can entrust it to a king. While this constitutes the only theoretical difference with Jean-Jacques Rousseau's concept in *The*

Social Contract, in both cases, this sovereignty of the collective remains inalienable: In the medieval version it is entrusted to an individual, whereas Rousseau solemnly rejects all representation. The medieval sovereign represents the group, and even embodies it, but he is not its absolute master or owner. While the Capetian king increasingly exhibited the tendency to set himself up as Higher Law, the Anglo-Angevin king, in greater conformance with early Christian thought, was only the servant of Higher Law, which itself resulted from a covenant between God and the bulk of his subjects. This would soon inspire the Thomist theorem by which all power comes from God through the intermediary of the people *(a Deo per populum).* It is not by chance that the ecclesiastical philosopher John of Salisbury wrote his major political work, the *Policratus,*[21] in the sphere of influence of the Anglo-Angevin dynasty. The work states (in IV, 7): "The prince is the servant of the Lord, but he fulfils his duty by faithfully serving his *camarades serviteurs** (of God and the Law), otherwise known as his subjects."

What we have, then, in the entirely feudal western Europe of the twelfth century are two political trends that, while barely visible to the contemporary observer, nevertheless strengthened over the course of the centuries. On one side is the centralist Roman current represented by the Holy Empire and the Capet dynasty, and the other is the current that could be labeled Germano-Celtic, represented by the Anglo-Angevin monarchy. There was very good reason for Eleanor's decision to break her union with the Capet king to marry the Angevin monarch: her personal tastes, ambition, and political awareness were all better served in the Anglo-Angevin context. There she could play a dual role: on the practical plane, it gave her the elbow room she needed to influence the march of events, and on the theoretical plane, it allowed her to symbolically represent this sovereignty as the incarnation of the group. Who better than a queen, haloed with great prestige, heiress of vast domains, arbiter of styles, mistress of arts and letters, and finally mother of a large family, would have embodied this group? She offered

---

*["Comrade servants." —*Trans.*]

her people the reassuring image of a mother making sure each of her children received what he rightfully had coming to him.

Eleanor's "divorce" was accepted by Louis VII because he had no other choice and because he hoped that the young woman would be satisfied with a remarriage based on love. It is true she made a love match the second time, but that was not all it was. It was only after much careful thought that the young queen of France took the path that would lead her to become an old queen of England.

3

QUEEN OF THE TROUBADOURS

What is true of heroes of legend is also true for those of history: once tradition takes possession of them, they are no longer their own people. Yet a tradition surrounding a historical figure cannot exist unless that figure enters the framework of what is most often a preexisting myth. Eleanor's legend shows that she corresponded to what she was expected to be; starting at this moment, epic and history were no more than a single reality with two faces.

Further, while Eleanor's political conduct fulfilled the context reserved for her, through her activity and, to a lesser extent, through the influence she wielded over writers of the time, she did much more in the arena of arts and letters. Far from inferior to what she held politically, this influence remains her most important contribution for all time. The woman who was queen by turns of both France and England and who was always duchess of Aquitaine and countess of Poitou channeled around her a remarkable range of intellectual energies.

This role as literary influence was one the first wife of Louis VII had already played in the French court. There she invited Occitan troubadours, which allowed fruitful exchanges between writers of different tongues and civilizations and consequently paved the way for the creation of an authentically French literature. Thus, the langue d'oïl of twelfth-century France would never have been so brilliant without Eleanor's direct contribution. It is perhaps, however, through a more subtle action that her influence expanded both during her lifetime and after her death. Because of her beauty, charm, and legendary aura, for example, she certainly inspired the writers who took her as model for their heroines.

On analysis, a chanson de geste such as the *Pilgrimage of Charlemagne* refers to a possible quarrel between the king and the queen, which is followed by the king's departure for the Crusades. In the chanson, Charlemagne quite presumptuously asks his queen: "Lady, have you ever seen under heaven a king who bears the sword and crown so well as I?" The emperor expects his wife to confirm his words, but she thoughtlessly responds that there is another king who wears the crown with greater ease. Charlemagne flies into a rage; he wants to know who this king is, for he wishes to go to him immediately in order to learn whether his wife is right. "We will bear the crown together to this leader and your counselors and friends will sit before you. I will summon my court of good knights. If the French share your opinion, I will accept it. But if you have lied, you shall pay dearly; I shall cut off your head with my sword of steel!" The queen is obliged to tell him that the king she has in mind is Hugh the Strong, king of Constantinople. At this revelation, Charlemagne decides to go on a pilgrimage to Jerusalem and determines to stop in Constantinople on the way.

The twelfth-century allusions are obvious. The text of this chanson de geste symbolically translates the queen's detached attitude toward Louis VII and the scorn she felt for his "monklike" behavior and timidity. The king of Constantinople is the twelfth-century Manuel Commenius, and an analogy can also be found with the legendary episode of Eleanor's love for Saladin. Because the *Pilgrimage of Charlemagne* was written at the time of the Crusade of Louis VII, it is not unlikely that the author used the queen of France as the model for Charlemagne's wife. This text is not the sole example of this modeling in the chansons de geste. In these tales contemporary events always peek through their pretext of the Carolingian world.

What's more, the *Pilgrimage of Charlemagne* is not a true chanson de geste. Rather, its marvelous or fantastic episodes make it more a courtly romance or at least a satirical adaptation of the ancient Carolingian epic for a more refined audience that had a keen hunger for enthusiastic descriptions of the East, however much these descriptions departed from reality. As stated by Rita Lejeune in her *Étude sur le role littéraire d'Aliénor d'Aquitaine* [Study of Eleanor of Aquitaine's Literary Role], "the epic is revised, corrected, and urbanized for women—and especially for one woman, Eleanor, whose cast of mind impressed itself on an entire society." Thus, there is good reason to claim that not only did Eleanor unintentionally serve as a model for writers but also that she inspired a new literary style that expressed ideas and feelings. Her role was considerable—and more so because she held sway at the French court, where everyone sought to please a queen who was open to criticism on many points but who was nevertheless worthy of admiration and enthusiasm.

Another chanson de geste, this one part of the cycle of Garin de Montglane rather than a chanson of the King cycle, also signifies the role Eleanor played in the fabrication of the female characters of the declining Carolingian era. The Anglo-Norman version of the *Chanson de Guillaume* dates from around 1160, and its principal episodes were later borrowed for the *Chanson d'Aliscans*. The central figure is William of Orange, a kind of Herculean hero who seems to have emerged from the most remote Celtic mythology. He can be seen as an equivalent of the Irish god Dagda, famous for his strength and gluttony. He is a Gargantua before the fact, and once we know that the Gargantua of Rabelais is a character of folklore inherited from Celtic tradition, we cannot help but note the permanence of myths through the various layers of a civilization. The *Chanson d'Aliscans* also had a double of William, the giant Rainouart, who fought with a *tinel,* "club." And it so happens that in the Irish epic, Dagda's favorite weapon is a club: one of its ends pummels and slays while the other heals and resuscitates, a symbolic image of the ambivalence of the deity who metes out both life and death. In another chanson from this cycle, the *Coronation of Louis,*

William fights with a Saracen giant named Corsolt, which reminds us of the Armoricain people known as the Curiosolites. In any event, this William—whom the oldest texts nickname *au courb nez,* "of the hooked nose," and who is called in the reworked versions "of the short nose" (because of a mistranslation of the adjective)—is a figure who, during the twelfth century, enjoyed success equal to that of the famous Roland.

According to the chansons, William has a wife named Guibourc who was once a pagan named Orable married to a Saracen king. After her husband was slain by the Christians, however, she converted and married our hero—which could well be an allusion to Eleanor's divorce and subsequent remarriage to Henry. With the character of Guibourc these chansons distinguish themselves. In contrast to the first chansons de geste in which women are merely insignificant shadows, Guibourc is at center stage; she is a strong, crafty, and intelligent woman who is a skilled politician and a formidable strategist. In the *Chanson de Guillaume,* when the hero returns from combat defeated and in complete despair, it is Guibourc who pumps him up so well that his morale is completely restored and he regains all his taste for life and triumph. To her husband, who weeps and laments the fact that he is too old, she responds: "Marquis! Milord! For God's sake, listen to me! Let me lie." In fact, she does lie, inventing an army that does not exist, promising the moon and stars to all the able-bodied men remaining in the fortress, and inventing a treasure that the Saracens allegedly hoarded in a cave. As a result, everyone agrees to set off on a new campaign, and Guiborc comforts Guillaume by seeing that he eats many dishes and drinks many beverages.

The episode could appear to be caricature. In fact, it is a caricature as are all the chansons de geste of the latter period. Yet the unflappable character of Guiborc owes much to the energy and tenacity of the duchess of Aquitaine. In addition, the *Chanson de Guillaume* stands out for transferring the setting of its episodes to central and western France—that is, to the states of Eleanor.* The chanson is written as if

---

*[Most of the others were set in the holy lands or the more southern and eastern French areas menaced by the Moors during the time of Charles Martel when the Moors were driven back from France into what is now Spain. —*Trans.*]

it intends to make Guillaume a kind of mythical ancestor of Eleanor while entrusting to Guiborc a role that the duchess of Aquitaine certainly could have assumed.

In the *Chanson d'Aliscans,* when Guillaume, fleeing before his enemies, asks his wife to open the gate to his fortress, she refuses outright, inventing every excuse and pretending she cannot recognize Guillaume. Yet she does all this for the purpose of arousing her husband's fighting spirit. In the chansons it was necessary to magnify the members of the family of Aquitaine. The poets who compiled various original elements to create the *Chanson de Guillaume* and the *Chanson d'Aliscans* have, consciously or not, taken sides with the queen-duchess in whom they saw not only a model for their female character but also an enthusiastic protector of arts and letters. At the time, they wrote only to please an important family, a great sovereign, a great queen, even if the content of the legend was originally alien to this kind of praise. Similarly, the theme of the faraway princess, which was closely connected to Eleanor, was adapted to the style of romance in the chanson de geste we know as *La Prise d'Orange* [The Capture of Orange], whose hero is also William. In fact, making ancient themes relevant to contemporary events was a style of the twelfth century. Charlemagne therefore symbolizes the Capetian monarchy. Arthur symbolizes (and brought back to life) the monarchy of the British Isles, thus foreshadowing Henry II Plantagenet. William of Orange symbolized both Henry II, Eleanor's second husband, and the family of the dukes of Aquitaine, all of whom bore the name William. At this juncture, these specifics were not merely coincidences.

Certainly, the involuntary or voluntary effect Eleanor had on poets and romance writers took place over a long span of time, but we know that it began during her youth and continued at the court of France. As the focal point of a society in search of itself, the young queen could not help but become an inspiration as well as a protector. The size of her legend also demonstrates that it is impossible not to think of her when we study the different works of the twelfth century.

Yet it was not in Paris where Eleanor had the greatest influence over the literature of her time. Her time of greatest influence was primarily after her marriage to Henry II and, more precisely, when she held court in Poitiers during the 1170s. This is quite telling of the great importance of this city in the formation of the literary works of the twelfth century, not only in the language of Occitania but also in French and even in Breton and Welsh.

In fact, Poitiers was the linguistic frontier of the French, specifically the Occitan, world. Additionally, because it lay in the Plantagenet sphere of influence, it conducted privileged relations with Normandy, Brittany, and England. It is well known that the queen-duchess drew to Poitiers all the finest minds of that time, including numerous poets and musicians. There she also enjoyed the company of her favorite son, Richard—and probably that of the mysterious Marie de France, author of the lays, who in all likelihood was a half sister of Henry II, and also the company of her daughter Marie, one of her children with Louis VII, who had been wed to the count of Champagne, Henry the Liberal. It was thus a particularly refined atmosphere in which Eleanor lived during those months when, having been abandoned by her royal husband, she and her personality truly reconnected with the emotions that had shaken her youth.

By all evidence, she had become acquainted with the legend of Tristan and Iseult at an early age. It has been proved that the famous Bréri—referred to by one of the authors of the *Romance of Tristan* and who was the *ille fabulator Bledhericus* [the writer Bledhericus] mentioned by Giraldus Cambrensis in his chronicles—lived at the court of the counts of Poitou. Eleanor's adolescence was rocked by the waves of Iseult's amorous passion for Tristan,[1] which truly depicts the violent love of a woman for a man, as made evident by the Irish archetypes of the legend. This exposure during adolescence might cause us to wonder if Eleanor did not try to materialize the myth of Iseult in her life in a kind of eternal return concept.* We might also see the adventures

---

*[The eternal return concept refers to the idea of the cyclical nature of existence—that everything comes back, again and again. For more on this, see the writings of Nietzche and Mircea Eliade, who reintroduced this element of pagan philosophy into modern philosophy. —*Trans.*]

attributed to the duchess of Aquitaine as illustrations of this myth. It is interesting to note that in every one of her claimed relations with men, Eleanor played the active role. In addition to the incarnation of sovereignty, was she not also the embodiment of the female freedom to do as she liked with her heart and body? After all, it is not Tristan who first casts eyes on Iseult in the original legend, but rather it is Iseult who forces Tristan to love her.[2]

The primacy of the woman demonstrated by Iseult's adventures and popularized by the poetry of the troubadours did not fail to leave its stamp on the mind-set of the court of Eleanor of Aquitaine in Poitiers. The entire immediate environment of the queen-duchess was female—and moreover, it was in this milieu that the personality of Richard developed. (Some believe his homosexuality was perhaps more psychological than physical.) Eleanor's daughter Marie de Champagne shared her mother's thinking on the importance of women in the new society born in the aristocratic class. In her daughter and her daughter's sister-in-law, Marie de France, Eleanor found reinforcement for her desire to promote femininity and redefine love both as a totality of being freely accepted by the woman and as a factor in being able to go beyond oneself morally, psychologically, and spiritually. This explains the debates that took place in this court of women that were most often centered on problems related to love and marriage.

Certainly, the actual existence of these famous courts of love has long been fuel for debate. A good part of the legend does not exclude the factual reality: Eleanor and her companions often gathered to judge an abstract case in which love raised serious problems that were considered to be insoluble. They judged these cases and on each occasion provided personal solutions dictated as much by their own sensitivities as by their reason. In short, at a time when justice was exclusively in the hands of men, this was a means of creating an "antitribunal" in which could play the feminine sensibility that was officially too far removed from the business of the kingdom. The courts of love were a manifestation of women's desire for independence in the suffocating, androcratic framework imposed upon them. These women found ways to use literature, poetry, music, and amusements to claim a status that they felt had been lost to them for several centuries. For this, Celtic legends and the quasi-adoration of Ovid, with all the pagan context emanating from his work, constituted a formidable weapon and forced a breach in a fundamentally gynephobic Christianity. Here is another possible explanation for Queen Eleanor's "bad" reputation: she was regarded as being chiefly responsible for the disruption of morals.

In fact, these courts of love were social games somewhat similar to what took place later with the Précieuses* of the seventeenth century. There is a strong resemblance between the court of Poitiers around 1170 and the salon of Mademoiselle de Scudéry. Eleanor and her companions never entertained the notion of replacing the established courts; rather, their activity involved taking positions on psychoemotional cases while amusing themselves as pleasantly as possible. In short, the courts of love were amusement for idle and refined women who were discontent with the crudeness of their husbands or lovers. After all, hadn't Henry II provided an example of coarseness by running up a large number of amorous liaisons while Eleanor held the dream of forming with him the ideal partnership that would dominate the world? In fact, she sought passionately to achieve this ideal coupledom, and her entire attitude toward the king of England proved her desire. When her dream was thwarted, however, she turned toward the imaginal and theoretical realm, instinctively finding the words that would enable the magic of love to work by first transforming the individual and then transcending this individual state toward one that was absolute. The remedy for the coarse love of men was courtly love, *fine amor,* conceived by several women of the elite—such as Eleanor—with the complicity of the writers and troubadours or romance creators the queen protected and inspired either directly or indirectly through the intermediaries of the women of her court.

---

*[The Précieuses was a witty group of writers and intellectuals, generally women, which frequented the salon of the Marquise de Rambouillet in the mid-seventeenth century. Its overly refined style highlights its qualities of wit and elegance. The playwright Molière wrote a satire of them in his play *Les Précieuses ridicules* (The Affected Young Ladies). —*Trans.*]

During the feudal era, it is perceived that there was a consistent emphasis on the brutality of mores—yet this is a far-too-simple description of a situation that is quite complex in reality. First, when we speak of brutality, we must determine what layer of society is involved. Next, it is necessary to analyze the different strata of twelfth-century society and take into account the fact that these strata often penetrated one another and cannot be absolutely classified.

Of course, we find the ternary vision of the Ancien Régime, which was really only an adaptation of Indo-European tripartition of a nobility, a clergy, and the people. The nobility, however, can be broken down into different categories, while the clergy included both nobles and commoners, and those called the clerks, the intellectuals, formed their own separate caste. As for the people, their category contained everything from the powerful bourgeois capitalists to the most miserable serfs.

Furthermore, it is impossible to complete this analysis without a geographical reference: The situation was obviously not the same in all the European countries and sometimes, depending on customs or the rights granted individuals or climate, it varied within a kingdom, a duchy, or an earldom. For example, in principle a peasant of the plains was more favored than that of the mountains, but in the final analysis, the mountain-dwelling peasant was more isolated and was thus freer and no doubt subject to decreased pressure from taxes and conscript labor. On the other hand, the lords of mountainous areas, such as those of Auvergne, lived miserably on their fortified rocks and had to satisfy their needs by ransoming travelers and pillaging from the peasants in the valleys, but the lords of the plains could oversee the efficient exploitation of their fertile lands.

Similarly, serfdom, which had been quite important during the tenth century, was not a general rule everywhere; for instance, early on it had been abolished in Armoricain Brittany, and by the twelfth century serfs had been freed in large number in other regions. Yet it should not be assumed that humanitarian reasons compelled the lords to free their serfs: Once the land no longer constituted absolute wealth—and we mustn't forget that it was the twelfth century that witnessed the ascent of commerce and industry in its craft incarnation—serfs no longer served much purpose. In fact, they were more of a burden to lords, who preferred to reach an understanding with free peasants who would better cultivate their lands. The Church, which has also been cast in a philanthropic light for both freeing serfs and protecting them in the famous *villeneuves* and *villefranches** that were created under its aegis in the shadow of the cathedrals and monasteries, also obeyed much more temporal motives. In fact, the immense holdings of the Church had more or less remained fallow and required hands to develop them. What solution would have been more practical than welcoming fugitive serfs and settling them where they were needed? Dating from this time are both the great clearing of wild lands and their transformation into agricultural use and—let us be honest—the origins of the wealth of the Church.

This all falls into the context of a veritable class struggle—but instead of concerning two social categories, the owners and the proletarians, as was the case in the nineteenth century, the struggle in the twelfth century consisted of three groups fighting for supremacy: the nobles trying to maintain the privileges they had acquired through strength of arms; the clergy trying to seat its spiritual power on a material foundation; and one part of the people, the bourgeoisie, trying to gain recognition for the economic weight it represented. This struggle is fairly well symbolized by the presence in certain cities of three towers: the keep of the castle; the steeple of the church, which became increasingly massive; and the belfry of the commune.

Because these three groups buffeted one another, the struggle took on varied and sometimes conflicting appearances through the play of alliances at various times defined by the objectives of the groups. The Church could use the bourgeoisie to attack the nobility; the nobility could use the clergy to thwart the bourgeoisie; and the bourgeoisie could reach an understanding directly with the nobles to reduce the strength of the Church. So we can see that the situation was not so simple.

---

*[Meaning "new towns" and "free (franchised) towns." —*Trans.*]

What is certain is that whatever their status and wherever they lived, the peasant class was at the bottom of the social ladder; the heaviest burdens fell upon the peasants, and they were despised by town folk and nobles alike. It was during this time that words such as *vilain* and *manant** began assuming their pejorative meaning. We need only look at twelfth-century romances to see the way knights treat rural inhabitants: these peasants were barely human beings, and it was not considered a crime to strike them down in cold blood for the smallest peccadillo or the slightest lack of respect.

A slight climb up the social ladder was represented by those who became castle servants, but while the castle sheltered people against want, it did not protect them from insults. The castle servants formed what was known as the *valetaille*.† They were needed, but their superiors never missed an opportunity to remind them of their sordid origins. These servants were obliged to put up with a great deal, yet those who managed to make themselves indispensable to their masters either through their intelligence or their manners could hope to receive rewards. Some of them who had caught the notice of Church men or nobles were sent to school and then became clerks. This was basically the only effective means available for intelligent peasants to move out of their social rank. These clerks immediately formed a sub-category because they belonged to the Church (even though they were not priests) but were dependent on the common class. Generally they worked in service to the nobles as tutors, counselors, or writers. These twelfth-century clerks (Peter Abelard remains one of the most striking examples) played an extremely important role in both the political and the intellectual arenas. They were chiefly responsible for the evolution of medieval society and effectively contributed to the changing mentality of the second half of the twelfth century.

The inhabitants of the towns and cities—both former peasants who had left the land through the practice of a trade and the descendants of

---

*[Meaning "villain" and "churl," respectively. —*Trans.*]

†[Meaning "menials" or "flunkeys." —*Trans.*]

former artisans—were able to obtain enviable positions. In fact, because of an improvement in the quality of life and greater security than was available in earlier centuries, consumption became greater in Europe, and it became necessary to satisfy a constantly growing demand. This led to the creation of numerous workshops, mainly for weaving, in Champagne and Flanders, which also had the effect of attracting to the urban areas a kind of wretched underclass whose fate was often depicted by the authors of that century, particularly Chrétien de Troyes. Because manufactured products needed to be distributed, commerce between cities and regions developed and enriched both the merchants, who brought back to the cities other products from their travels, and the lords of the lands through which the merchants traveled, because they demanded a tithe in return for guaranteeing the safety of the roads. An entire system of local taxes and duties was thus created, permitting some nobles to consolidate almost staggering fortunes.

The real winners from this activity, however, were the artisans and merchants. In the cities they had comfortable houses built for them, which gave masons greater opportunity to work. The Crusades had allowed them to establish contact with faraway lands, and consequently commerce had been extended to the far side of the Mediterranean, which literally flooded Europe with silk, oriental fabrics, spices, and luxury goods. The merchants and artisans were therefore the most active class and the one that accumulated the largest fortune. With all this newfound wealth, they wished to have the right to charters, thus the bourgeoisie were set on claiming their autonomy in the towns that, until that time, had been the property of the lords. Initially, the lords were quite reluctant to cede anything, for they did not wish to deprive themselves of an appreciable source of revenue or to allow this kind of challenge to the principle of their sovereignty.

As circumstances evolved, however, and the nobles experienced a growing need for the support and money of the bourgeoisie, charters were granted to free the cities from the tutelage of lords, and the bourgeoisie was conceded the right to form a political community. Of course, the nobles received something in return: the charters were in fact bought by the bourgeoisie, and various clauses set limits to the commune's power. This does not mean, though, that this emancipation of cities in the twelfth century was not a veritable revolution. It began quite early in Occitania before continuing soon after in northern France and then spreading throughout Europe.[3] In the Holy Empire it sometimes attained unthinkable proportions, as we can see in the number of free cities that behaved like actual sovereign states. As for the queen, we have seen how Eleanor, who, as a young woman, reacted harshly against bourgeois demands to organize as communes in Poitiers, subsequently enthusiastically granted charters to the towns and cities of her domains. She had matured and realized that history could not move forward without the support of the bourgeoisie, the true keeper of capital.

In this regard, Eleanor's own domains formed a typical example of economic prosperity. While wars, which were always a latent possibility, had hindered the success of some regions, at least in Poitou and Aquitaine—and even in Brittany, which was a Plantagenet dependency at that time—the economy flourished. Water mills, which used natural energy, were countless, and they not only permitted the grinding of grain but also powered the bellows and drop hammers of the smithies, milled colorings and dye products, brewed beer, beat hemp, pressed sheets, and turned the saws of carpenters. An entire range of artisanal activity that verged on the industrial was connected to using the waterways. This also allowed the creation of water reserves in the form of ponds and millraces, which could serve as fisheries, for fish were a large part of the daily diet. Among the various agricultural products in the regions, the Bordelais vine provided a harvest much appreciated by the inhabitants of England and guaranteed the wealth of the landholders and ship owners that specialized in the wine trade. The general prosperity of Aquitaine inspired intense construction activity that, through both community and noble donations, was accompanied by the building of new religious establishments almost everywhere, giving Aquitaine a reputation that few other regions at this time could rival.

This rise of the bourgeoisie had consequences in every sphere, first through profoundly altering the relations within the three traditional classes. We know that the Capetian kings relied on this bourgeoisie to get around the nobility. The Plantagenets did not operate systematically in this way, but, when granting charters to the bourgeoisie of the cities, they made sure to specify that the communes were responsible for their own defense, thus freeing the royal army from this duty. In addition, they added one significant detail to the articles: the bourgeoisie had to furnish a contingent for the royal army if it was necessary. Further, upon seeing the enormous advantage these bourgeois militias gave his adversaries, Philip Augustus rushed to copy their example. Obviously, this was risky: arming the bourgeoisie was akin to letting the fox into the henhouse. Previously, the nobility held a monopoly on arms; thus arming another group meant a removal of one of their distinguishing features. We know that eventually these bourgeois militias prevailed over the knighthood, and Henry II had already forced a breach in the nobility's arms monopoly by hiring mercenaries for a good number of his expeditions. The nobles believed, however, that these mercenaries presented no risk as long as there was money to pay them, whereas an armed bourgeois class could very well demand political rights.

Further, this was a time when cities proliferated, which increased the size of the bourgeoisie. Whereas the nobility saw its position becoming stagnant, this new class of society felt the promise of a future that nothing could truly darken. It is common knowledge that Karl Marx saw this rise of the bourgeoisie and the liberation of the cities as the starting point for modern capitalism. We must admit that on analysis this assertion is correct and that the birth of a city-dwelling bourgeoisie in the twelfth century was the first step on a long road that ended with the French Revolution and, consequently, the "liberal democracy" now found in Western countries, whether sometimes tinged with conservatism, as in France and the United States, or social democracy (a tragically paradoxical term to the extent that it involves a negative compromise between Utopian socialist doctrine and realist democracy), as in Germany and Great Britain.

The Church could not escape this ferment. Since the edict of Theodosius, which made Christianity the official religion of the Roman Empire, to some extent the Church had forgotten its original doctrine based on humility and universal love and had sunk into an intransigent sectarianism that was propped up on an increasingly extensive temporal power (which grew with the conversion of new lands). Mainly under the Merovingians, the Church—heir to the imperial administration, the sole power of stability at a time of troubles and confusion, and the keeper of science and culture—was a considerable force that could not be opposed rashly. Charlemagne grasped this so keenly that he divided the world between the pope and himself. His successors, emperors and Capetian kings alike, were less fortunate in their attempts at conciliation, and there were always delicate disputes to be settled between them and the power established in Rome, primarily concerning the nomination of bishops and the imposition of various taxes. In addition, as the high officials of the Church took on an increasingly political role in the countries where they performed their duties, the problem of dual allegiance arose: Did bishop, archbishop, and abbot owe obedience first to the pope or to the king? The feudal oath had seemingly arranged matters nicely—but only seemingly, because the Church, with its international branches, found itself beyond all constraint and made no secret about it.

Just like the popular or common class, however, the Church did not offer the picture of a unified block. With rare exceptions, the high offices went to nobles, who maintained close ties with their original class. The lower clergy, on the other hand, the Church men of the countryside and the poorest towns, was of popular extraction. Country priests, who were quite close to their parishioners, often led a wretched existence. They were barely educated, and in fact they were more like peasants than priests. Numerous ecclesiastics were married, officially or not, and no one found it shocking. They contributed only to maintaining a vague spirituality in a world where pagan survival fiercely resisted the Church and was often embodied in local forms of worship and traditions that could not be uprooted. Between these lower ecclesiastics and the high dignitaries of the Church there was a stark difference in both fate and mentality.

Furthermore, this lay clergy that was subject to temporal influences and was dependent on kings and princes was opposed by a regular clergy that was directly dependent on Rome through the intermediaries of the leaders of the congregation. This regular clergy was also better established than the lay clergy, and the wealth of the Church made its way to all its different levels. It formed a world apart, in both the Church and in the era, which did not prevent it from playing a significant moral and pedagogical role. This was also the wealthiest fraction of the clergy, for as a rule, noble and regal donations went to abbeys. In fact, monasteries were founded or richly endowed to ensure the salvation of the donor's soul or to atone for some almost unforgivable sins, and, consequently, the holdings of the monks became exorbitant. Never before the twelfth century were as many orders founded and monastic buildings constructed. This was the height of monachism's triumph throughout western Europe. As a result, it is quite difficult to get a clear view of this large mass of congregations, brotherhoods, and isolated orders and separate the wheat from the chaff. In fact, a good many foundations were due to deep faith and a perfectly respectable mystical inspiration. Twelfth-century monachism produced great saints, as no one can deny, but along with them there were also a good many creations that were intended to ensure the material prosperity of individuals whose vocations were dubious to say the least. During the Middle Ages, the profession of monk was filled by many who, having no other means of making a living, exploited the great mystical tendencies of the era.

The third ecclesiastical group was that of the men generally labeled clerks. They, too, formed a world apart, but of course, they were part of the Church and even served as its most beneficial leaven. Whether priests or simple laymen, they formed the cultural heart of not only the Church but also the entire society. They were responsible for the education of both the great and the regular folk, and because of this, they were in contact with all strata of society. These men were also what we might call internationals; they knew no borders and the Latin language they all spoke allowed them to make themselves understood wherever they went. They were of all origins—commoners, bourgeoisie, and nobility—and their solidarity with each other often led them to push their own interests instead of those of the masters they allegedly served. Finally, they were often in positions that made them arbiters. In actuality, some were advisors to princes and kings, and, because of this, they were intimately involved in the political life of the countries where fate had sent them. This was how the monk Suger came to be the most heeded counselor for Louis VI, then Louis VII. He was a clerk and a formidable statesman, neither of which interfered with his wise administration of the abbey of Saint-Denis. Likewise, Thomas Becket was the confidant and most trusted friend of the Capets' adversary, Henry II, before the well-known rift that terminated their relationship so tragically. Becket had gone from being a brilliant clerk to being the equally uncompromising archbishop of Canterbury.

Of course, there were clerks of all stripes. If ever anyone should write a history of the clerks of the twelfth century, it would be quite colorful and diverse, to say the least. A good number of them were the worst miscreants on earth. They had found this the means of leaving their original class and living well, for the privileges given clerks allowed them to lead quite pleasant lives that were either devoted to study and literature or, when they were instructors, were filled with constant travel or were simply quiet, if they served in some sinecure where material wants did not affect them. In any case, the clerks truly formed a caste apart that had branched out into society thoroughly and deeply and that kept the extraordinary powers that culture and science inspire whenever the majority of the populace, nobles and commoners alike, are almost illiterate.

It was over this society of clerks that Eleanor of Aquitaine ruled, just as she ruled over educated women and courtly knights. She herself was the student of clerks who had passed on to her a substantial cultural legacy (from both Occitania and antiquity) and had shown her the way to further her knowledge. She remembered this education all her life and never ignored the counsel from a member of this class. Nor did she ever fail to bestow her favor on those who were the most loyal upholders of cultural tradition. When she was in the midst of clerks, the queen-duchess felt as if she was with family. She was a member of their "guild," and no one dreamed of declaring this shocking. After all, wouldn't this feeling be perfectly normal for someone who was William the Troubadour's granddaughter?

Even though she maintained such friendships, Eleanor never lost sight of the fact that she belonged to the aristocracy. Yet the nobility of which she was part was also in the midst of drastic change. To see the entire picture, we need to familiarize ourselves with the crude mores of the previous era, especially in the north, for with respect to Occitania in the south, considerable progress had already been made among the nobility by Eleanor's time. Yes, the nobles of the earliest feudal era were brutes whose sole concerns were war and hunting and who surrendered to their basest instincts without thinking of emerging from their intellectual squalor. Yes, the lords—and kings—of the early feudal era did not know how to read or write; they had better things to do than stick their noses into grimoires and cultivate an interest in fine literature. The times were hard. They had to lead, fight, ensure that there was a constant food supply in their lands, and protect their domains. In this kind of jungle where the strongest always came out on top, the rule of life was always to outdo your foes in violence. These obscure times, this "dark age" was a period of great uncertainty during which the fate of entire peoples hinged on battles that pitted a thousand fighters against each other—and the lords were right there in the front ranks, fighting and risking their lives.

Thus all things related to reading and writing and all the useless belles-lettres became the preserve of the clerks. Being familiar with all of this constituted their profession and what they were paid to do. This is how the clerical caste, keepers of the permanent culture, were able to win a preponderant place in social life.

Yet the clerks' strength was not something the lords of all ranks regarded with no concern. Because of their inability to do without clerks, they were able to envision a time when these clerks would gain the upper hand, and, partially in an attempt to avoid this, they began to educate themselves. Thus culture did not remain the private domain of the clerical guild but instead was shared with those who had a claim to ruling the world. In Occitania, the dukes and counts were the first to grasp the importance of an education intended for aristocrats that would enable them direct access to culture. Eleanor's family is living proof of this. Eventually, the northern kings made an effort to regain the ground they had lost. It is common knowledge that Henry II constantly endeavored to spread culture among his knights and nobles and encouraged by every means the creation and diffusion of literary works. This was the origin of that courtly aristocracy for whom Béroul, Thomas of England, Chrétien de Troyes, and all the Anglo-Norman clerks wrote and upon whom trouvères lavished their treasures of charm and poetry to impart a dimension of life that was fine and good. In this regard, the legendary hero Tristan, who was simultaneously an unbeatable warrior, an excellent diplomat, a good prince who befriended the common people, a brilliant debater, a competent harpist, and a refined poet, admirably sums up the ideal of the noble knight of this new generation.

At this time the nobility officially held authority. The king was one of the barons chosen by his peers, and, therefore, he belonged to this class and was distinguished from it only by his right to have the final say over it. Nevertheless, as we have seen, this power was a heavy burden. On the one hand, it was constantly necessary for nobles to defend against potential rivals, hence they had to have recourse to noble or clerical allies; and on the other hand, nobles had to be prepared to justify themselves to everyone. Thus, a kind of religious-mystical concept of nobility appeared that stressed the idea of the sacred service the nobles performed for the good of the community—and suggested that they did this with divine blessing, which forestalled the problem of usurpation by force from any uprising.

Exactly who were these nobles originally? They were warriors, of course, who had won their domains in battle either by annexing lands or receiving them as fiefs in reward for their service. Kings or princes selected some nobles for their management skills, but this was fairly rare. The rule of war still outweighed all others, and the large fiefs most often were carved out in blood.

In the twelfth century, this nobility was organized in a way that presented an unshakeable facade. Theoretically, feudalism permitted a perfect hierarchy: at the top of the pyramid was the king, followed by dukes, counts, and simple lords. It might seem quite similar to a military system in which all the ranks are clearly established and divided up along the hierarchical ladder. In reality, however, it was nothing of the sort. A simple lord could be more powerful than a count, and a duke more powerful than a king. Furthermore, given the complexity of inheritances, a duke could be a count and a lord at the same time, and even then he might not be dependent on the same suzerein or sovereign, which only further complicated matters. In practice, the feudal pyramid betrayed its rickety nature, for it was still the strongest and most audacious who prevailed.

The nobles, however, could not remain isolated. They formed communities bound by interest and sealed their accords with the feudal oath. They thereby formed disparate bands that could fiercely oppose other groups. Wars were reignited. The Church attempted as best it could to codify these shifting moods with the Truce of God, the Peace of God, and especially the Crusades, which made use of the energy and aggressiveness of these men who were unable to let go of the notion that war was the sole means to assert personality and obtain additional riches.

It is at this stage that chivalry entered the game. In the beginning, knights were minor nobles at the bottom of the feudal ladder, generally sons who had lost any right to their family's inheritance for one reason or another. Their entire fortune consisted of their horse and their arms. These knights rented (so to speak) their services to a slightly richer noble who needed reinforcement. Those who had the good fortune to defeat an enemy first collected war booty: the arms and horse of the defeated knight as well as a ransom for him if he had been captured rather than slain. It should be noted that it was much more to the knight's advantage to capture rather than kill his foe. In addition to this booty, a knight's master might reward him by giving him lands, in return for which the knight became the tenant vassal of a fief. This arrangement enabled some knights to establish themselves and become nobles in their own right.

It is obvious that perpetual struggles among nobles and the necessity of defending domains against enemies or simply against pillagers or highway brigands favored this warrior caste that was little separated from a group of mercenaries. Indeed, the knights formed a caste that was structured and transformed into a veritable institution. Feudal society needed knights, and it therefore created them. Thus, numerous commoners and adventurers who had lived in the shadows were able to infiltrate the warrior caste by serving knights either as simple valets or squires. In fact, once these men had displayed their martial abilities, they could themselves claim admission into the brotherhood if they found sponsors, or godfathers, and if they fulfilled the complicated rites of initiation that formed the apprenticeship of knighthood.

It should be noted that this caste did not position itself outside feudal society but instead integrally respected all its rules. Knights were in the exclusive service of the individual to whom they had sworn an oath of fealty. The situation could become quite tricky, however, when circumstances forced a knight to swear an oath to several lords. To remedy this state of affairs, the code of liege-homage was instituted. In the event of an internal and horizontal conflict in the hierarchical ladder, this code gave preference to one of these lords over all the others. Eventually, the Church also became mixed up in the matter, taking moral responsibility for the knights and governing them according to a code that was not only practical but also spiritual. Besides his mission of aiding his immediate suzerain, the knight thus had to obey a certain number of much larger imperatives, in particular the demand to take a stand against injustice wherever he found it.

The knights were thus pushed in the direction of becoming a police-like militia that was charged with protecting everyone's property, aiding widows and orphans, supporting the rights of the weak, and laboring for the supreme suzerain, meaning God. The fact that they were charged with this divine mission gave them unique importance on the moral plane but placed them in a somewhat borderline rank.

The consequence was quite visible in the twelfth century: The knights found themselves to be an autonomous social group that was aware of both its mission and material significance. Once they grasped this, it was not long before the knights considered playing an equally important role in the political sphere—which they did many times, influencing the march of events with their demands.

The knight caste could act thus because, consisting of active nobles ready to tempt all, it had a noteworthy coherence. Like the clerk caste within the Church, the knight caste was distinguished by its commonly held rules and motivations. Instead of being a fraternity of knowledge, however, it was a fraternity of arms that eventually had a tendency to become a fraternity of power. A knight never acted on his own; instead he acted in the name of the entire community of knights that he represented when he was in action and that, at risk of his own life, he had to lead to its greatest glory. Ultimately, it was not for king or some suzerain that the knight undertook the struggle, but for the whole of his caste. This mentality, as we can see, appeared in the romances of the Round Table, which means it was a reality in the latter half of the twelfth century. It also partly explains why the caste of knights was so important and so necessary but, at the same time, so alarming to the political power held by the king or the great lords.[4]

At her court of Poitiers, it was to this caste of knights that Eleanor turned, just as she turned to the caste of clerks. Her political strategies required these quarrelsome and ambitious knights just as they needed countless clerks to spread a humanist culture to the four corners of the kingdom. While she was queen of the troubadours, Eleanor was also queen of the knights. In addition, because of interactions in this complex twelfth-century society, numerous troubadours were also knights. The queen's intention was clearly to gather around her the two large, active forces of the era. But to what purpose?

It is likely she meant to reconcile them, and to achieve this, she used the fundamental assumptions that contributed to the transformation of men and women's mentalities. Indeed, as the long period of women's effacement was generally considered to be a thing of the past at this time, why not take advantage of the new mind-sets that were being born? As we have seen, Eleanor was a woman of remarkable intelligence and one who knew how to calculate in advance the return on a policy. This is not to say that she was entirely guided by self-interest; she firmly believed that an aristocratic society *should*—here it is a notion of duty—be cultivated and refined: to the extent possible, she strove to transcend the fundamental desires and instincts of the knights and clerks in order to offer both castes a more brilliant future. Further, she knew she held the most advantageous position to prepare this future. In the company of the women of her court—her daughters figure strongly among them—she set up a charm battalion of sorts that, in its energy and determination, left nothing to be envied when compared to any elite corps of Poitevin knights.

In history nothing is gratuitous. Eleanor has too often been treated as a frivolous queen, no doubt because she was concerned with dress style, parties, and fine amor. People tend to forget, however, that all is connected and that everything from clothing and artistic styles to issues of amorous casuistry (case-based reasoning) can very easily correspond to social necessities and material realities. The image of an era will only be depicted fragmentarily if we confine ourselves to recounting military expeditions and the political aims of the rulers of that era. In the final analysis, these rulers have authority only if they benefit from a large consensus of the people they govern. This, more than at any time before, is the case for Eleanor's era. To understand this period thus requires understanding its cogs—and fine amor became one of those cogs.

Eleanor's intention was to form a new society based on respect for the oath of fealty, perfect knowledge of the world and its secrets, the fine appearance of one and all, luxury, and prosperity. This is obviously a kind of Utopian ideal that brings to mind those Celtic legends of the Land of Fairy, where there reigns a mysterious woman who has quasi-divine powers at her command, a woman who is the heiress of the ancient solar deities and who radiates all her charm and magnetic powers throughout the world. Eleanor never lost sight of the fact that she was the *azimant* (magnet) of the troubadours. At her court in Poitiers, she would have liked to feel herself at the heart of a closed and perfect world from which all wickedness was banished. This is the myth of the Isle of Avalon coming back to the surface and can also be seen, in the following century, in the large romance of the *Prose Lancelot,* particularly in its description of the strange world of the Lady of the Lake. In this romance, Eleanor's dream manifests almost consciously, as if the authors hung onto the nostalgia for this briefly glimpsed moment. Perhaps it was also the world of the countess of Poitou that the clerk Ulrich von Zatzikhoven has in mind when he says, in his German version of the Lancelot legend: "She was queen, the best who had ever lived until then. She was a maid full of wisdom. She had ten thousand women with her in her land that had never known men or the laws of man. All the women had robes and cloaks of silk with gold brocade . . . all year long, this land was covered with flowers as if it were the month of May . . ."[5]

Here we are obviously in the realm of Utopia. This is the domain of the fairies, an unreal world that corresponds to a gynecratic ideal that was asserting itself among the women of the nobility of the twelfth century now that they understood how they had been intentionally deprived of authority. Because their revolt could have no other outlet except dream and poetry, however, they strove to draw the greatest possibility from these. Since remotest antiquity, storytellers and chroniclers have cited a land entirely governed by women, as is shown by the legend of the Amazons, for example, or by Aristophanes' satire *Lysistrata.* Yet no attempt to truly feminize society had ever succeeded. The misfortune that dogged women and their desire to be if not superior to men, then at least their equals, weighed heavy on Eleanor and her companions. We have seen that the queen of England had succeeded in making her voice heard on her own behalf—but what needed to be done to extend this personal and solitary conquest? It is to be thought that because all other means of persuasion were revealed as inoperative, women of the time decided to make use of another secret weapon inherent to their charm and even their condition: fine amor.

There has been much debate on the origins of fine amor. The name courtly love or Provencal love is insufficient to explain a distinct phenomenon that appeared in the aristocratic milieu of the Christian West during the twelfth century. First, we must put this phenomenon into context. The whole populace was never affected by this concept of love. It affected only the aristocracy, and, even then, only the most evolved and refined experienced it consistently, although often in a purely theoretical state.

It is important to recall what characterizes this courtly love, for Eleanor of Aquitaine appears to be at the heart of the debate. Because of the existence in Arab lands—especially Persia—of a precious kind of love poetry in which women were often given high standing, some have claimed that fine amor was of Muslim influence. Examples of this tie are certainly not lacking, and because fine amor first made its appearance in Occitania, where there were close ties to the Muslim world, there are legitimate grounds for accepting this theory of Islamic origin. Yet this connection takes either too literally or too superficially the Muslim love poems of this era. In fact, a good many of these poems are actually poems of mystic love in which the symbolic love language seemingly referring to woman in fact designates worship of a hidden deity who can be known only through a human experience. Further, analysis of Islamic love poems reveals that while they openly glorify the beauty and perfection of woman, in reality, they are lyrical offerings to a woman-object who is honored with words and gifts but is carefully kept on the sidelines and imprisoned in a harem if necessary. While she may be queen of the harem, she is not the absolute mistress that is known in certain courtly texts.

Furthermore, as refined as it must have been at that time, Muslim society does not explain the gynecratic tendencies asserted within the context of works inspired by courtly love. The symbolic value of the poetry of the troubadours is more complex than mere exaltation; it is truly worship of woman. In addition, this work is lyricism that is rightly considered as the first manifestation of the originality of the medieval mind. It is thus going out on a limb to claim that courtly love was of Arabic origin, even if it is undeniable that Occitan poets had contact with the Muslim poets of Spain. Indeed, contact doesn't always mean profound influence.

There has also been discussion of the many Celtic components in the code of love that comes out of the literary works of the twelfth century and that can be found in the theoretical book *The Art of Love* by Andreas Capellanus, another protégé of Eleanor of Aquitaine. The question is too broad to be dealt with fully here, but we can assume that the permanence of Celtic legends concerning the primacy of women and their moral and social role was not foreign to this new mind-set. More than a deification of the woman, fine amor was a social formulation, the charter of a feminist demand, thus prefiguring the theories of the seventeenth-century Précieuses and its "map of the amorous sentiments," as well as contemporary movements that aim to liberate women and recognize their specifically female identity. Among the Celts, especially the Irish and the Bretons, women enjoyed privileged status, at least in theory, in comparison to what they had among other peoples during this era. There is a strong temptation to see in courtly love theories a survival, or rather a renaissance, of a Celtic mind-set that is more favorable to the female condition.[6] The fact that we know that divorce was possible in Christian Ireland in the heart of the Middle Ages and that women retained significant rights when their marriages were dissolved should prompt us to accept this hypothesis as infinitely probable. We can see abundant traces of it in courtly literature—that is, essentially in Arthurian romances and all the cycles connected to them.

What is perhaps more important are the mystic-religious components of fine amor and their relationship with the construction of an ideal society. In fact, the appearance of the courtly themes coincides with the prodigious development of the cult of the Virgin Mary, who had become the model for all women and occupied the place once held by ancient female deities of the Mediterranean religions as well as those of the regions bordering the Atlantic Ocean, including druidism. At this time, it was believed that the Virgin Mary, who was presented as an anti-Eve ("one woman was humanity's ruin, one woman will be its salvation"), had come to prepare a new age in which love would replace hate. The mother of Jesus—the symbol of motherly love—gave birth to a son who incarnated universal love, thus reconstructing the old dream of the Golden Age or a lost Paradise, the Garden of Bliss where man and beast lived peacefully together in an eternal spring. In this notion is another Isle of Avalon, the famous Insala Pomorum, where illness, old age, and death are not known and where fruits—in fact, the only available food—are forever ripe.

Who rules over this blessed island? The fairy Morgana, incarnation of the original mother goddess, rules. In this Promised Land, as the Irish call it, we find the most favorable conditions for the establishment of a society without classes and, more important, without a hierarchy. We find a concept dear to the poets of Celtic lands: that of a horizontal society that establishes the bonds between family and tribe according to affective relationships of a complex nature that are dictated by the desire not to give any social category an advantage it could use to the detriment of another group. The powerful advantage that emerges from such a concept is that of a nonmandatory cohesion of a group not bound by imperatives of defense. Groups that form for defensive purposes require an enemy to maintain their cohesion. The spirit of Rousseau's *Social Contract,* at least when it is read literally in its entirety, appears quite clearly in this society: Relations between people are the consequence of a reciprocal acceptance of an affective order instead of an obligatory order. This horizontal society—as can be glimpsed in the stories about the Isle of Avalon, the Promised Land, the Land of Fairy, and the Island of Women—is, for the Celts, the materialization and visualization of a Utopian state that is later cited by Thomas Moore. This Utopia was specifically rethought in the twelfth century in the context of an aristocratic society that had only recently emerged from a crude and somewhat anarchic feudalism.

Thus originally there was the will to change society and bring out its feminine element, which had been repressed by patriarchal society. No legend provides a better illustration of this occultation than that of the city of Ys. The image of this cursed city and its princess Dahud (meaning "the good witch") sinking beneath the waves is one of a society that has been cast into the depths—into the darkness of the unconscious. Yet this kind of civilization is fated to reappear, for the legend tells us that Ys will return the day Paris is covered by water. The meaning is clear: if Paris represents androcratic society, Ys represents the occulted gynecratic society that is ever present in collective memory.

To what extent did fine amor summarize an attempt to change society this way in the middle of the twelfth century? It did so through its attempt to establish new social relationships based on emotional feelings and love. In fact, parallel to the oath of fealty sworn by a vassal before his suzerain, by which the two organized service and exchange, there was now an oath binding the wife of the suzerain to her husband's vassals through the love that the lady necessarily inspired in the knights serving her husband.

Some will say that it is a long way from the religious mysticism of certain literary texts to this sociological notion. Yet if we analyze the conditions under which the ritual of fine amor operated, we can see the equivalence. The first rule of fine amor keeps married couples out of this game. As will be the case with the later habitués of the Précieuses, love and marriage are absolutely incompatible. It should be noted that in the twelfth century, most often marriages were only public acts intended to unite not two people, but two fortunes, two domains, or two kingdoms. Even if it could be proved that Eleanor had married Henry II out of love, the principal motivation was the union of the western provinces in a more powerful state that could effectively oppose the claims of the French king-suzerain. Therefore, with marriage removed, what remains in fine amor is love. But what kind of love?

Scholars of the Middle Ages, especially those from the beginning of the twentieth century, viewed in the love uniting a knight and a lady (the wife of his suzerain) a moral and spiritual bond that was always platonic and that made it possible to keep the largest number of knights around the lord, who could therefore place greater trust in their loyalty. Because the Church had given fine amor its blessing (based on the criteria of its rules), no doubts could be harbored about the theoretical nature of courtly love, which of course introduced considerations about the beneficial role of such a custom with regard to morality and politics. Pushing this line of investigation further, we discover an interesting kind of asceticism in the tradition that is analogous to that which is still practiced in certain forms of tantric Buddhism and that gave rise to an entirely spiritual vision of this love.

The reality, however, was quite different. Given the light cast by Andreas Capellanus's book *The Art of Love* and others, both works in prose and verse, from the courtly era, we can only be astounded at the irritating mania these experts of the past exhibit in their attempts to pass off courtly heroes as little saints. In fact, there is a very subtle eroticism in the poetry of the troubadours and in the romances by Chrétien de Troyes—in particular, in *The Knight of the Cart,* which the countess Marie (who was herself inspired by Eleanor) inspired the trouvère from Champagne to write. This eroticism, which Rẹné Nelli has proved is genuine, can be readily summarized: Everything is based on revelation and initiation. The act of revelation is important in that it involves a choice. Indeed, the knight, who was the future lover, had to choose the woman who would be his lady. Generally his eyes were drawn to the wife of his lord because she was his natural, "legitimate" mistress. Yet given the fact that the feudal system assumed complex ties between vassals and suzerains (and that a vassal could have several suzerains at the same time), the choice was actually much more free. Considerations of beauty, wealth, and reputation all entered into the picture. A knight could love a lady only if she was worthy of love, if her radiance was such that there was no shame in swearing a veritable oath of allegiance to her.

Of course, all the literary texts stress the exceptional beauty of the chosen woman, though this has become somewhat cliché. (The beloved woman could be only the most beautiful woman in the world, and never had anyone encountered her equal in beauty and wisdom.) Yet this excessive declaration was necessary to the game. For the knight, because courtly love involved transcending himself through an act that turned his earlier life upside-down and paved the way for a new future, the idea of beauty and perfection was indispensable—and all the more so when the reality was different.

Thus the knight had to choose. Yet the lady, too, had total freedom to accept or inspire the homage of the suitor. She could refuse outright a knight that didn't please her or, conversely, act in such a way as to compel him to love her. This is the case with Iseult, who falls in love with Tristan first and thereby inspires his love. This means of proceeding is incontestably Celtic, and there is no lack of models in early Irish epics.[7] What is noteworthy is the freedom allocated to the woman: rather than being the prisoner of a decision made by a man, at the last, it was she who decided.

While choice is important for the knight, who thereby displayed his intentions toward an ideal of beauty and perfection, this choice was much more noteworthy for the lady, who built a veritable network of men around her. Her suitors—for it was rare to have only one—were all knights in her service and, consequently, in the service of the collective entity for which she had become the symbol and whose chief executive was her husband, the lord. By this reckoning, the political aspect of fine amor was as important as its mystical or religious aspect.

We should not lose sight of the fact that during the twelfth century, knights formed a relatively closed caste that gradually discovered the power it represented. The lords, the holders of the domains, were nothing without them. These knights began dictating their law to their suzerains, thus making them "constitutional" sovereigns, and Henry II realized this perfectly, for after selling his support to his suzerain, the king of France, on numerous occasions he found himself the plaything of his vassals' whims. It was therefore necessary for every lord to hire the services of loyal knights, and the lords therefore not only tolerated but even encouraged the institution of fine amor. It was completely within their interest that the oath of fealty, which they were due, should be mirrored with an oath of amorous allegiance that drew the lord's vassals even more fully into his orbit. Hence the scant amount of jealousy displayed by the great lords of the twelfth century when their wives accepted the homage of their suitors.

For their part, the knights saw this institution as a means of climbing the social ladder. The higher the place occupied in the hierarchy by the chosen lady, the higher their own rank would become. We know that many knights owned only their horse and equipment, when they were not obliged to use them as collateral.[8] Material interests thus commanded the service of love.

This is also why the figure of Arthur, in the stories of the Round Table, is never ridiculed despite Guinevere's infidelity. The theme of the cuckold king, which clearly appears in these stories, belongs to a very ancient tradition and refers to magical-martial rituals in the same way as the improperly named right of first night, or lord's right.[9] In the Irish epic *The Cattle Raid of Cooley,* King Ailill, informed that his wife, Queen Mebdh, has been caught redhanded in an adulterous affair with the hero Fergus, merely says that it is necessary for the success of the expedition. This, however, does not prevent the king from reacting jealously. Further, this theme of the cuckold king (or cuckold lord, as we might call it in the framework of twelfth-century fine amor) is connected with that of the sacred prostitute and necessary adultery.

Once the system was established, the process followed its own course. The knight had to blindly stick to the code that he had accepted through his choice. He first had to show proof of his discretion and that he respected the honor of his lady, and he had to court her assiduously. Most important, he had to show himself capable of performing feats of prowess for the love of the woman he had chosen. It is in this sense that fine amor formed an excellent engine for heroic action. It permitted the knight to show not only his lady but also others and himself that he was capable of exceeding what he had done in the past. It is common knowledge that the pride of the knighthood was at issue whenever the actions of one of its members was involved. In the romances of the Round Table, then, the fact that the heroes often send their prisoners to Queen Guinevere or to another lady of high standing proves the importance of male warrior activity performed in the name of the lady.

All of this refers to initiation rites that are both amorous and martial. Here again, the original model is Celtic. The Irish story *The Education of Cuchulainn* shows us the hero leaving his homeland to learn combat methods and feats of magic as well as feats of sexual prowess from warrior women who have a greater resemblance to witches or infernal goddesses than to members of the human race.[10] The same is true in another Irish tale, *The Childhood of Finn,* in which the hero is raised and educated by women like this.[11] There is also the Welsh Peredur, who attains his full valor and ability to perform great deeds from the witches of Caer Loyw, who, ironically, also permit him to defeat them at the end of the story of his adventures, for he is the sole person to know all their secrets, including the magic spells that are in such full supply in the ancient traditions.[12] In these three cases, magic, sexuality, and the warrior arts are intimately connected, illustrating an initiation of young men and their preparation for adulthood in which sex, death (the power to kill), and the challenge (the magic that necessarily interferes with the established order) are the necessary components. This is again what we find in fine amor, albeit in a more refined form that is more consistent with twelfth-century taste.

The stages of this initiation are quite simple though: The knight attained the next stage and a reward after a feat of prowess. The reward perhaps consisted of a simple gaze from the beloved, but this nonetheless encouraged the knight to continue his efforts, for he now knew he was on the right path. From the gaze he moved to the fleeting touch of his and his lady's hands, then to the chaste kiss. If he could prove his perseverance in his actions and his obedience to the counsels (more like orders) of his lady, he would win other rewards: for instance, he might be invited to enter his lady's chamber and converse with her. From one rendezvous to the next (time does not exist for those in love), he would gain the right to satisfactions that ordinary morality censures but which the twelfth-century Church did not appear to have condemned.

These satisfactions cannot be described by the word *platonic.* Truly, they involved sexual relations: First, the lady granted her lover sight of all or part of her body, then the two caressed, which eventually became increasingly precise and intimate. The lover might also lie in bed with the woman who granted him his long-awaited reward, but while this love play often ended in orgasm, never, at least in the context of strict fine amor, did coitus take place, for it was banned for reasons that were much more magical than moral: It was believed that the penetration of the woman's body by the male organ of a lover was sufficient to produce a kind of pregnancy that adulterated the legitimate lineage of the woman's husband. It is important to remember that all of this occurred in a context that remained androcratic, and the reigning social system was one of hereditary transmission through the male lineage. Therefore, it was impossible, even when the relationship went quite far in the way of sexual relations, to authorize complete union—all the more so because contraception was worse than rudimentary at that time, thus permitting fears that sexual intercourse would be followed by effects harmful to the purity of the race.[13]

We should not at all believe that the initiation of the knight would stop with the victory of this love. Quite the contrary, it continued, for the love inspired by the lady obliged the knight to resume his efforts unceasingly and pursue his attempt to achieve transcendence, which would give him the opportunity to obtain his reward. Chrétien de Troyes's *The Knight of the Cart* is quite explicit on this point. Lancelot earns the queen's displeasure because of his momentary hesitation before climbing into the infamous cart that is his sole means of reaching Guinevere again. He therefore poorly performs his service to love and thus does not deserve the reward he expects for freeing the queen. The requirements of fine amor could never be transgressed. Obedience to the lady was absolute. We can see this again in this same Chrétien text when, in the tournament that pits Lancelot against Meleagant— who is himself a symbol of death in the original myth and a symbol of anticourtliness here—Lancelot must fight his worst, according to Guinevere's directives, which means he must fight like a coward when his pride bids him be courageous. In short, in this extremely significant episode, Guinevere has made Lancelot her plaything; he is merely a marionette whose strings are pulled by the queen. As a result of fighting like a coward, Lancelot is the laughingstock of everyone until the moment when the queen issues the order for him "to fight his best." Only then can he show the full measure of his skills and carry off the victory. This is a victory at great cost, however: he has both exceeded himself and renounced himself. The system of fine amor is no longer just a simple series of rituals; it is a veritable philosophy.

This philosophical system was built to seduce a woman as cultivated and intelligent as Eleanor of Aquitaine. She may even perhaps have inspired certain of its details. It is beyond question that she contributed to the spread of a doctrine that, by nature, she could only approve. The privileged situation in which she found herself in Poitiers made her a kind of arbiter of mores and mentalities. There is no doubt that she had no trouble making herself heard when she involved herself in settling a difficult problem of love, and there is no doubt that she made herself the accomplice of all those poets that converged upon the ancient city of the Pictones.* In fact, when we examine in depth the duchess's cultural activity, we cannot help but be surprised by her energy in protecting and encouraging inventions of any kind. Further, because culture is inseparable from the social life of an era, we might state that she had a decisive influence on the triumphant thought of the twelfth century in the West.

In addition, Eleanor's personal activity was inseparable from the actions first of Henry II, then from her son Richard the Lion Heart. We know that the Plantagenets definitively launched the Arthurian tradition in Europe, and though they did so for political reasons, their efforts were nonetheless essential in transmitting knowledge of the epic world of the ancient Celts.[14] It cannot be denied that Eleanor influenced Henry and Richard, and consequently she shared responsibility for the spread of the myth of Arthur, with all its secondary political and social elements.

If more proof is needed of Eleanor's role in all of this, the testimony of Andreas Capellanus confirms the importance the queen had in crafting the doctrines of fine amor. The author of *The Art of Love,* which he wrote at the end of the twelfth century at the request of Marie, countess of Champagne, was in fact a frequent guest of Eleanor. He knew her quite well, and in his treatise on amorous casuistry, which was vaguely

---

*[The Poitevins' Gaulish ancestors. —*Trans.*]

inspired by Ovid, he records themes and debates that must have been dear to the queen-duchess and her companions. It is he who mentions the courts of love, those female tribunals of which Eleanor was, both literally and figuratively, the uncontested sovereign.

These courts of love probably date from as early as 1152, from the beginning of Eleanor's reign if not in Paris then at least in Poitiers when she lived there alone for many months after her marriage to Henry, at a time when he was greatly occupied with the succession of Normandy and England. They also took place in the travels of the court itself held by the new queen during her expeditions to the different cities of her vast domain. Andreas Capellanus depicts her surrounded by the two Maries, her niece Isabelle of Vermandois, and another protector of the troubadours, Ermengarde, viscountess of Narbonne. Of course, poets were granted admission to these female tribunals and offered advice on all questions up for debate. In the interest of providing a brief history, we should note that out of the twenty-one "judgments of love" mentioned by Andreas Capellanus, six are attributed to Eleanor; five to Ermengarde; and seven to Marie de Champagne, who appears to have excelled in this art. All evidence shows that Eleanor's eldest daughter shared the same opinions as her mother and was enthused by the same causes.

But *The Art of Love* by Andreas Capellanus and the courts and judgments of love are only manifestations, albeit deeply vital ones, of a philosophy that animated the intellectual society that was more or less protected by Eleanor. As we have seen, there was a typically Celtic aspect that overlay the feminist movement of the twelfth century—at least philosophically. As to what gave it shape, this was incontestably due to the poetry of the troubadours that are wrongly labeled Provencal—the majority were from Auvergne or Limousin—and who were widespread not only in the Occitan territories but in the north as well. The troubadours were the first to compose poems to the glory of a fictional or real lady, extolling her beauties and merits. These *ensenhamens* contributed to the spreading of an image of woman entirely different from that of the preceding centuries. The first ensenhamen, dating from 1155, is dedicated "to a great lady," and it is certain that the author, Garin the Brown, lord of Châteauneuf-de-Randon, in fealty to Ermengarde of Narbonne and vassal once removed of Eleanor, had in mind the queen-duchess when he composed his poem. It should be pointed out, incidentally, that the Randon family played a far from negligible literary role at the time, particularly by the canal of their court in Puy, where, based on various testimonies, they enjoyed the "sport of the sparrow-hawk" recalled by Chrétien de Troyes when he wrote *Erec and Enid*. From this we can conclude that even if the trouvère from Champagne, Chrétien, did not actually stay in Puy, he had knowledge of what went on there.

Another important ensenhamen was composed between 1170 and 1180 by Arnaut-Guilhem of Marsan and is known as *The Knight Desirous of Pleasing the Ladies*. We know it was written in one of Eleanor's states, perhaps Gascony, and, as can be seen in the poem, very clearly influenced what went on in the court of Poitiers.

In addition, there were other society literary formats of the time that enjoyed rapid popularity. The *tenso,* which is a kind of debate, was practiced throughout the Occitan region since the beginning of the twelfth century. Derived from the tenso was the *partimen,* or *jeu-parti,* a poem dialogue between two poets, each of whom defended an opposing thesis regarding a problem related to amorous casuistry, of which the intellectual elite never seemed to tire.

It is worth noting that the first jeu-parti in the French language, written around 1180, occurs between one of Eleanor's sons—Geoffrey, duke of Brittany—and the trouvère Gace Brulé. In another jeu-parti, this same Geoffrey exchanges French couplets with a troubadour speaking Occitan. This work could be seen as illustrating as well what was taking place in Poitiers and eloquently translates the linguistic and cultural blend at work there. While it could be claimed that these literary forms were at best no more than distractions on the part of Eleanor and the noble ladies who kept her company, no one can deny the immense repercussions these amusements sparked in the intellectual world of that era. Here again, Eleanor was at the center of a transformation that went beyond herself and touched the whole of Western civilization.

If we accept the contention that the Plantagenets truly created the literary tradition of the French language by their encouragement of Angevin, Norman, Breton, Poitevin, and English poets and writers, we must clarify the subtleties of this argument. Of course, in his pursuit of an imperial politics covering England and the Continent, Henry II developed the myth of King Arthur, the uncontested and uncontestable coordinator of various peoples. Nevertheless, while the king gave the order and while he opened wide his strongbox to command the writing of books, it is also true that Henry II was primarily a warrior-king more concerned with keeping his vassals in line than with satisfying his literary inclinations. In fact, there was never a sovereign as anticourtly as Henry II, and the court of London was much less affected by courtly ideas than that of Paris. Indeed, Henry resided more on the Continent than on the island he had inherited. It is likely, then, that the literary and artistic renaissance of the twelfth century, while proceeding from Henry, was more the work of Eleanor as well as the king and queen's son Richard (who was also a poet).

In any case, courtly literature essentially developed between the years 1152 and 1174 as a harmonious synthesis of the doctrine of the troubadours, Breton folktales, and French dialectic. When Eleanor temporarily vanished from the political stage in 1173, literary production slowed to a trickle instantly, proof that the queen-duchess played an important role in its occurrence. As we've learned, at that time Eleanor was held prisoner in Winchester and Salisbury, and there was no longer any literary capital in the states of King Henry. It was not until the death of the king that the formidable literary explosion continued and largely overflowed its original framework to overrun Europe. Here again, Eleanor's presence alone at the head of the Plantagenet empire seems positive. After all, hadn't the granddaughter of William IX borrowed on her own behalf and "with usury," as Rita Lejeune says, the courtly opinions of the Troubadour who kneeled before his lady? In fact, the word *dame* [lady] comes from the Latin *domina,* meaning "mistress." Would not Eleanor then be the ideal and all-powerful mistress?

We still need to look at how Eleanor behaved specifically toward the poets and writers of her era and identify who these writers were. Alfred Jeanroy, one of the first French medievalists to systematically study troubadour poetry, states: "The frivolous and vain Eleanor could cast only a friendly gaze upon the distributors of glory who were the troubadours. Although we know the name of only one of her protégés, we can declare that poets and minstrels swarmed around her."[15] We should certainly qualify Alfred Jeanroy's harsh judgment of the "frivolous" queen—which she most certainly was not—and we can determine that the poetry of the troubadours was laudatory only in appearance, but he does acknowledge the fact that Eleanor reigned uncontested over the literary world.

The protégé mentioned by Jeanroy is obviously Bernart de Ventadorn. Legend makes him the suitor, even the lover, of Eleanor, but even if this is not true, we do have to admit that he was certainly the queen's favorite and that she is present in many of the poems by this Limousin troubadour.

Yet he was not the sole poet to benefit from Eleanor's largesse. The greatest names of twelfth-century poetry are natives of her states: Jaufré Rudel, Cercamon, Marcabru, Arnaut-Guilhem de Marsan, Peire Roger, Peire d'Auvergne, and Bernard Marti. With the exception of Jaufré Rudel, who died at an early age, the others knew one another and met and criticized each other, as can be deduced from certain debates and jeux-partis. It is even more than likely that these troubadours celebrated Eleanor under various pseudonyms, as was customary then, or with allusions that we cannot grasp. In addition, despite the specific character of the work of each, we can determine that all these poets share a certain unity of style. Their concept of love is identical, which has prompted the somewhat hasty judgment of troubadour poetry as cold and impersonal and the description that it was more a literary game than the expression of authentically experienced feelings.

We should not forget, however, that in this writing we are in the presence of a poetry of the court intended for a privileged milieu: the tone is intentionally heavy, and the object of the collective brilliance of the poet-courtiers corresponds admirably to the object of their individual brilliance. In short, Eleanor could very well be the mistress of these narrators, idealized and clad in all imaginable qualities. This assumption of the ideal by a real woman is not a unique phenomenon. We need only read the poems by Gerard de Nerval in which the Virgin Mary, the goddess Isis, the poet's mother, and all the women he has known take on the face of one Jenny Colon. It is simply poetry, and it is the art of the poet to transpose the feelings and sensations of a real person onto an imaginary or inaccessible figure, as Queen Eleanor was for the majority of these poets.

Of course, at the end of the century, when Eleanor was still queen though an old woman who ruled only by her legend and the renown of her former beauty, the formulation of the poets became a literary genre that utilized many stereotypical elements. Yet the same holds true for any innovation: from a sincere reality it becomes a style that is followed blindly to the point of seeming ridiculous. Even more, the poetry of the troubadours became a formal poetry under whose colors its authors also disguised their religious concerns, thereby designating as their lady the Cathar religion, which was officially under the Church's attack.

What also distinguishes the troubadours who were loyal to Queen Eleanor is the jeering tone they happily employ and the invectives they hurl when their passion turns into jealousy or anger. Found in this poetry are all the subtleties of amorous psychology that were later embraced by the frequenters of the seventeenth-century salons of the Précieuses. So many lovers' quarrels, so many inflamed protests, so much jealousy, and so many tears find themselves in these verses by circumstance, yet these shows of emotion never fall into platitude. It is not at all surprising that the beloved woman should be pilloried by her suitor if she dares look at another man or even if she flirts too much with several friends. All events in these poems transpire as if Cercamon, Marcabru, Peire d'Auvergne, Bernard Marti, and the others, jealous at the sight of Eleanor serving as the target of desire for all the men of their time, had found through their writing a way to express their resentment and bitterness. In this behavior and the poets' response to it we cannot help but be reminded of the attraction exercised by Queen Guinevere over King Arthur's knights.

Earlier we discovered that Andreas Capellanus's *The Art of Love,* which is an admirable summary of the courtly theories that were so dear to Eleanor, is freely inspired by Ovid. It is certain that the queen-duchess, who had received a thorough education during her childhood and adolescence, must have contributed to making stylish the authors of *Metamorphoses* and *The Art of Love.* Ovid's influence is also quite visible in an anonymous work from 1155 that is still quite close to the traditional epic genre: the *Romance of Thebes,* which, when we study its language, reveals itself to be of Poitevin origin. This influence is even more visible in the *Romance of Aeneas,* which dates from around 1160. The name of the author of this romance is not known, but we do know that he belonged to the Norman literary school that was shaped in the Plantagenet court. This book is a skilled adaptation of Virgil, but its success and its originality stem from an added episode—amply exploited—concerning the turbulent love of Lavinia and Aeneas. All the structuring themes of courtly love are concretely exhibited in this work: the complaints, the moans, the moral sufferings, the inner monologues—nothing is missing. It is a forerunner of the *Romance of Tristan,* which beats all the competition in the arena of delicate and refined casuistry. In this *Romance of Aeneas,* it is obvious that literary inspiration has come from the theories of Ovid, and that these ideas could not leave readers or listeners indifferent, for in them are all the major questions that can be asked concerning the relations between lovers.

Ovid's tangible influence in narrative works such as the *Romance of Thebes* and the *Romance of Aeneas* is even more obvious in the poetry of Bernart de Ventadorn and that of his contemporaries. From this milieu of Occitan poetry came the French authors of *Pyramus and Thisbe* and *Narcissus,* spurious works of antiquity constructed on the same themes. As for *Philomena,* by Chrétien de Troyes, we know this author wrote many works inspired by Ovid that are now lost but which Chrétien must have composed from the viewpoint of the Aquitaine court. Also constituting an important literary event in the years 1160–1165 is the monumental *Romance of Troy* by Benoît de Sainte-Maure.

In fact, Sainte-Maure does not mention Eleanor's name, but we do know he created his work with her in mind, thinking it would please her. It can be shown that Eleanor is "the rich lady of a rich king" to whom he dedicated the romance.[16] He even presents his apologies to this rich lady, for he makes his heroine Briseis a model of female fickleness. It so happens that anyone can recognize certain features of Eleanor's character in the figure of Briseis, even if these features are borrowed more from legend than from the actual history of the queen-duchess.

These romances illustrate the desire of Eleanor's entourage to bring classic antiquity within reach of a larger audience. Once the domain of the clerks, this Greco-Roman tradition (which appeared in Latin, for the Greek language, the language of heretics, was unknown in the West) strongly entered cultural life, at the same time taking on all the innovations of fine amor. In this way, culture crossed over the walls of the monasteries and convents and through the doors of the great universities to mix with aristocratic life—an occurrence of considerable importance. If Eleanor was indeed one of the principal artisans of this rediscovery of a culture and its expansion, we should pay homage to her as one of the most significant women of the Middle Ages. As noted by Rita Lejeune, it is hard to believe that "tens of thousands of verses in the classic triad* emerged by chance in the space of a few years in the wake of her court. There was undoubtedly conscious intention, official patronage, and a distribution of roles." In fact, all of this seemed organized, planned, as if Eleanor and her entourage sought to provide the Plantagenet empire with an extraordinary cultural dimension.

Eleanor is also responsible for two major works of the twelfth century, the *Romance of Rollo* and the *Romance of Brutus,* both attributed to Master Robert Wace, canon of Bayeux and in the queen's service. This is proved by an early-thirteenth-century account written

---

*[The classic triad here refers to the three-line works of Celtic Wales and Ireland that were resurrected by the courtly poets. —*Trans.*]

by Layamon following the death of Eleanor. In fact, Layamon says it was Eleanor to whom Robert Wace offered, in 1155, his *Romance of Brutus,* which is a French adaptation of the *Historia Regum Britanniae* by the Latin-writing Welshman Geoffrey of Monmouth. In addition, in his prologue, Robert Wace clearly indicates his intentions: he wishes to write the history of the kings that have ruled over England and Normandy—in other words, the history of the predecessors of Henry II. This is why this Norman clerk began by freely translating the most important British work to synthesize a complete series of traditions, particularly the Celtic tradition of the isle of Britain, which would justify the union of the English and French crowns. The plan Wace suggested (and followed) was to write the *Romance of Brutus* as a kind of preface and then provide the true history of the Normans in the *Romance of Rollo* (Rollo was the first of the Norman dukes) and eventually make his way to Etienne de Blois, Empress Matilda, and ultimately the Plantagenets.

It is quite odd, though, that the *Romance of Brutus,* whose purpose was to laud the Plantagenets, was dedicated not to Henry II, but to Eleanor. We should accept as fact that Eleanor not only received this work but also that she ordered it written. Because Wace could have begun his enormous work only before Eleanor's "divorce," this order speaks volumes about the interest the duchess of Aquitaine took in the history—even the legendary history—of the Britons long before her marriage to Henry II. Thus, while we cannot afford to neglect the obvious role of Henry II in the diffusion of Arthurian legends, we must allow that Eleanor is equally responsible for reasons that might well have been different initially but that eventually converged with those of her spouse.

The *Romance of Brutus* directly precipitated an entire series of romances on Arthurian subjects—but we must not forget that Wace was aiming elsewhere. The Britons did not interest him excessively and he regarded them as fabulists ("Britons often tell tall tales"), yet he used them to demonstrate the actual predominance of the Normans. In this regard, his *Romance of Rollo* clearly corresponds to his convictions, and he dedicated it to both Eleanor and Henry, emphasizing the queen over the king ever so subtly. In this dedication we find that he was more attached to the brilliant granddaughter of William the Troubadour, in whom he found a woman capable of appreciating refinements of thought, than to his natural lord, the bellicose Plantagenet, who was more concerned with waging war than with valuing literary works. It is tempting to claim that when Eleanor was imprisoned by Henry, Wace was disgraced. In fact, he had not yet finished the *Romance of Rollo* when he was copied by colleague and rival Benoît de Sainte-Maure, to whom Henry II entrusted the task of writing a chronicle of the dukes of Normandy. Yet the possibility of this disgrace is bolstered by the fact that it seems another individual—Chrétien de Troyes—was disgraced at this same time. Although Chrétien was not a direct dependent of Eleanor, he was a dependent of her daughter, Marie de Champagne.

Chrétien de Troyes in fact poses a problem. We might legitimately wonder if he was related to the ducal family of Normandy. He may, in fact, have been a cousin of Etienne de Blois, and it would have been through this channel that he made his way into the Plantagenet sphere of influence and thus that of Eleanor. While it is difficult to determine the validity of this, it is nevertheless incontestable that Chrétien had close and sustained contact with the court of Poitiers. Where else would he have gained his extensive knowledge of British legend if not at Poitiers, where a person was as likely to meet a Celtic bard as an Occitan troubadour?

We know that the early works by this trouvère from Champagne were fairly numerous, but none survive except a vapid romance entitled *Guillaume d'Angleterre* [William of England]. He certainly wrote a *Tristan,* which would be the first to date in French, but his earliest Arthurian romance to survive is *Erec and Enid,* the subject of which must have been well known in England, for there is a Welsh version with a basic outline that matches Chrétien's work but comes from a different source. Chrétien's *Erec* is later than Wace's *Brutus,* which he skillfully exploits, and may also assume a scholarly origin or at least a deliberate intention to connect an Arthurian episode to a coherent overview, which may have been accomplished by the *Romance of Brutus.*

It is interesting that *Erec* is full of allusions to events in Brittany. In fact, in the story there is a transposition of the 1166 engagement of Geoffrey Plantagenet, son of Henry II and Eleanor, to Constance, heiress of Brittany, then five years of age. In addition, the reception of Erec into his own lands—which takes place, as if by chance, in Nantes—brings to mind Geoffrey's welcome as duke of Brittany in May 1169, and in the luxurious description of Arthur's court we can see an echo of the plenary assembly held by Henry and Eleanor on Christmas that same year in Nantes, where Erec's coronation supposedly took place. There can be no doubt about the Armoricain influences that permeate *Erec*—if Chrétien did not personally witness the facts he adapts, he owes knowledge of them to the people who surrounded Eleanor or who had taken part in these events.

Other passages from this romance also show that Chrétien was aware of all that took place in the court of England, and numerous details suggest he was familiar with the isle of Britain. Indeed, in the romance *Cligès,* presented as something of an anti-*Tristan* tale (perhaps this is an homage to Eleanor as an irreproachable wife, much as *Tristan* is a glorification of conjugal love), Chrétien de Troyes is not miserly with geographical details, all of which are accurate—which shows the author knew England from having actually visited it.

Yet this fact does not give us authority to conclude, a priori, that Chrétien lived in Eleanor of Aquitaine's circle of influence—but other elements scattered throughout his work give us good reason to determine this. It is evident that Chrétien immediately enrolled in the school of troubadours to compose his lyric poems. It was in their works that he learned the rudiments of courtesy or courtly manners, with the essential difference that he adapted this courtesy from the lyric genre to the epic or narrative genre. In fact, one of his chansons is directly inspired by a well-known Occitan model: the famous *Chanson d'Alouette* [Song of the Lark] by Bernart de Ventadorn. From this we might presume that he knew Eleanor's protégé and that the two men met as a result of some connection to the queen-duchess.

Ovid's influence on the two poets is also an important element to consider in determining Chrétien's involvement in Eleanor's circle. While it is correct that Chrétien composed *Ovidiana* before 1170, he could have written its contents only at Eleanor's court, where these themes were de rigueur. It was only later, after Eleanor was imprisoned by her husband, that Chrétien followed Eleanor's daughter Marie to the court of Champagne where he wrote *Lancelot* and *Yvain* for Marie. Indeed, *Lancelot* is still completely imbued with the atmosphere of the courts of love and the casuistry of the troubadours. In fact, it is reasonable to believe that Chrétien de Troyes forged his first writing in Eleanor's entourage. This is what medievalists usually call the Tristan period of the trouvère from Champagne—and this Tristan period must have been equally important for other poets.

We know that the legend of Tristan became widespread early on in Occitan literature. The two main French texts on the Tristan legend, by Béroul and by Thomas, while different in spirit, are both written in Anglo-Norman and were composed for an audience more accustomed to the Plantagenet court than that of the Capets. While Béroul's *Tristan* is essentially more popular, it is as loaded with details borrowed from the amorous casuistry of the troubadours as the work of Thomas. Thomas's *Tristan,* however, in presenting the thesis that love is stronger than anything that would constrain it, is more in line with the concerns of Eleanor's entourage and consequently has a direct bond with that milieu. Whichever form it takes, though, the theme of Tristan bears the mark of Eleanor in the way it is handled by the two principal authors of the romance. To be fair, to the authors Béroul and Thomas as well as the anonymous Oxford author of *Tristan's Madness* we should also add Marie de France, whose *Lai du Chevrefeuille* [Lay of the Honeysuckle] is utterly imbued with a courtly atmosphere.

In fact, it clearly seems that Marie de France—about whom we know nothing except that she was the bastard daughter of Henry's father, Geoffrey Plantagenet—pursued her worldly and literary career in the shadow of Eleanor of Aquitaine, her sister-in-law and counselor. All of the work of Marie de France bears the stamp of the discussions and judgments of Eleanor's court. The most varied episodes, indubitably borrowed from Brittany tradition, are handled in the strictest courtly style, and the author's moral speeches refer most often to the well-known problems of Andreas Capellanus, who dealt with them purely theoretically.

Here again, in Marie's lays we can feel the obstinate presence of the lady who is the ideal mistress, the woman who is so renowned and so widely heeded that she contributes to giving a concept to love through the blossoming of works that together are so many subjects for meditation. We can conclude that without Eleanor, there would not have been any courtly literature, at least in the French language, and the majority of Celtic legends relating to love would have remained unknown to the educated Europe of the twelfth century. A queen with a passion for love and poetry lent her ears to the Breton storytellers who crisscrossed her Continental lands and island holdings and thereby triggered a process unique in literary history: the resuscitation of a centuries-old myth and its rejuvenation by poets whose genius appears in the grandiose fresco that they left us. Tristan, Iseult, Arthur, Guinevere, Lancelot, Gawain, Merlin, Yvain, Laudine, Luned, Vivian, and Morgana are all names that were transformed into universal symbols, and we owe their remembering to Queen Eleanor. Without her, they would remain nothing but shadows. It is clear that the duchess of Aquitaine, countess of Poitou, protector of arts and letters, was also the uncontested queen of the troubadours.

4

THE LEGEND OF ELEANOR

A quick skim over the principal stages of Eleanor of Aquitaine's life throws light on a certain number of incontestable facts. Next to these facts, however, there are a great many suppositions that, taken together, create a complete portrait of the woman who was queen of two countries. There are many uncertainties concerning the exact role Eleanor played, and gaps in our knowledge only excite the imagination. These uncertainties and gaps largely form Eleanor's legend, which has been peddled since the twelfth century by chroniclers and writers who could not remain impartial regarding the duchess of Aquitaine and thus transformed and adapted all that they did not like to create a veritable artistic object. As a result, we know that the figure of Eleanor far exceeds the actual woman she was. During her life and after, she was quickly made into a heroine of courtly romance, a particularly colorful symbol of the ideal woman of the twelfth century.

Of course, we also have to take into account the antipathy and even hatred that Eleanor inspired. The chroniclers of the north had little love for her: She was the foreigner, one who did not behave like other women and whose attitude was scandalous, even if there was actually nothing reprehensible in her behavior. She became for them one of those avant-garde women, a southerner whose mystery was heightened by ignorance and who had to be denounced because she brought about a profound transformation of mores. The same was true for the "English" chroniclers (who were most often Norman). They had little affection for their queen who, in their eyes, was guilty of taking a greater interest in her Aquitanian domains than in Normandy and England. For them, too, she was the foreigner. What's more, especially during the period of her imprisonment, one means of paying court to Henry II was to speak ill of Eleanor, inventing sordid stories about her. All of this took shape in the context of the literary renaissance of the time, in the milieu of the poetry of the troubadours or the verse inspired by their example as well as in the midst of the spread of courtly romances in which all the Celtic legends concerning women were given substance in character types that often resulted from the adaptation of contemporary models.

It is true that for three reasons the duchess of Aquitaine fascinated the intellectual elite of her time, a fascination that began with her marriage to Louis VII: First, as confirmed by many authors, Eleanor was extremely beautiful, and this beauty did not wane with age. Next, she was an extremely cultivated woman—a rarity at this time—and possessed a keen intelligence that she exhibited every moment of her life. Finally, she was a powerful woman, the holder of sovereignty over a large domain and perfectly aware of the political role she could play. Because of all this, it is not surprising that Eleanor became the center of a legend that was constantly revived and rounded off and that, though unverifiable in full, was based on a few fragments of reality.

In fact, it is through studying the principal anecdotes in which Eleanor appears as a legendary heroine that we are able to paint her complete portrait. The first anecdote concerns a possible liaison between Eleanor and her young uncle Raymond before her marriage. As we have noted, they seemed to share a great affinity in part based on culture, poetry, a taste for the arts, and ambition. When William X left on pilgrimage, it was Raymond to whom he entrusted guardianship of Eleanor and her sister. Eleanor and her uncle often spent time together, sometimes alone, particularly when they went horseback riding. From there it is only a step to imagining they shared something more than great affection and common tastes—and this step was quickly taken. Later, when the relationship between Eleanor and Louis VII turned sour in Antioch, it was not long before various people dredged up this old complicity between Eleanor and Raymond, with Raymond suffering accusations that he was a disturbing factor to the couple's harmony and that he had gone further with his niece than an uncle should go.

We can never determine whether or to what degree these accusations were true. All we know is that it was the king's jealousy that motivated his decision not to follow the battle plan drawn up by Raymond and to bring the queen with him to Jerusalem after a somewhat precipitous departure. We must remember, though, that here is an epic and mythological theme that certainly played a role in the formation of Eleanor's legend: incest.

We must also remember that the twelfth century was a period in the Middle Ages that was the boldest in the evolution of mores and was, theoretically at least, the most immoral in the sense of rejection of traditional morality and movement toward another morality that was more flexible and less bound to Christian imperatives. This was the era that witnessed the development of the legend of Tristan and Iseult, the absolute triumph of a love that rejected all taboos. Incest lurks constantly in the story of Tristan, although the authors do not formally allude to it: Iseult is Tristan's aunt by marriage. Marc, Tristan's maternal uncle, is a father substitute for Tristan and plays this role with the orphaned nephew that he wishes to make his heir. In this the equivalence to Phedre is obvious. Further, when we seek out the Celtic origins of the legend of Tristan, we encounter again and again the theme of transgression of the taboo against incest.[1]

From this history, it was therefore tempting to imagine a liaison between the niece Eleanor and her uncle Raymond—and all the more so given the many historical examples of such incest. After all, the Byzantine emperor Manual Commenius, who gave such a magnificent welcome to the Crusaders, caused a scandal by openly displaying a tumultuous liaison with his niece Theodora in defiance of custom and transgressing current social taboos. Of course, only exceptional people in the image of the ancient gods and heroes could carry out such incest; it remained dangerous for common mortals—only superhuman people could assume its many consequences. Inventing a liaison between Raymond and Eleanor therefore placed the two of them on a higher level where the laws governing the masses no longer applied. This was a kind of deification of the couple, and primarily served to charge Eleanor with a certain aura. During the development of the notion of amorous initiation of the knight by his lady, some might have thought the lady should also have been initiated by someone older belonging to her very family. Even when she was very young, Eleanor was already truly the lady—the domina, the mistress not only of knights and troubadours but also of the kings and princes over whom she exercised her sovereignty. This archetype is found again in the literary transformation of the figure of Queen Guinevere, wife of King Arthur.

Outside of this incontestable mythological aspect, however, the love affair of Raymond and Eleanor falls entirely in the realm of the feminist claims of the time. In fact, Eleanor's entire life in its historic framework is an illustration of this ascent of feminism. Indeed, courtly love itself preaches woman's freedom outside marriage. During the twelfth century, marriage was felt to be a form of slavery for women, and in any case was incompatible with love. Marriage was only a social action; it was necessary for procreation and inheritance and to guarantee society's balance inasmuch as the family constituted the essential base of any human group, no matter its nature or size. During this time, however, there was a realization of the ambiguous nature of marriage. Christianity tolerated it merely as an outlet for sexuality and the sole possible exit from the problem of the continuation of the species. The great battle between love and marriage began in the West and has not come close to ending. A liaison between Eleanor and her uncle therefore existed in favor of the freedom of young women to do what they wanted with their hearts and bodies outside of any religious or political constraint. Though in the context of a well-organized society a woman was not free to marry as she pleased— that was decided by paternal authority—she could assert her independence in her attitude toward the man who was her betrothed before marriage and her husband after marriage. According to the courtly spirit of the times, the husband gave children to a woman, but it was her lover who gave her personality.

It is impossible to examine the real or imagined adventures of Eleanor without referring to the courtly philosophical abstract, for Eleanor incarnated the courtly woman. Yet was she aware of the role she played? Yes, surely, for ever since childhood she found herself in a milieu where questions of love were considered important and were debated passionately. The granddaughter of William the Troubadour, the inventor of *trobar clus,* that refined and precious hermetic poetry that shook up lyricism and led to the development of amorous casuistry, could not have remained insensitive to the problems of love, for from this angle, such problems caused people to ask questions related to the very nature of femininity. In addition, in this troubadour poetry imbued with Islamic mysticism and originating in Spain was the image of the ideal woman, a notion of Celtic origin. According to this notion, the ideal woman was beautiful, cultivated, an enchantress, and foremost a symbol of sovereignty and freedom. Eleanor was all of these.

Another characteristic episode, this time with the young Saldebreuil, was supposed to have taken place during the period when Eleanor was queen of France. It is well known that during the tournaments over which Eleanor presided many knights wished to fight for her (that is, to wear her colors). It was a custom (of Occitan origin, incidentally) to pay homage to the beauty and nobility of a lady by performing feats of prowess for her. Yet even if it is true, which no one can either prove or refute, the episode of Saldebreuil is filled with underlying meanings that are scabrous and make the alleged occurrence akin to the legend that developed around the theme of Eleanor's sensuality. In fact, the queen had a reputation as a sensual woman, which the austere French court deemed unacceptable, and because she was a sexual object for those around her, she thereby contributed to the development of others' sensuality.

Here is what is told regarding the episode with Saldebreuil: One day, as a game, Eleanor asked her knights who among them would wear only one of her shirts (that is, would be entirely nude save for her shirt) during battle with an armored adversary. The young Saldebreuil—an Aquitanian—immediately stepped forward, and during the course of the combat, he was wounded. Eleanor then cared for him quite attentively, and when she went to dinner clad in the blood-spattered shirt, the king was quite annoyed.

Whether this anecdote is true or not changes nothing of substance: regardless, we find ourselves in the presence of the phenomenon of fetishism. Saldebreuil's behavior is no different from that of the fans of many show-business stars who become trancelike when their idol sings on stage and then keep as precious relics pieces of his or her clothing after the star tears them off and tosses them to admirers. Though this phenomenon more often affects young women than young men, it remains to be determined what passes through the mind, both conscious and unconscious, of young men in the presence of a female idol.

The sexual components of this behavior have been proved by depth psychology, and many individuals, both male and female, share this penchant for fetishism to various degrees.[2] It is simply an attempt for intimate contact with a loved person or a person for whom you have great admiration.[3] If actual contact with this admired person is impossible, fetishism serves as a substitute; if an individual is unable to touch this person's body, he or she touches the clothing that is theoretically permeated with the idol's body. This tendency—which is quite common, by the way—can go quite far in some cases, including certain acts that are somewhat hastily labeled depraved[4] and that in ultimate cases become transvestism.[5]

In Saldebreuil's case, this fetishism is accompanied by a process of identification with the lady represented by Eleanor. It is the lady herself who fights as the knight wears her shirt in direct contact with his skin, and if he wins, it is the lady who gains the victory through him as an intermediary. Yet there are more troubling components: the combination of sex and death causes additional excitement for the knight, who knows he may be killed but who believes that being killed while wearing the shirt of his beloved lady would be the highest degree of voluptuousness. In the story of Saldebreuil, however, the role Eleanor plays is that of the tyrannical, demanding, and cruel mistress. She does not hesitate to place her knight-lover in danger knowing full well that he is at a physical disadvantage and is risking much. In so doing, however, she reaps proof of absolute love, for the knight-lover accepts sacrificing himself for her.

In this deconstruction we are in the area of courtly philosophical abstract, which we will soon examine with regard to *The Knight of the Cart,* written by Chrétien de Troyes and largely inspired by Marie de Champagne, daughter of Eleanor—in other words, inspired by Eleanor herself. The lover's total obedience to the mistress is necessary in order for the knight to receive his just reward. In the instance of Saldebreuil's tale, Saldebreuil's reward is the queen's physical care. Eleanor's victory is displayed by her exhibitionism in appearing at the dinner clad in the bloody shirt. She thereby demonstrates that she is desirable and beautiful and can obtain whatever she wants from those she has commanded to perform heroic actions. In this legend, Saldebreuil will no doubt subsequently be added to the list of the queen's lovers.

This is the logical conclusion of the knight's amorous initiation undertaken by Eleanor. In the context of the anecdote such as it is recorded, Saldebreuil, like many of the knights surrounding Eleanor, loves her because she is beauty, perfection, and sovereignty. His eyes are blinded by the moral light that emanates from this woman. Yet the queen must choose those of her suitors who are capable of loving her madly. She subjects all of them to a test and gives them her shirt as a security deposit and as strength to the candidates. This is the first stage of the initiation: contact through an interposing object. The second stage is made up of the care the queen gives the wounded knight. Many knights were content with a simple kiss or a mere touch from the hand of their lady, but to reach this point they had to deserve their reward, follow the rules of the art of love, and obey their lady in all things. Saldebreuil satisfied the test imposed upon him and thereby received his reward. Implicit in this is the promise that should he later pass through other stages of initiation and show himself to be the perfect lover, he would obtain much more. This is why legend took possession of this episode, and because there was a desire to make Eleanor a new Messalina, it was concluded that a liaison existed between her and Saldebreuil—but who really knows?

In any event, with all due deference to those who wish to see courtly love as a purified and platonic love, we know that the intellectual elite of that time was haunted by eroticism. The poetry of the troubadours is undeniably erotic—whether subtly so or otherwise—and the context of the romances of the Round Table is bathed in a refined but perfectly carnal eroticism. The image left by the twelfth-century chroniclers of Eleanor could only be dependent on this context. In short, Eleanor was woman in all her wholeness, and as such she was the object of the avowed or repressed desires of a certain number of courtiers or poets. The fact that the queen was attacked for her morals proves both the attraction she exerted from the erotic perspective and the disapproval she inspired in those around her who were little used to such freedom of mind and body. It is well known that woman is the center of desire and repulsion, the object of pleasure and disgust. In the context of the twelfth century, during which there developed the cult of the Virgin Mary, Eleanor represented both salvation (although toward a dubious Paradise) and perdition (as a satanic being). It could not be otherwise in this era; everything that did not conform to the norm or that rose above the ordinary smacked of fire and brimstone. As such, the shadow of the devil enveloped the queen in his halo of mysteries.

The reputation of Queen Eleanor caused a scandal because of her behavior—both real and imagined. The author of a rhymed thirteenth-century chronicle, Philippe Mousket, depicts her undressing entirely in front of her barons after the Council of Beaugency and telling them, without an ounce of modesty:

> See lords,
> is my body not delectable?
> The king said I was a devil!

Further, if we believe the thirteenth-century preacher Étienne de Bourbon, she was harshly scolded one day by Gilbert de la Porrée, then bishop of Poitiers, because she had paid him the friendliest compliment on the beauty of his hands and it was somewhat risqué in its innuendo. Yet is this a truthful detail or part of Eleanor's legend? Regardless, Eleanor is not only an important figure but also—and especially—is the symbol of the women of her time. These women sought to free themselves from the tutelage of men and wanted to dominate the world. In this context, any means to the end are acceptable, particularly the sensuality Eleanor inspired, which ensured that words were heard. This was in fact how Eleanor became the target of many in Europe. When she married Henry II, the author of a German satire consecrated in his verses the impertinent expression of his desire: "If the whole world belonged to me, from the wide sea to the Rhine, I would use it all up to get the queen of England resting in my arms." This anonymous poet only said out loud what many of those surrounding Eleanor were thinking in silence.

The Crusade in which Eleanor took part permitted the legend to take shape and develop. Because the chroniclers did not have a great deal to say about the queen of France at the time of this expedition, the storytellers made up for it in spades. One of the most famous legends concerning Eleanor during the Crusades, although it is of later provenance, is that which portrays her at the head of a troop of women fighting the Saracens.

There was obviously a need to justify the presence of Eleanor and the wives of the other barons in the Crusader army. It was said that Eleanor wished to accompany the king of France, but this is hardly likely, although it was well within the queen's character to have the notion of taking part in a military expedition. It so happens that the presence of the queen and numerous women on a religious and military expedition was shocking. The chroniclers tell us that the prevailing atmosphere in the army was not much in accord with the sacred purposes of the Crusades. Therefore, either to justify Eleanor's presence or to show her in a still more formidable and more diabolical light, she was transformed into the queen of a troop of Amazons that swooped down and harassed the enemy but also—and this was the flip side of the coin—assumed risky initiatives that put the entire army in peril.

Nevertheless, portraying Eleanor astride a steed at the head of a band of women cavaliers was also a rather romantic image. This contributed further to shaping the notion of the ideal. In this portrayal, she was not merely cultivated, beautiful, and intelligent but also was the legitimate holder of sovereignty and the woman who fights, the warrior-empress who knows how to inspire the masses and lead them to feats of blessed prowess. In the same way that she subjugated Saldebreuil (who happened to be in the troop of Crusaders) by making him fight for her whatever the danger, she stirred up the courage of the soldiers— many of whom were her own vassals—for a good cause.

Yet this image of Eleanor leading an armed troop does not really conform to that of the courtly woman who might be satisfied to inspire the prowess of knights but who would never take part personally in any kind of battle. In *The Knight of the Cart,* by Chrétien de Troyes, Queen Guinevere, kidnapped by Meleagant, king of Gorre, patiently waits for one of the knights in her service, Lancelot or Gawain, to free her. While the lady is the keeper of sovereignty, it is up to the knight to take action. Even if the woman of the twelfth century held a rank that made her a war leader, she never took part personally in a battle.[6] It wasn't until the fourteenth century that a woman rode at the head of a troop: Joan of Flanders, known as Joan of the Flame, wife of the claimant to the ducal crown of Brittany, Jean de Montfort, who distinguished himself at Hennebont by feats worthy of the most hardened warrior. Further, we can add Joan of Arc.[7]

At the root of all of this is memory of the Amazon legend as well as a series of correspondences to Celtic heroines, mainly those found in the Irish epics. There is no lack of women warriors in these tales. First, there are queens such as Ness, the mother of the famous king Conchobar,[8] and Medbh, queen of Connaught, a formidable figure who is the heroine of several stories, particularly *The Cattle Raid of Cooley.*[9] These women obviously held supreme authority, but in addition they took direct part in battle at the head of their troops, often appearing like unleashed furies. The same holds true in history with the adventure of Queen Boudica, who bitterly fought the Roman legions in combat.[10]

On another level, but in a context that pushes these elements back to a pre-Celtic period, there is also much mention in the Irish epics of women warriors who are more or less witches or magicians and who teach young men the art of war. Generally, these warrior women live in Scotland, where the future Irish heroes go to receive initiation in order to perfect their knowledge of the military arts. In addition to weapons training, including magic tricks that can be used to surprise the adversary, these warrior women also provide sexual initiation. They contract temporary "marriages" to the young men who come to board with them. For example, this is what is told in the text *The Education of Cuchulainn,* in which the future defender of Ulster leaves his fiancée, Emer, to go to Scotland, where he learns warrior techniques and experiences sexual initiation at the hands of women warriors whose appearance is similar to that of witches and whose names, Scatach and Uatach, mean, respectively, "she who causes great fear" (or "she who protects") and "the most terrible one"—names that speak volumes about their characters.[11]

We also have the hero of Leinster, Finn, who is hunted as a child by his father's killers and is taken in to be raised and educated by women warriors akin to magicians, who make him an uncommon individual ready to face any danger that he might meet.[12] The same is true of the Welsh epic *Peredur* in which the hero receives an initiation in weapons training from the witches of Caer Loyw, who teach him infallible means for triumphing.[13]

This theme of the woman warrior reappears in the legend of Eleanor leading her band of Amazons. Nevertheless, the erotic aspect is not missing from this legend, just as it is not absent from the Crusades legend of the love affair of Tancrede and Clorinda.[14] War and sexuality are inseparable, but in the case of Eleanor and the Amazons, instead of being promised as a reward the women of the cities they conquer, the warriors are led in battle by their own wives, who thereby excite both the warriors' martial and sexual fervor. It is no cause for surprise then that the chroniclers allude to a certain disorder in the Crusader army after this.

The presence of women in the midst of the Crusader army did in fact hinder military operations—yet we have no proof of Eleanor's participation in battles or of the participation of other barons' wives. It is likely that these women were carefully kept away from the front as a separate group under the close supervision of the knights and that anything other than this is merely invention. Oddly enough, though, this invention fed into the ancient myths and served to integrate them into the twelfth century. It seems that every effort was taken during Eleanor's lifetime to make her personality mythic or legendary to the maximum extent possible in order to create from her an exemplary model of woman as it was seen in a certain intellectual milieu of the twelfth century. In this way, Eleanor provided an ideal opportunity to show a woman in full possession of her entire personality. This effort was obviously successful, for over the course of the centuries, numerous authors have simply shrugged off the historical data and attached themselves to this legendary aspect of the duchess of Aquitaine.

The events that took place in Antioch during this same Crusade began new legendary inventions. Recall that while we do not know anything of what actually transpired here, according to the evidence, the queen cheated on her husband on one or more occasions. There can be no other explanation for the king's exacerbated jealousy, the definite rift between the couple, the precipitous departure from Antioch, and the subsequent attempt made by Pope Eugenius III to reconcile them. Poisonous comments also moved at a brisk pace. The possible liaison between Eleanor and her uncle Raymond of Poitiers was dredged up again, as was the episode with Saldebreuil. Other names were also mentioned, but first and foremost, talk dwelled on an attempt made by the queen to flee with a handsome Saracen, the sultan Saladin himself, who, we can recall, was less than twelve years old at the time.

An anonymous author, the Minstrel of Reims, has left us the most detailed narrative about this affair, although he confuses the city of Tyre with Antioch. According to him, on her arrival in Tyre, Eleanor heard people speaking about the sultan Saladin and took great pleasure in listening to what was said about his beauty, generosity, and courage. She thus fell in love with him before ever laying eyes upon him and soon started corresponding with him. With great courtesy he accepted the messages sent by the queen of France, and on hearing what was said about Eleanor's beauty, imposing presence, and intelligence, he too fell desperately in love. He responded to her messages with valuable gifts and a letter in which he confessed his great love. Eleanor answered immediately, suggesting that he carry her off so that they could marry—for this was one means of getting away from a husband whose monkish qualities she appreciated less and less.

Allegedly, still using messengers, they perfected an escape plan. Saladin armed a galley that left the port of Ascalon for Antioch. This galley with Saladin himself on board arrived shortly before midnight. Eleanor left the place where she had been residing, and, accompanied by two maidens who helped her carry two chests stuffed with gold and silver, she headed to the ship, which was docked at the point the queen and the sultan had agreed upon. But—there is always a but in matters like this—another of Eleanor's attendants found out about the affair, and seeing her mistress sneaking away toward the port, she ran to the king's room, woke him, and said, "Sire, misfortune is about to befall you! Madame plans to leave for Ascalon, and Saladin and his galley are in port awaiting her. For God's sake, Sire, hurry!" Stupefied by this news, the king leaped to the foot of his bed, dressed, and equipped himself. He then assembled his men and raced off to the port. There he caught the queen, who had already set foot on the galley, and brought her back immediately to her chamber. Once in the bedroom, the king asked her why she had sought to flee. The queen answered him, "In the name of God, it was because of your malice, for you are worth no more than a rotten apple—and I have heard so many good things about Saladin that I love him better than you. Know this well, in truth though you may hold me you will never take your pleasure of me."

Historically speaking, this anecdote does not hold water, but the elements composing it are fairly significant, and it is likely that they translate, in veiled fashion, the profound causes of the quarrel between the king and queen. Eleanor had tired of Louis VII for various reasons. He behaved too much like a monk, either by lending a sympathetic ear to the clerks or by acting somewhat timidly in his intimate relations with his wife, which surely did not earn her sympathy and left her sensual needs unsatisfied. Eleanor also had a tendency to think the king incapable of providing her with descendants. Eleanor wanted to be a mother—but during all the years of their marriage to this point, Eleanor had given birth to only one daughter. Then there was the king's character, which was extremely austere, markedly less than brilliant, politically mediocre, and not skilled in matters of war. He simply was not the kind of man she required. This explains the words the Minstrel of Reims puts in her mouth: "You are worth no more than a rotten apple." We know that during her stay in Antioch, Eleanor envisioned separating from her husband; she even put forward the argument of consanguinity that had not occurred to the king of France. Further, it is not impossible that she had considered running away with another man. There was no lack of fine matches in Antioch, for the finest flower of European chivalry was then in the immediate area.

What is absurd about this story, however, is the intervention of Saladin. As we have seen, this could actually have been only the sultan Nured Din, which in itself is quite unlikely. It is also hard to envision Eleanor, an ardent Christian despite her temptation to stray, running away with an infidel. Saladin was thrust into this legend because, at the time it was put down in writing, this sultan was the best known of all the Saracen foes of the Crusaders. During the Third Crusade he was pitted against Richard the Lion Heart, whom he greatly esteemed. He had a reputation for generosity and courtesy, great ambition, and unbounded courage. In an attempt to explain the rift between Eleanor and Louis, he was the ideal figure to put between the husband and wife and thus was turned into the cursed Muslim who was responsible for Eleanor's "divorce."

What is truly interesting in this anecdote is the fact that Eleanor falls in love with Saladin because of his great qualities without ever laying eyes upon him, and Saladin feels a strong love for her when the messengers sing her praises. Love engendered in this way is a literary theme started by the troubadours that eventually enjoyed great success in all courtly poetry, both in Occitania and in the north. In fact, this theme appears much earlier in ancient Celtic legends, particularly in Ireland, and often involves a hero or heroine, who, having heard the praises of the merits and beauty of someone, offers this person his or her love before ever seeing the individual. This occurs in the very odd *Story of Derbforgaille,* in which the heroine, a kind of fairy with the power to transform into a swan, hunts down the hero Cuchulainn to tell him she loves him and wishes to be his.[15] The same idea can be found in *The Voyage of Art, Son of Conn.* In this story, the hero sets off in search of the woman who has been promised him. Though he has never seen her, he already feels a strong love for her. After numerous adventures that are all initiatory ordeals, he eventually finds her on an enchanted island where she is guarded by her cruel family members and dog-headed beings.[16] In Welsh epic this theme is found in the narrative of Culhwch and Olwen. Because of magic, the hero has fallen in love with a young woman about whom he knows nothing—not even where she is.[17] As for the folktales from Brittany, many of them center around the search undertaken by a young hero to find the princess of the sun, the queen of mighty deeds,[18] or the daughter of a mysterious king.[19]

In the poetry of Eleanor's time, this theme is brilliantly illustrated by the troubadour Jaufré Rudel, singer of *The Distant Love.* A legend that grew after Jaufré's time maintains that he was a prince of Blaye who had fallen in love with Melissandra, countess of Tripoli. He had never laid eyes upon her, but her charm and beauty were extolled. He set sail for the East, became ill while at sea, and reached Tripoli on the brink of death, but the countess, who had been informed of this, ran to his bedside, and the troubadour died in the arms of the woman he had always loved. This touching story, which served Edmond Rostand for his play *La Princess Lointaine* [The Faraway Princess], was obviously invented and was based on some of Rudel's poems addressed to a distant woman he never names:

> Love of a distant land
> for you my heart is aching

and I can find no remedy for it
lest first I make my way
drawn by love's intoxication
into the orchard, behind closed curtains,
with the companion of my desire . . .

The poet bemoans his current condition and asserts that he cannot live without the presence of this mysterious woman:

My heart's desire is unending
for she I love more than all
and I fear to lose her
by desiring her too strongly,
for it stings worse than a thorn,
that pain soothed with love play
for which I seek no sympathy . . .

The poet then imagines leaving for distant lands in search of the woman who occupies all his thoughts:

What joy shall be mine, when I ask her,
for love of God, this distant shelter,
and if it pleases her, there I will find haven
next to her, although I have come from afar,
then with sweet words, distant love so close to her,
what splendid joys shall be mine!

The poems of Jaufré Rudel offer a clear parallel both to the theme of the distant love and the love affair attributed to Eleanor and Saladin. What makes all of this more odd: we are now certain that this distant princess, the object of Jaufré Rudel's desires, is none other than Eleanor herself.[20] The troubadour was one of the many people who were in love with Eleanor and celebrated this impossible love in his own way, taking pains, like his colleagues, to refrain from providing details that might identify the lady. Yet the reference to Blaye in the fictionalized life of Jaufré and to certain details concerning the Second Crusade are extremely troubling. Further, the general atmosphere of the poems by the so-called prince of Blaye are well within the tone of the amorous casuistry that developed during this time around the queen of France. In addition, Jaufré Rudel was not the only person to compose enflamed verse about and for Eleanor.

It is important that we note, however, that the legend of Eleanor and Saladin was not invented by chance but to illustrate a literary theme that was in vogue with the entourage of Eleanor, protector and lady of the troubadours. In fact, this is one of the ways in which the mythology of Eleanor was shaped during a century that was rediscovering the power of symbols.

In addition to the intellectual and literary aspect of the legend surrounding the queen are its moral and social aspects. Here again we find a feminist agenda: a woman's right to do anything she chooses with her body and heart unhindered by constraints—especially marital constraints. We can remember that this was also the time of Abelard and Heloise, very real people who left behind letters of great significance. In one of her letters, in fact, Heloise said, *amorem conjugo, libertatem praeferebam*—"I would prefer love to marriage and freedom to slavery." We would be hard-pressed to find a better summation of the attempt by twelfth-century women to free themselves from male tutelage. When the Minstrel of Reims has Eleanor utter the stinging retort to the king that he is more vile than "a rotten apple," these words are simply a solemn affirmation of a woman's right to choose freely her own destiny. In addition, at this time the sacrosanct institution of marriage was entirely challenged: according to the theoreticians of courtly love, as it was later to the seventeenth-century Précieuses, marriage was nothing more than a social act, a temporary situation, as are all contracts of this nature. Here again, beneath these medieval attempts at women's liberation we find a Celtic notion, for women of the ancient Celts not only enjoyed greater freedom but could claim full assumption of their personality in a society that considered marriage a temporary and easily dissolved state.[21] Eleanor's plans for escape and future marriage to Saladin, even if invented, are pieces of propaganda in favor of liberalizing morals. Romances such as *Tristan and Iseult* only extended this demand.

Eleanor's "divorce" and her almost immediate remarriage to Henry Plantagenet inspired a complete flood of stories: Walter Map[22] and Giraldus Cambrensis[23] reported that the queen of France enjoyed intimate relations with Henry's father, Geoffrey the Handsome, before her marriage was annulled. Walter Map describes it as consensual adultery on the part of Eleanor whereas Giraldus Cambrensis puts forth the view that Geoffrey made himself the queen's lover by force. We can see, however, that the two chroniclers agree on one point: the queen had relations with the count of Anjou—but there is still a wide gulf between the rape described by Giraldus Cambrensis and the voluntary liaison reported by Walter Map. It should be pointed out that both these men are generally considered to be gossipmongers. Walter Map was a Norman in fealty to Henry II, and he might very well have been trying to please his master, who then had chilly relations with Eleanor. What's more, he did not care for Eleanor and revealed her supposed turpitude. Meanwhile, Giraldus Cambrensis, who was Welsh, was quite detached from events taking place on the Continent and was ever ready to pass on a salacious anecdote about those he regarded as enemies of his people. It is beyond doubt that the "revelations" of these two chroniclers are only tall tales.

In addition, an important figure who holds a desirable place on the world's stage is always exposed to this kind of calumny, and Eleanor was no exception to this rule. If her liaison with Geoffrey is a legend—and the facts show that it is—it is not mythological but rather is simply political. This tale allowed certain authors to vent their spleen against both Henry II, who was little liked by his vassals and companions because of his authoritarian and brutal nature, and Eleanor, who was the foreigner whose manners were judged to conform little to those of Normandy and England when she was at the French court. At its base, this venting represented an old quarrel that could be classified as the permanent antagonism between north and south. The north, stamped by a strong Germanic heritage and relatively unurbanized, with little familiarity with belles-lettres and luxury, was somewhat jealous of Occitan wealth and, of course, was envious of a more advanced and refined civilization than existed in the lands where Saxon or the langue d'oïl was spoken.

Whatever the basis of the dislike, many in the north believed it was imperative to sully the duchess of Aquitaine, and fuel to further this endeavor could be found in even the most minor event. It is certainly well known that Eleanor had contact with Geoffrey Plantagenet before her "divorce," and her conversations with him may have decided the future course of the queen of France. We must remember that there can be no gossip without a kernel of truth at its origin—but the chroniclers were deceived in seeing amorous intrigue in what was actually a political plot. Following the principle that money is lent only to those who are already wealthy, because so much had already been said about this daughter of the devil, there was no reason not to dish out more. At that time, after all, it was unforgivable for an intelligent and willful woman also to be beautiful and to make no secret of her sensual nature.

With the adventure between Eleanor and Bernart de Ventadorn, we are back in the arena of poetry and mythology. The most famous troubadour of the twelfth century was the son of a soldier and a kitchen girl of the castle of Ventadorn (or Ventadour) in the Limousin region. The lord of the castle, Ebles de Ventadorn, was a poet himself and loved to surround himself with musicians and artists. He had noted the gifts of the young boy and saw to it that he received a thorough education. This was how Bernart became a poet in turn and came to compose songs in praise of his benefactor. Now Ebles had an extremely beautiful wife, and it is said that Bernart fell in love with her and dedicated impassioned poems to her, which was not at all to the liking of the lord, who soon had the troubadour driven out of his domains.

Then, as we are told by the anonymous *Life* of Bernart, which is just as fanciful as that of Jaufré Rudel:

[H]e left and headed toward the duchess of Normandy, who was young and of great merit. He was an excellent judge of talent and honor and wrote songs about the duchess's glory. She found the songs and verse of Bernart much to her liking and welcomed and honored him, giving him gifts and doing whatever might please him. He stayed long at the court of the duchess and fell in love with her—and the lady fell in love with Bernart, who wrote many beautiful songs about her. King Henry of England, however, wed her and took her away from Normandy to England. Then Bernart remained on the Continent, sad and unhappy.

There are some major historical errors in this legend. It maintains that Eleanor was already duchess of Normandy before her marriage to Henry II and that he was already king of England. Nevertheless, this does not disallow the fact that after being urged to leave Limousin, Bernart de Ventadorn may well have gone to Eleanor's court, probably in Poitiers. He was already sufficiently well known by his songs that the doors of the most important noble houses would be open to him. It is therefore beyond question that Bernart knew Eleanor at the time of her marriage to Henry. We do not know just how long he remained in Eleanor's retinue. The thirteenth-century troubadour Uc de Saint-Circ insinuates that the king of England took umbrage quite quickly at the passionate poems Bernart addressed to his protector, and it is not impossible that Henry forbade the queen from keeping the troubadour in her vicinity.

In any case, the seed for this legend can essentially be found in Bernart's poems. Some of them are "sent" (in the address that ends the song) to the king and queen of England and most often to the queen alone. Nevertheless, this does not present any kind of convincing proof, for it was a widespread custom at that time for the troubadour to dedicate his works to the lady of the lord who protected him—a woman who, in accordance with courtly poetics, could not help but become the lady, the crystallization of all beauty and virtue and a living symbol of physical and moral perfection. In fact, Bernart makes direct allusion to Henry in five of his songs and designates Eleanor by title only once (he calls her queen of the Normans)—but we should not forget that according to troubadour tradition, the lady of their thoughts was never named. Instead, they designated her under a *senhal,* or nickname. In this instance, the senhal for Bernart's lady is *mos aziman,* or "my magnet."

There has been much debate about the identity of this magnet of the Limousin troubadour. Taking into account that eight poems of Bernart's English period allude to the aziman and that three of these are dedicated to her, it was eventually accepted that the magnet was none other than Eleanor, natural suzerain of the troubadour and inspiration for many other poets. This identification has been rejected by some modern critics,[24] but their arguments are not persuasive and it can be stated that Bernart de Ventadorn truly wrote some of his most beautiful songs for Eleanor.

From this can we conclude that there was actually a love relationship between Eleanor and Bernart de Ventadorn? Here again, we are reduced to speculation. Of course, it is possible to cite the famous poem in which Bernart, addressing his aziman, beseeches her to give him the command to go to her chamber "where one gets undressed." It is true, that a bit further on, he asks her only to permit him to "abase himself on his knees" to take off her shoes, but anyone who is aware of the refined eroticism of the troubadours will find that this detail only reinforces the notion of a liaison between the queen and the bard of Ventadorn. Further, what of the constant allusions to the story of Tristan and Iseult in Bernart's work? Bernart compares himself to Tristan,

> who suffered many sorrows
> for Iseult the Blonde.

This is obviously proof that the legend of Tristan had become a literary theme in vogue. Its popularity was probably even greater because Eleanor, to a certain extent, embodied the figure of Iseult, a woman who had loved outside the bonds of marriage and who justified adultery. It can never be stated enough that the romance of Tristan and Iseult was, in a climate of full Christian austerity, a plea in defense of adultery and a glorification of sin as well as just one more argument in favor of women's freedom to love whom they liked, outside all moral and social restrictions. The allusion to this legend necessarily takes on a certain meaning in Bernart's work, even if he was not the actual lover of Eleanor. He may well have been her paramour on an ideal plane—and this is more than likely—but his poems have an accent of sincerity that goes beyond the simple technique employed by the troubadours to sing of love and the grief it causes. We cannot help but be struck by the ardor and beauty of the poem in which Bernart evokes his separation from his beloved lady. Though she is far from him, nature serves as a link between them:

> When the gentle breeze blows
> out of your land,
> it seems that I am breathing
> the wind from heaven,
> because of my love for the comely one
> to whom I have surrendered,
> in whom I placed my passion
> as well as my heart,
> for all women have gone from me,
> for her, so strongly she has charmed me . . .

The end of the poem curiously offers us a solution to the question concerning amorous relations between the queen of England and the Limousin troubadour. Here is what Bernart says:

> I am he who nothing troubles
> the good that God had given him:
> Know well that in the week
> when I left her side,
> she told me quite clearly
> that my songs pleased her.
> May every Christian soul

enjoy such joy as I did
and as I will again:
for it was only then that she declared herself.

Perhaps this strophe can be interpreted as the troubadour's reminiscence of his farewells with Eleanor: there had never been anything between them, but at the last minute the queen declared her feelings, which she had never done before. The text is quite specific here. We can thus assume that the love between Eleanor and Bernart actually existed but never became concrete. Furthermore, as all of this took place during the early years of Eleanor's marriage to Henry, it is not likely that the duchess of Aquitaine, deeply in love with her husband, would have been tempted to commit adultery.

Nevertheless, the Bernart–Eleanor couple became a symbol. The poet is the knight servant, he who cannot live except by the lady and for the lady. Eleanor is the mistress: tyrannical and absolute, unique and perfect, it is toward her that all gazes should be drawn. Sketched here is the face of Queen Guinevere in the Arthurian romances that were directly or indirectly inspired by Eleanor and Henry II. This absolute mistress is also the all-powerful mother who provides her children with the food they expect. This nourishment is symbolic; it is the strength that will enable the son to achieve the goal of all courtly initiation, the feat of prowess, and it is this feat, once achieved, that will make her son-knights perfect lovers. The legend of Eleanor and Bernart de Ventadorn is far from being devoid of all historical basis, but it primarily explains the characters in the diagram related to problems of love: the lady, the lover, and the husband.

The troubadours' philosophy sought to resolve the antipathy between love and marriage, but they did not succeed, for the result of all their songs and jeux-partis was that love as a vital and involuntary emotion could never coincide with marriage, a social and planned action. Nonetheless, the relationship between Eleanor and the man called the king of the troubadours could be nothing if not fortuitous: it flowed out of the necessity both had to find words appropriate for singing of the love sickness that resulted from this social repression. This was one more occasion for the duchess of Aquitaine to become more than ever the queen of troubadours, she who was honored above all reason, albeit in veiled terms:

> Lady, I am and shall be yours,
> given in your service.
> I am your man, by sworn oath
> and have been since before;
> and you are my first joy
> and thus shall you be my last joy
> so long as my life lasts. . . .

These impassioned words seem to conform to the ideal Eleanor imagined. In the center of the world a beautiful woman is surrounded by the world's most splendid society and receives the homage of all knights in love with her. This is very like the myth of the queen of the fairies, absolute mistress of the fate of men. In a medieval context that was always receptive to the supernatural, a woman such as Eleanor, about whom so many human adventures were assumed, could not escape some extra-human adventures as well. This is how rumor spread that because she was not content to play Messalina among men, she had welcomed the devil into her bed, and out of this bizarre passion her son Richard was born.

Why was Richard and not the others pegged in this way? It is because Richard was the English king who gave the French (meaning the supporters of the Capets) their greatest fear. If Richard had survived, he would likely have completely isolated the kingdom of France and probably absorbed it, making England and France one kingdom. He was handsome, intelligent, courageous, a polished diplomat, an excellent poet, a tireless worker, ruthless in his judgments but flawlessly fair-minded. In short, to the Capets and Philip Augustus, he was a formidable adversary. Nevertheless, he also possessed the downside of his virtues: if he was tireless in his work, he was equally so in debauchery, and his morals were considered "against nature." When Richard was freed from the German prison, Philip Augustus sent a letter to John Lackland warning him that "the devil was back." Bernard of Clairvaux, who knew Richard only when he was young, made the curious observation that "he comes from the devil and to the devil he will return."

All of this means simply that the origin of the legend concerning Eleanor's relations with a devil are to be sought in the character and reputation of Richard. Yet in fact it is not that simple; we must take into account other elements, both political and mythological. During the Middle Ages, there was widespread belief in incubi and succubi—the demons that assume male or female shape and slip into people's beds to tempt them and persuade them to commit the sin of the flesh.[25] This belief goes back quite far in time and can be found in apocryphal biblical texts such as the Book of Enoch, which discusses fallen angels who coupled with human women. In telling of the birth of Merlin, Geoffrey of Monmouth explains incubi in his *Historia Regum Britanniae:*

> In the books of our philosophers, and in a great many histories, I have found that several men have had like origin. For, as Apuleius informs us in our book concerning the Demon of Socrates, between the moon and the earth inhabit those spirits, which we call incubuses. These are of the nature partly of men and partly of angels, and whenever they please assume human shapes, and lie with women.

Also in Geoffrey's work, Merlin's mother, an innocent young girl, explains what happened to her.

> I know nobody that begot him of me. Only this I know, that as I was once with my companions in our chambers, there appeared to me a person in the shape of a most beautiful young man, who often embraced me eagerly in his arms, and kissed me; and when he had stayed a little time, he suddenly vanished out of my sight. But many times after this he would talk with me when I was alone, without

making any visible appearance. When he had a long time haunted me in this manner, he at last lay with me several times in the shape of a man, and left me with child.

This text dates from around 1135, and on the orders of Eleanor and Henry II it was translated by Robert Wace in his *Romance of Brutus,* thus forming the literary starting point for the Arthurian legend and the legend of Merlin the enchanter. With regard to Richard, the reference to Merlin's birth is obvious: it was expressive of a wish to make Richard a new Merlin, but while the enchanter shared the nature of demons yet used his power for good, Richard was definitely classified as diabolical.

This is not the only reference we find to Merlin in Eleanor's life. On several occasions claims have been made that Eleanor was designated in the prophecies attributed to Merlin in the *Historia Regum Britanniae.* We know that these prophecies, which were incredibly popular not only during the twelfth century but also in the following ones as well, were invented by Geoffrey of Monmouth, probably on the behest of the Anglo-Norman dynasty. While it is true there was a historic Merlin—the bard Myrddin, a native of northern Britain, meaning lower Scotland—and while it is true that numerous legends circulated about him, the intention behind these prophecies is openly political. They were a means of combining the independent tendencies of the Celts of England (essentially the Welsh and inhabitants of Cornwall) with the interests of the Norman monarchy against the Saxons. The Plantagenets were doing nothing less. They encouraged the spread of everything Celtic as a support for their unification policy and used reference to Celtic ancestors as a means of thwarting the obvious unwillingness of the Saxons to accept a government they regarded as foreign.

The reference to Merlin's prophecies dates from the time when Eleanor was still queen of France. Louis VII had brought her to the Council of Sens, which had been convened to judge and condemn the doctrines of Abelard. We can remember that Jean d'Estampes described the queen as the great eagle mentioned by Merlin whose wings would stretch over both England and France. By all evidence this anecdote was invented after Eleanor became queen of England, but it is no less significant of the mind-set of the Anglo-Norman clerks and their desire to connect Eleanor's fate and Celtic mythology.

This eagle theme was exploited on numerous occasions. In an appeal addressed to Eleanor when she was held prisoner by Henry II, the chronicle of Richard the Poitevin declares: "Tell me, eagle of the two heads, tell me, where were you when your eaglets, flying out of their nest, dared raise their claws against the king of Aquilonia?" He follows this later with a quote borrowed from Geoffrey of Monmouth: "You, the eagle of the broken covenant, for how long shall you protest before your wishes are granted?"

This was also the time when these extracts from the prophecies were circulating throughout the Plantagenet empire: "Albany [Great Britain] will be angry. . . . Between her jaws there will be found a bit that was forged in the Bay of Armorica. The eagle of the broken covenant will paint it with gold and will rejoice in her third nesting." This is an allusion to Eleanor's captivity, the death of Henry II, and the freeing of the queen by her third son, Richard. The chronicler Ralph de Diceto interprets the prophecy this way:

Eleanor the queen, who had been kept in prison for many years, received the power from her son to decree as she wished in the kingdom. Thus, this time made clear what had been ambiguous in the words "the eagle will rejoice in her third nesting." She is called "eagle" because she spread her wings over two kingdoms, that of the French and that of the English. But divorce for reasons of consanguinity separated her from the French, and she was separated from the English by imprisonment far from her husband's bed. Her captivity lasted sixteen years. Therefore, she was the "eagle of the broken covenant" for each side. And when it is added that "she will rejoice in her third nesting," it should be understood to mean that the first son of Queen Eleanor died in childhood; Henry, the queen's second son, reached royal status only to show his hostility to his father, and he also died; Richard, her third son, who is meant by the "third nesting," fought to exalt his mother's name.[26]

We should also remember Henry Plantagenet's interpretation of a painting in the palace of Winchester that depicted eaglets attacking an eagle: the king viewed this as his sons rebelling against him. All this goes to show that the eagle was a widespread symbol regarding the Plantagenet royal family. Anyone wishing to explore Merlin's prophecies in detail will find many other lyric passages that, because of their inexact and ambiguous nature, could also apply to Eleanor and her family. For example, these phrases are found in the prophecies:

> Next . . . shall come the ram of the castle of Venus, with golden horns and a beard of silver. It will breathe such a fog from its nostrils that the entire surface of the island will be overshadowed by it. In the days of the ram . . . women shall become snakelike in their gait, and every step they take will be full of arrogance. The castle of Venus will be restored and Cupid's arrows will continue to wound. The source of the River Amne will turn into blood and two kings will fight each other at the Ford of the Staff for the sake of a lioness.

It is obviously tempting to see Eleanor in the lioness for whom fight two kings—the kings of France and England. It is difficult to see "the castle of Venus restored" as anything but an allusion to the famous courts of love over which Eleanor presided. Yet interpretations of this nature can be carried quite far, and the prophecies of Merlin, like all other predictions of this kind, can be interpreted however we like and especially as political circumstances demand.

The main point to consider in the legend concerning Eleanor's alleged sexual relations with the devil that led to Richard's birth is the obvious connection they have to the story of Merlin. In fact, this detail is an intrusion into history from the world of fairy. The world of Merlin was one of dream and phantasmagoria in which all the ancient beliefs were crystallized. At the same time, stories abounded on how the ancestress of the Plantagenets was an evil fairy. Some undoubtedly asked why Eleanor couldn't have had her fairylike aspect as well. She enjoyed hearing the stories of the extraordinary adventures of Arthur and his knights. She ordered books written on the "matter of Britain." Once again, she embodied the feminism of that era. In the name of women's freedom, then, why refuse her the right to enjoy relations with the devil? This was not viewed as incredible by her contemporaries, who were ever ready to find the diabolical in women. What's more, as the author of the *Romance of Merlin* said about the fairy Vivian, "woman is more cunning than the devil." With her uncommon personality and her almost "infernal" beauty, Eleanor met all the requirements of at least a wife of the devil if not a demoness.

The best known of all the legends concerning Eleanor, and the one that certainly enjoyed the greatest success, is the legend of her relations with Rosamond Clifford, the young mistress of Henry II. We know that the king of England was no model husband. He had married Eleanor only to further his ambitions and to add her domains to his holdings. He was unfaithful to her, and it was largely to avenge herself of her husband's gradual abandonment that Eleanor incited the rebellion of their three eldest sons against their father, which was the reason for her many years of imprisonment. As Giraldus Cambrensis says: "Once he had imprisoned his wife Eleanor, he who had formerly practiced adultery in secret no longer had any care and acted for all to see and hear, openly and without shame, with the Rose du Monde [Rose of the World], who in this instance was rather a Rose Immonde [Rose of Impurity]."

According to the chronicler Higden, Henry adored Rosamond, and because he was exceedingly jealous, he wished to keep her far from the world—from both potential rivals and the possible vengeance of the queen—and thus had a palace built in Woodstock, not far from Oxford, in the form of a maze. It was extremely difficult to enter this castle, for it was well guarded on the outside. Once inside, though, a person found himself in the presence of an inextricable tangle of corridors that went nowhere, with mirror-covered walls that contributed to leading astray any who did not know the exact route. It was in the middle of this rather phantasmagorical palace that Henry had apartments built for Rosamond, and with the exception of a few handmaidens confined there with her, only Henry could enter.

It is easy to see that this story is told completely in the spirit of twelfth-century fairy tales, especially those by Marie de France, which constantly feature old husbands who hold prisoner their young and pretty wives. This is especially the case in the famous *Lay of Guigemar,* in which the hero makes his way by sea to the home of his love, which is a tower completely isolated from the world, mirroring the will of a jealous old fogy. Thus, the invention here is obvious, although it is true that the palace of Woodstock was renovated around 1170 to serve as a royal residence in accordance with blueprints that indicated both an Occitan and Eastern influence.

But to resume this history—or rather, legend: Having been warned that her husband was hiding his mistress in the palace of Woodstock, Eleanor made her way to England and managed to use gold to corrupt one of the masons who had built the castle. She was able thereby to obtain a detailed map of the maze. Profiting from Henry's absence, she took twenty men of arms with her to Woodstock, and there she hid her companions in a grove and presented herself alone at the gate to the palace. The porter had no suspicion for an unescorted woman and lowered the drawbridge, whereupon the men of arms stormed out of the grove and easily overpowered the porter and the several guards who served with him. The queen then made her way through the corridors, using the directions the mason had provided. In the first corridor she counted eight doors and pushed through the ninth. Here she found herself in a new gallery consisting of oblique and perpendicular entries. At the third crossing, she turned right and counted twenty-five steps. Here was located a trap door, which was barely visible. She lifted it and went down six stairs. She now found herself in a small, dark cellar. She followed the wall to the right three times the length of her arms, climbed up a new flight of six stairs, and made her way into a long hallway. Then, without hesitation, she headed toward the last door on the left.[27]

Eleanor entered a chamber, and there she found the fair Rosamond, lying on a bed covered with furs and drapery. The queen seized her by her hair, which Rosamond wore quite long and unbound, and stabbed her with her sword, satisfying both her vengeance and her hatred for the woman who had stolen her husband's heart.[28]

Of course, this story is completely false. In 1177, Rosamond died in a convent to which she had retired, at about the same time when Eleanor was held prisoner and strictly guarded. It is likely that Eleanor had long since abandoned any thought of winning back her husband and thus had no reason to nurse a deadly hatred for this young woman, whom she knew in reality to be much more Henry's victim than accomplice. This, however, did not prevent the legend from spreading and emphasizing the evil role played by Eleanor. Throughout all Europe, in every language, people voiced regret for the unfortunate victim of a bloodthirsty queen. A passage from the medieval English ballad "Fair Rosamond" is characteristic of this:

> The queen went to where Lady Rosamond was to
>   be found,
> There where she lived like an angel . . .
> Take off that dress, said the queen,
> throw off that rich and costly garb
> and drink this potion of death
> that I have brought for you!

Rosamond attempts to plead her cause, but Eleanor remains pitiless and inflexible and Rosamond is forced to drink the deadly mix:

> Then lifting her eyes toward heaven,
> she asked mercy for herself,
> and drinking the violent poison,
> she immediately surrendered her life. . . .

In consequence of the many ballads composed around this theme, Rosamond became a veritable romantic heroine and was celebrated by numerous poets and writers not only in England but also throughout Europe. In 1707, Addison borrowed the subject for the libretto of an opera, and in the nineteenth century Franz Schubert used it for a ballet that became famous. As in the tragedies of Jean Racine, what we see in this tale is the clandestine struggle turned violent between two kinds of women: the timid young girl, a prisoner of her fate; and the passionate, jealous, and authoritarian older woman. This is probably what seduced the poets and the public, who are always predisposed to accentuate the Manichean aspect of dramatic situations.

If this story was meant to blacken Eleanor's reputation, it was completely successful. The duchess of Aquitaine had gone from being a mad virgin to being an adulteress and a witch and, finally, to being a murderess. Though she had left unease and alarm in her wake and triggered a veritable adoration on the part of her regular companions, Eleanor also unleashed ferocious hate for herself, and it is this hate that wins out in the majority of the legends concerning her. Paradoxically, however, her figure emerges ever larger from this mud used to bury her, for in the final analysis, such stories turn out to be additional homage to her extraordinary character and uncommon personality.

The famous "Confession of Queen Eleanor," another medieval English ballad about the queen of England, circulated at the time—and it is loaded with slander about her:

> Queene Eleanor was a sick woman
> And sick just like to die,
> And she has sent for two fryars of France
> To come to her speedily.
> The King[29] called downe his nobles all,
> By one, by two, by three:
> "Earl Marshal,[30] I'll go shrive the Queene,
> And thou shalt wend with mee."

The earl Marshal is somewhat ill at ease. The king's suggestion torments his conscience. He tries to beg off but eventually capitulates to his master's wishes. The two then dress as monks and go to the queen's bedside, where they both assure her they are really French not English monks, then she begins her confession:

> "Oh, the next sin I did commit
> I will to you unfolde;
> Earl Marshal had my virgin dower,
> Beneath this cloth of gold."
> "Oh, that was a vile sin," said the King,
> "May God forgive it thee!"
> "Amen! Amen!" groaned the Earl Marshal,
> With a heavie heart spake hee.
> "O don't you see the two little boys,
> Playing at the football?
> O yonder is the Earl Marshal's son
> And I like him best of all.
> O don't you see yon other little boy,
> Playing at the football?
> O that one is King Henrie's son,
> And I like him worst of all!"

The king can take it no longer. He shouts that this little boy is his favorite. Then:

> The King plucked off his fryar's gowne,
> And stood in his scarlet so red,
> The Queen wrung her hands
> And cryed that she was betrayede.
> The King lookt oer his left shoulder,
> And a grim look looked he;
> "Earl Marshal," he said, "But for my oath,
> Thou hadst swung on the gallows-tree."[31]

It is obvious with this ballad that we have entered the realm of pure fantasy. Certainly, William Marshal—for this could be only him—was a faithful companion of the royal couple since the beginning of Eleanor's second marriage, but nothing allows us to assume intimate relations existed between him and his king's wife. As for Eleanor's virginity, she had lost it long ago, long before knowing Henry and his right-hand man. Here again, the intention is to sully Eleanor by drawing a portrait of her as a voluptuous and unscrupulous woman who had multiple love affairs. Of course, Eleanor's behavior always permitted such assumptions, but outside of the historical element attached to these inventions, these kinds of stories lead us to examine Eleanor's legend in its most mythological aspect.

We cannot help but be struck by the fact that, with the exception of the case of Rosamond, this legend always involves incest and adultery. In fact, the stories of Eleanor could be entitled all together, "Adultery Considered as One of the Fine Arts." The hate and distrust she inspired is not sufficient to explain the number of love affairs attributed to the queen-duchess. For an explanation, we must refer once again to the context in which these real or fictitious adventures were developed and then go beyond Eleanor the individual to reach what she represents.

In the many commentaries inspired by Eleanor's life, one name often surfaces as a label for the woman who was twice a queen: Messalina. This comparison is extremely inexact with respect to the Eleanor phenomenon; indeed, nothing could be more incorrect than to make her equivalent to the wife of Emperor Claudius. Messalina was truly a nymphomaniac (even if the stories told about her are exaggerated) who spent her nights in Roman brothels to satisfy what was a somewhat perverse sensual appetite. Eleanor's case is entirely different—and the adulteries she is assumed to have committed are far from being proved.[32] She was only a woman asserting her right to freedom. In fact, this is exactly what her detractors were unable to tolerate and forgive her. Whenever a woman displays too free an appearance, the general tendency is to consider her a woman of light morals, truly a prostitute. This is all the more true when a woman marries a younger man; she thereby earns accusations of licentiousness and perversity.[33] In the soci-

eties that govern us—and this was also true in the twelfth century—
the woman who does not confine herself to a lower status and has a
forward personality is necessarily considered outside accepted norms,
and the good conscience of the group expels her into the shadows of
guilt.[34]

In addition, with the figure of Eleanor we touch on the theme of
sovereignty. In the Celtic tradition, which resurfaced in the twelfth
century not only on the British Isles but also in Brittany and Occitania, this sovereignty is incarnated by women. By marrying Louis VII,
Eleanor brought him her own domains of Aquitaine and Poitou. By
"divorcing" him, she took back what was rightfully hers and then gave
it to Henry II when she married him. She was thus truly a keeper of
sovereignty, and throughout her whole life she arranged matters so that
everyone knew it. It was therefore natural for her to make this temporal
sovereignty the symbol of power set into motion by man. In Irish tales,
the future king always leaves in quest for a woman and can become
king only when he has won the woman destined to be his. The same
is true in the folktales of Brittany, in which we often see a poor young
man of an ordinary background enduring numerous adventures that
are actually initiatory ordeals to become a prince or king who marries a
woman he has literally won. Folk tradition has kept intact the symbol-
ism of the ancient mythologies.[35] In the same fashion, an impotent king
is not capable of ruling, for his authority symbolically resides with the
woman who is the keeper of sovereignty.

This is nothing more or less than the social aspect of the *hierogamos,*
the sacred marriage between the mortal and the goddess. In the Babylo-
nian epic, when the goddess Ishtar invites Gilgamesh to couple with her,
it is to transmit to him some of her power. Gilgamesh refuses for various reasons, but the sense of the hierogamos clearly appears. The same
is true in the *Odyssey* when Ulysses refuses to share the bed of Circe as
long as she refuses to promise to cause no harm to his virility—for contact with the goddess, meaning sovereignty, can end with castration if
the mortal (meaning the man) is incapable of withstanding the infinite
nature of the deity. Thus only the elect—the initiates, those who have

shown proof of their valor—are capable of assuming the heavy responsibilities of sovereignty.

In traditional tales, particularly in ancient Celtic narratives, the woman who holds sovereignty is considerably sexually active. She shares her bed with many men, and when married, she is necessarily adulterous. A typical example can be found in the Irish legend of Queen Medbh. This epic heroine, the queen of Connaught, has married King Ailil—and it is through their marriage that she allowed him to become king. Without her he is nothing—and, incidentally, even with her he does not amount to much, for he is often restricted to being a mere presence in any battle in order to ensure victory and to being satisfied with the role of the theoretical center of a horizontal society.[36] The actual engine of popular action is the queen, who animates energies and desires and for whom all means are used for achieving her purpose. This is the quasi-permanent justification for her adultery. When she has need of a warrior's services, she promises him (with the gentle euphemisms of the Irish texts) the "friendship of her thighs," or the "friendship of her hips." Yet she is not content with a promise alone; she keeps her word. For example, in the great epic *The Cattle Raid of Cooley,* Medbh strays quite often from the troops with the hero Fergus, who is one of their most indispensable lieutenants. Her husband, King Ailill, pushing his jealousy to the background, deems it wise to explain to his companions that "it was necessary for her to act this way to ensure the success of the expedition."[37]

This concept of the adulterous queen is quite ancient and evidently refers to the myth of sovereignty: the woman who embodies this sovereignty must share it with men who act in her name but who need some kind of transmission of power through sexual union. Masculine desire is necessary to stimulate bellicose enthusiasm and thus actions that benefit the collective. The queen, who embodies the collective, should incite this masculine desire. This is the case in what is improperly called courtly love: the lady, the object of the knights' desire, excites them to accomplish feats for her. Yet if there is no complicity between the lady and her potential lover, nothing can happen. Contact with the gods was essential for the heroes of classical antiquity to attain the full development of their potential. Contact with the queen, the keeper of sovereignty, was indispensable for Celtic heroes to perform the sparkling feats that benefited the queen—in other words, the collective. The same is true in the context of twelfth-century fine amor, and Eleanor of Aquitaine clearly embodies the central figure in this system.

It is not at all surprising, then, to find so many allusions to the queen's adultery in the legends her contemporaries drew for us. These are not actual incidents of adultery but instead are perfectly symbolic and in accord with what Eleanor represented in the context of the society of that time. She was the royal prostitute who bestowed her powers on whomever she chose in the best interests of the community. This is the historicized image of the great goddess who also whores in the temple, for this great goddess is alone capable of giving the means of triumph to those audacious few who accept the challenge of physically coupling with her.

We shall see how important this image is in the case of Eleanor when we examine how she served as model for Queen Guinevere, the faithless wife—for she could not be otherwise—of King Arthur of ancient Celtic legends.

5

FROM GUINEVERE
TO MELUSINE

The image of Queen Eleanor that history has left us has been distorted by storytellers and scandalmongers. We have seen how and why the legend of a frivolous and adulterous Eleanor developed, and how and why there was a systematic desire to transform her into a Messalina despite the fact that there was no proof to allow confirmation of this image. Here we see definitively that no historical figure can escape myth. It percolates through all time with an active tenacity that reduces—or transcends—those whom history has placed at the center of the world's stage. History is nothing but the narrative of a mythology that is constantly being updated by the whim of circumstances.

We can find the components of the Eleanor legend in the concerns of the time. The first concern was political: when Eleanor was queen of France, she ultimately had to be removed through "divorce" because she caused discomfort in the powerful Church's moral order, which had been established for centuries and which ruled over the French monarchy. The Church in fact rejected Eleanor because it suspected her of seeking a profound transformation in northern feudal society. Once she was separated from Louis VII and remarried to Henry Plantagenet, it was obviously necessary for the Church and the French crown to discredit her by any means possible. It was unacceptable that a former queen of France could triumph and become more powerful than when she was married to the French monarch. At the same time, the quarrel between the Capets and the Plantagenets appeared as an essential ingredient of the political balance in Europe. After all, a nation is not formed with words: it is necessary that a king manipulates the people he rules—and what more skilled manipulation is there than the development of aggressiveness? Regarding the Capets and Plantagenets, it was thus a matter of prime importance that each side felt attacked by the other. Eleanor, the former French queen who had gone over to the enemy, provided a wonderful subject for discord.

Another concern of the time was religious. It may seem surprising to claim that Eleanor was a religious symbol, but this is what emerges from analysis of her legend, for from the moment a woman is given heroic dimensions by the voice of both poets and the people she moves from human to supernatural. If we take into consideration the Christian mysticism of the twelfth century, there was a notion that woman would eventually save humanity from diabolical powers and reveal the path to God. The cult of the Virgin Mary, intermediary between God and men, is evidence of this profound desire to hoist one individual to the top of the hierarchy, from whence she becomes a unique model. Suffering humanity was a woman; the Church was a woman, the bride of Christ. Reaching God, therefore, required passing through a woman— and how does a person pass through woman if not by loving her and seeing her as crystallizing all aspirations, even those most repressed and inadmissible? Eleanor, queen of legend, symbolized the earthly love through which could be gained access to the love of the lord, whether it was the feudal sovereign or the lord of lords, God himself.

A third concern of the time was clearly mythological. There was a need for the myth of Eleanor in the twelfth century in a world torn by the permanent battle between good and evil. A principle of femininity was revealed in the symbolic image of woman, which, until now, had been eliminated from Continental European Christian culture. Until this time, woman had been reduced to the roles of reproducer and servant under the leadership of a phallocratic Christianity because she bore the guilt for Eve's sin. The strangulation of the feminine myth therefore established the proper conditions for this myth to reemerge more violently than it ever would have otherwise. Eleanor constituted an excellent support for a myth that simply needed to take on form. This was the legend of Eleanor of Aquitaine, queen of the troubadours, but also queen of men of good will who no longer knew what needed to be done to live in peace with each other. This explains the stereotyped images of Eleanor that we find not only in the literature of the time but also in the various works that extended this literature over the course of the following centuries.

In reading this literature, however, we must follow practices of decryption. In the same way that numerous troubadours named Eleanor only in ambiguous or analogical terms, literary works passed on the idealized portrait of the queen of the court of love. Eleanor can therefore be found in three principal literary characters: Iseult, Guinevere, and Melusine—three legendary heroines who, in one form or another, have left their stamp on Western tradition.

We have seen how the legend of Iseult and her affair with Tristan formed an excellent theme for discussions of love. We know that Eleanor must have become familiar with this legend early on and encouraged its diffusion and that the legend of Tristan and Iseult is a kind of glorification of adultery, hence a challenge to marriage. It can be reasonably assumed that wishing to break her marriage to the king of France, the duchess of Aquitaine favorably regarded the fate of Iseult, who was torn between her duty and desire. Iseult's love specifically showed evidence of the power of woman by proposing man's quest for woman.

Eleanor could not help but recognize herself in Iseult—and the poets made the same identification. This explains how numerous portraits of Iseult found in Béroul, Thomas, and the work of many later writers were conceived on the model of Queen Eleanor. The solar nature of the figure of Iseult also lent itself quite readily to the queen. Iseult, a solar deity of the ancient Celts, permitted the illumination of the lunar symbol of Tristan. This acknowledged Eleanor's primacy and thrust to the forefront her dazzling renown. Thus legend came to the aid of history by imparting the elements history needed to make a strong impression on people's minds.

Eleanor's legend made her the heroine of a romance. At this time, who could untangle the true from the false and believe Eleanor was innocent of all the amorous adventures attributed to her? Tristan and Iseult provided an admirable example that swept away traditional values: they carved out a niche in sacrosanct marriage and defied the Church, which ferociously guarded conjugal unions when it did not think it wise to annul them for political or economic reasons. In fact, this seditious undertaking (the poets' identification of Eleanor with Iseult) used the figure of Eleanor to demonstrate the incompatibility of love and marriage—and, at least going by Béroul's version of the tale, followers of the story might ask what use there was in respecting the laws in force when God protected lovers and guarded them from all their enemies. If God was the first to sweep aside the laws, how could it not be the same for poor humans? Béroul certainly repeats throughout his text that Tristan and Iseult are in love only because of the potion they drink by accident, but an attentive reading establishes the truth: Tristan and Iseult would love one another without the help of the potion. This conforms to the legend's Irish archetype, *The Pursuit of Diarmaid and Grainne,* in which the magical desire of the heroine is enough to inspire the man's love. The potion is a convenient invention to make acceptable a situation that Christianity could find only scabrous.

In addition, the Iseult of the French writers is a courtly queen. She is cultivated and refined. She is also—and this is extremely important—a magician who heals poisoned wounds, which shows a trace of the supernatural powers in her archetype. She rules over a court filled with young and well-educated knights, and her servants are of noble birth. Her handmaiden Brengaine depicts none other than the ancient Welsh love goddess Branwen, daughter of Llyr and sister of Bran the Blessed. When we are told, then, that Brengaine, mistaken about a container, inadvertently gives Tristan and Iseult the potion to drink, we must read between the lines. It is clear that the handmaiden poured the contents of the vial into the silver *hanap* on the orders of the future queen of Cornwall—and though this is obviously a symbol, we can see its clearest meaning as that of the union of two individuals that nothing can keep apart, especially not the prohibitions and laws that govern common mortals. In the context of this twelfth-century aristocratic society, love was not made for the manual laborers; only people of quality were capable of love.

This is what emerges from reading the songs of troubadours and the texts relating to Tristan and Iseult. The caste system, the omnipotence of the knighthood, and the ambiguities of the feudal system all combined to craft a doctrine valid for its initiates. When Queen Iseult finds herself in the Forest of Morois dressed as a peasant, she feels ill, and if we analyze Béroul's text in detail, we will see that therein lies the true reason she abandons Tristan and asks to reconcile with King Marc. It is a long way from Grainne of the Irish story to Iseult of Béroul or Thomas, and in the story of Iseult all takes place as if the wife of a contemporary king was used as a model. What is significant in the version by Thomas is that it is not Cornwall over which Marc reigns but England, and its capital is London. No one will deny that Thomas, called Thomas of England, sought to pay homage to his lord, King Henry II. In his work he gives boundless praise to the city of London, richest in the world—but while performing his duty as loyal servant of Henry, he also uses this opportunity to identify Queen Eleanor as Iseult the Blonde.

We might object on the grounds that Eleanor never experienced a situation comparable to that of Iseult. Yet the authors did not seek to craft this identification historically but on the grounds of courtesy (courtly manners) and renown. This clever mechanism was also another opportunity to emphasize the confrontation of the rival English and French crowns. Further, a Tristan in love who was also a knight serving his queen made a fairly appealing symbol for the bonds that traditionally connected Eleanor to her vassals. By himself he represented chivalry in service to the queen-duchess. Thus it is easy to find the political context beneath the mythological one—and the two can never be separated in any case.

As described by the French writers, all of whom were Eleanor's subjects, Iseult is an idealized and transcended Eleanor, magnified by a myth that makes her even more extraordinary as well as more inaccessible. Iseult is an homage paid to the tenacity and assurance Eleanor displayed throughout her life.

Yet if we truly seek to uncover Eleanor's face beneath the heroines of the courtly romances, one figure eclipses all others: Guinevere, wife of King Arthur. Everyone knows the legend. Guinevere married Arthur before he reached the height of his glory, and, if we go by the text of the *Prose Lancelot,* she at first showed herself to be a model and efficient wife—which did not prevent her from having impassioned admirers, in accordance with courtly styles and the laws of fine amor. Because she undeniably represents the sovereignty that Arthur puts into operation, she finds herself at the center of the court, but at first only to the extent that she draws gazes from knights who have sworn an oath to her husband. To a certain extent, then, she justifies and stimulates the zeal of all those who have decided to stand by the side of a great king.

We must note the kind of admiration Guinevere evokes. She is the image of a goddess come down to earth for the good of all. She may also represent the mother who gathers the community of her children around her, all of whom are joined by bonds of interdependence and endowed with perfect equality. This is what the Round Table symbolizes, for originally it was not a table at all but a gathering of warriors around a hearth.[1] Because they were seated in a circle, no one was preeminent; everyone was the equal of his neighbor, and the queen alone possessed distinguishing features. The authors of the Round Table romances put this situation to good use; they spell out the broad outlines of an ideal, communitarian society that is reserved, of course, for a privileged or initiated class—a society that finds its natural itinerary through exploitation of sensibilities and emotional relations. In sum, the Arthurian world was a great dream whose principal tenets were sketched out in the very real court that Eleanor held to a certain extent everywhere she reigned but especially in Poitiers.

Of course, the wisdom of Guinevere did not last. Once the knight

Lancelot arrived at the court, all the queen's moral commitments were broken by the strength of the passion that united her to the man who became the "best knight of the world." In the *Prose Lancelot,* the exclusive passion Guinevere holds for Lancelot is revealing of a certain mindset: if there is adultery and it is real, it is for the good of the cause. The love between them becomes almost symbolic. Lancelot by himself represents the caste of knighthood that is faithful to the king and queen, for this adulterous love is a result of prowess: the bed of the queen is the vehicle for Lancelot's heroism, which on all points conforms to the code of fine amor.

In addition, because Lancelot occupies a privileged caste by himself, we can see the same theme of sovereignty shared between the king and the lover of the queen that we have seen in the Celtic epics of Ireland. Yet in the *Prose Lancelot,* Arthur plays no positive martial role. He is satisfied to send his knights to the four corners of the world on missions that are not always well defined, and he thus acts only as the pivot of the ideal society whose broad outlines have been drawn for us. Arthur is passive, and only his presence serves as guarantee of the legality of all that is achieved. The model here is incontestably Irish; there are several Irish tales that depict the king as content to attend battles in which he will not participate. It is explained that his presence is necessary for the success of the battle, but it is useless for him to take up arms himself. In sum, Arthur is similar to the king in the game of chess: he is indispensable but plays no active role. The queen in chess, meanwhile, is the uncontested mistress of operations; she is the only one who can move in any direction or put to work the faithful knights and other pawns of the chessboard.

Despite the adaptation made by the authors of courtly romances, the character of the ancient Guinevere, whom the Welsh called Gwenhwyfar, persisted and evolved more when it contacted the amorous casuistry of the troubadours. If we crosscheck the different versions of the legend, particularly the archaistic texts that follow the *Prose Lancelot,* as well as analyze the Welsh texts, we can see that Guinevere is not a woman whose heart would be satisfied with a single love. She has many lovers in addition to Lancelot, which is made even more evident by the fact that the early Arthurian legend did not include the figure of Lancelot, who was added only later, probably by Chrétien de Troyes.[2]

This unfaithful queen who shared her favors among many lovers— including the seneschal Kay and the king's own nephew, Gawain— embodies the theme of sovereignty. Symbolically, sovereignty can belong only to the community and not to the king alone. This conforms not only to Celtic tradition but also to the feudal system in which the king is nothing without his vassals and theoretically can make no decisions without the consent of his military. Rather than being a democratic principle, this is simply aristocratic, with power being equally divided between the king and his vassals.

This also serves to confirm the importance of women even in an entirely patriarchal world. The success of Queen Guinevere as a fictional character stems from the fact that there was identification of the legendary queen with the real queen who embodied feminism during the twelfth century. Given that the legend manufactures an ideal society out of whole cloth, it could only be expected that a woman who is uncommon for her beauty and moral authority, and for her exactions, should be placed there. Yet from the mythological perspective that serves as the basis for all Arthurian romances, there is nothing shocking about the various unions between the queen and the king's knights.

When Chrétien de Troyes took possession of the legend, however, he was unable to retain Guinevere's character as sacred prostitute. He worked for Eleanor and Marie de Champagne, who were his protectors, and it was unthinkable that he would give the public a portrait of women that was so open to criticism. Therefore, in his *Lancelot,* or *The Knight of the Cart,* Chrétien de Troyes struck at the very root of the problem and eliminated from the character of Guinevere everything that could be recognized as harmful to Eleanor's reputation. He melted all Guinevere's lovers into a single knight, Lancelot, and justified this adultery with the imperious passion that united the two lovers. Here he was plagiarizing the legend of Tristan and Iseult, making Guinevere a new Iseult. This did not prevent him, however, from retaining in

Lancelot some highly ambiguous passages about the relations Guinevere maintained with other knights. In fact, one episode places heavy emphasis on the bonds uniting the queen with Kay, and another shows Gawain in love with his aunt. There are also the relations of Guinevere with the man who kidnapped her, Meleagant: the least we can say is that these are fairly disturbing. The original version describing Meleagant's abduction of the queen can be followed on the sculptures of the cathedral in Modena in Italy,[3] which are supposed to recount the love affair of Guinevere and the king of the "land from which none return." This was no kidnapping; it was an elopement.

As he portrays Guinevere, however, Chrétien de Troyes makes a living portrait of Eleanor, both psychologically and physically. Arthur's queen is a great beauty with inestimable charm, great intelligence, and perfect courtesy. Chrétien gave her curious praise not in his *Lancelot* but in his final work, *Perceval,* where he says in the voice of Gawain:

> Not since the first woman was formed from Adam's rib has there been a lady so renowned. She deserves it well, for just as the teacher instructs the little children, my lady the queen instructs and teaches all who love. From her descends all that is good in the world, for she is its origin and source. No one leaving my lady may go away discouraged, for she is what each person wishes and she has the means to please him in accordance with his desires. No man performs any righteous or honorable deed unless taught it by my lady, nor will anyone be so unhappy as he who leaves her side bearing his grief with him.[4]

A dithyramb like this needs no commentary. It is quite evident that the woman described by Gawain is none other than the powerful queen-duchess Eleanor, whom the author sees as the absolute mistress of the knights. This is one more argument in favor of the theory that Chrétien was one of Eleanor's regular guests. Added to this is the fact that the whole of *Lancelot* is constructed upon the theme of indisputable sovereignty: only the queen is right, only the queen is beautiful, only the queen can reward those who deserve it. When Chrétien de Troyes wrote *Lancelot,* during the years around 1170, he frequented the court of Poitiers; it was thus perfectly normal for him to use his protector as a model for a female character of such great importance as Guinevere. Later, when he had entered the service of the earl of Flanders and wrote his *Story of the Grail,* Chrétien remembered the woman who made it possible for him to know both the most authentic Celtic legends and the refinements of amorous casuistry as it was practiced at the court of Poitiers.

With Chrétien, then, the sworn servant of Eleanor, the broad lines of the portrait were drawn. In the *Story of the Grail,* Chrétien depicts Perceval's arrival at the court of King Arthur just as a knight has stolen Guinevere's chalice and insulted the king. Guinevere's chalice holds a symbolic value: it represents both the queen's femininity and her power of sovereignty. Because the king is incapable of acting after the theft and because the seneschal Kay—the only one who wishes to avenge this affront—has been pitiably thrown from his horse, it is up to the young Perceval to avenge the queen. Thus, the first entrance of the future Grail hero into Arthur's court is characterized by a gesture of allegiance to the queen. Here again is a sign of the oath that every knight of the king should swear to his lord's lady. Guinevere is more than ever the fictionalized portrait of Eleanor.

Chrétien de Troyes's continuers went even further. The mythological adventure of the abduction of Guinevere by Meleagant and her freeing by Gawain and Lancelot as told by Chrétien in 1170 in *The Knight of the Cart* has become in the prose adaptations an illustration of Eleanor's captivity on orders of her husband, King Henry, and her deliverance by Richard the Lion Heart, the king-knight who served as the model for Lancelot. In this comparison a mythological theme was used to develop a political position—not at all extraordinary given that myths can be made relevant to any context.

Comparisons can also be made between the hate-filled rivalry that characterizes the relationship of Guinevere and Morgana in the *Prose Lancelot* and the inexplicable animosity that existed between Eleanor and Constance of Brittany, wife of Geoffrey. Louis's jealousy with respect to Eleanor during the Crusade can be seen again in an archaistic Arthurian romance, the *Romance of Yder.* Here King Arthur, wishing to have a clear heart about his wife's fidelity, asks her who among the knights present she would choose to be her husband if some misfortune took his life. Guinevere tries to avoid answering the question but is finally obliged to admit that she would choose Yder. The king is then gripped by a morbid jealousy of this knight and on several occasions sends Yder on adventures that might lead to his death.

We can see, then, that in the stories of the Round Table, Guinevere symbolizes the theme of sovereignty with which Eleanor's contemporaries invested the queen-duchess. In the final section of the great Arthurian cycle *La Mort d'Arthur* [The Death of Arthur], it is truly Eleanor, at the height of her glory, who is the star. At this time she was fifty years old but still retained all the bloom of her beauty, and in the tale Lancelot of the Lake is more in love than ever with her counterpart, Guinevere, forgetting for her sake all his other duties, all his scruples, and all his moral and religious commitments. Lancelot is the model knight, the queen's ardent fan, and she is the divine figure who does not age and assures immortality to those who obey her in a blind and almost mystical fidelity. We know that the portrait these authors give of the legendary Guinevere was directly inspired by the characterization of Eleanor that contemporary chroniclers composed around 1170, when she was queen of the court of Poitiers.

Indeed, Guinevere's success was linked to that of Eleanor, for with Eleanor's personal actions and patronage she contributed to the launching of the Arthurian legend. No matter that the face of the archaic Gwenhwyfar was somewhat distorted in this game; the legend left us the souvenir of a great lady who was not merely content to rule over her states but who also wished to remain the sovereign of the arts and literature of her time.

It is important to remember that throughout all of this, Eleanor was countess of Poitou. In fact, this was her first title. Interestingly, the earldom of Poitou served as the frame for the development of another legend: the story of the fairy Melusine.

Of course, it was not until much later, actually in the fourteenth century, that literary works introduced to Europe the strange story of Melusine of Poitou. The first author to tell the tale was Jean d'Arras, a sworn servant to Lusignan, who composed a grand romance that was intended to highlight the merits of the family he served. He was then followed by Couldrette, who composed a rhyming chronicle on the same subject, emphasizing still further the mythological elements that permeated the legend.

Melusine is in fact a mythic figure that goes far back in time, and while no one is sure how to determine her exact origins and whether they are in Scotland or Scythia, it is incontestable that since the early Middle Ages, Melusine has belonged to Poitou folk tradition. The places marked by the legend, the oral tales that describe her as a figure of fable, the superstitions that we can detect throughout the region all indicate a deep belief in Melusine that owes nothing to two literary works about the character. To the contrary, these literary texts only give body to all the oral traditions that had circulated up to that time.

The broad outline of the legend is simple. Melusine, Meliot, and Palatine are the three daughters of the Scottish king Elinas and a mysterious young woman, Pressine, whom he met on the banks of a spring and who never wanted to say who she was or where she was from. Elinas eventually discovers her secret: she is a fairy—but because this was something he should not have known, Pressine curses him and disappears to the Lost Island, taking their three daughters with her. After fifteen years, however, Melusine decides to avenge her mother and, after gaining her sisters' complicity, uses her magic powers to imprison her father in an inaccessible place. Furious upon learning her daughters had exacted their revenge without her, Pressine strikes them with a curse that falls most heavily on Melusine, who instigated the plot: every Saturday, she becomes a "serpent up to her waist," and if someone wishes to marry her, he must never learn her secret.

Melusine then leaves the Lost Island and travels to Poitou. There she meets Raimondin of Lusignan on the banks of a spring, saves him from a dreadful predicament, and marries him on the condition that he must never seek to find out what she does on Saturdays. Ten robust sons are born of their union, but each is afflicted with a strange physical defect: for example, Urian has an eye in the middle of his jaw and Geoffrey has an extremely long canine tooth, hence his nickname Geoffrey with the Large Tooth. One day, carried away by his curiosity or jealousy and perplexed by the fact that each of Melusine's absences corresponds to the quasi-magical construction of a church, monastery, or castle, Raimondin follows his wife into the cave where she retreats every Saturday. There he sees Melusine, with the lower half of her body resembling a snake, bathing in a green marble tub. Melusine perceives Raimondin's presence, and she wails. Her arms lengthen and turn into wings, then she finally disappears into the air as she utters a terrible cry of sorrow.

This is obviously a very ancient myth. In it, Melusine seems to be a double of Pressine: she is the goddess who bestows her favors upon a mortal on the condition that she is never seen as she really is. This theme was widespread in classical antiquity as well as in the so-called barbaric civilizations. What is interesting for us, however, is that certain details are reminiscent of the history and legend of Eleanor, whose unruly vassals, we should not forget, were the Lusignans.

First, in both the tale and in history, there is a woman builder. We know that Eleanor took pains to see to the construction of handsome monuments in the Poitou region and in the city of Poitiers specifically. She knew how to find the money required for this, and it is but a small step from this to the conclusion that she could employ magic. The tale was also homage paid to the woman who had been the protector and benefactor of Poitou. Finally, the exile suffered by Melusine recalls the period during which Eleanor was queen of France and was thus exiled in a land that was not her own. For both women, their fathers played a key role in their future actions. Melusine got her revenge on her father; Eleanor, who had no need to get revenge on William X, resolved instead to continue his work and maintain the grandeur and prosperity of her states. As for the ten children of Melusine, they could be compared to the ten children that Eleanor had with both Louis and Henry.

We can conclude that the Lusignan family, one of the most powerful in Poitou, took pains to encourage the spread of literary works on the subject of Melusine, for this provided their lineage with a magical ancestor—a well-established practice at this time. To paint a picture of a fairy known to everyone in Poitou or at least a fairy about whom everyone had heard, a model had to be used that was at least somewhat plausible—and what more prestigious model could there be than the famous countess of Poitou, queen of France and England, who left so many signposts in popular memory?

Furthering this comparison, the marriage of Melusine and Raimondin seems to be a clever adaptation of that of Eleanor and Henry II, for just as Melusine promises Raimondin the return of his fortune and the enrichment of his country, Eleanor brought to her husband the great wealth of her domains, her own intelligence, and her will to power. In legend as in history, then, it is a woman who gives a nobleman the opportunity to become rich and powerful. The ambiguous character of Eleanor easily permitted such an adaptation.

But this comparison is truly intriguing in the sphere of myth. Melusine is a kind of incarnation of the goddess mother of the first days: she resembles Morgana from the romances of the Round Table and Ceridwen of Welsh traditions. Morgana is the lady of the Isle of Avalon, where she reigns over an ideal matriarchal society. Ceridwen is the lady of a castle located in the middle of a lake. Melusine, meanwhile, comes from the Lost Island governed by the fairy Pressine. Morgana is capable of transforming her shape—she can fly in the shape of a crow, while Melusine, although an aquatic being, finally flies away in the form of a bird. Ceridwin is a veritable sorceress: she knows how to brew in the cauldron of science and inspiration and, more important, knows how to shift shape as she pleases into a fish, a bird, or an animal of the land. Melusine, like Morgana and Ceridwen, comes from two worlds, both earthly and divine—though some might say she comes from the infernal world, but this is a clandestine attempt to criminalize her. Morgana and Ceridwen, two figures of Celtic mythology, found their match in the corresponding historical figure of Eleanor once they were reintegrated into a medieval context.

Like any other mythological hero, Eleanor is nothing other than the incarnation of desires projected upon an easily retained and easily discerned image. All of the context for Melusine as well as Morgana and Ceridwen can be found in the broad outline of Eleanor's legend: the queen was made into a familiar of the devil, for it was typical in the Middle Ages, when all that was incomprehensible was automatically relegated to the demonic, for this exceptional woman to be seen as an infernal being. It had been forgotten that the devil, etymologically speaking, is he who casts himself across, he who reverses the movement of the machine set in motion at the dawn of time.

One of the greatest aspects of the myth of Melusine is that it asserts that a woman could save a country from disaster. Here we find a notion of the female messiah, one corresponding to the worship of the Virgin Mary that developed across western Europe beginning in the twelfth century. Indeed, Melusine is a Virgin Mary intended for the use of pagans in the countryside. In folktales from all countries there are many examples that make equivalent Our Lady and the fairies, heiresses of the ancient mother goddesses. Eleanor played the role of fairy or savior with both the king of France and the king of England whenever the opportunity presented itself, if only as protector of her vassals, who were alarmed by attempts to usurp their rights. Snared in the trap of power, Eleanor magnificently extricated herself through her intelligence and audacity (which is not the element least responsible for her legend). She was the woman who dared take off one crown in order to wear another, so why not raise her to the rank of fairy? After all, the authors of the two romances about Melusine did so more or less consciously.

Given Eleanor's features, Melusine is therefore the protector. According to the legend of Poitou, after Melusine vanished she sometimes returned on certain nights to help her children and to contribute to some construction project. She is always present even if she cannot be seen. These are characteristics of a deathless heroine, and in this regard she can be compared to King Arthur, who was also deathless, for legend tells us that he lies in a state of hibernation on the Isle of Avalon, from which he will return one day to free Britain from foreign control. Melusine is therefore the feminine aspect of Arthur, much as Eleanor was the feminine aspect of the power held by Henry Plantagenet. Further, according to the story of Melusine, despite the transgression committed by Raimondin, the fairy does not lose her powers and instead establishes a veritable complicity between herself and the people of Poitou. How could this not be seen as an adaptation of the affection that the Poitevins always gave their countess after the transgression committed by Henry—that is, Eleanor's exile and imprisonment? Like Melusine, Eleanor disappeared from center stage because of a husband's transgression. The coincidence is too exact to be the work of chance.

The similarity between a certain notion created around Eleanor and the actualized concept of Melusine is strengthened even further by consideration of the symbolic values of the two figures. Melusine is a siren. Her familiarity with water is an indication of her fertilizing nature. She is also a fish and thereby possesses a dual nature. Because water is the origin of all life, Melusine is therefore the goddess of beginnings. Melusine–Eleanor gives life because she is ambiguous. While she bestows life, by virtue of the fact that the deities of life are also the gods of the dead, she is necessarily alarming, for the siren leads human beings beneath the waters of the river or of the sea after charming them with her songs. The Otherworld is often depicted beneath the water of a lake or the sea, and to whomever is imprudent enough to linger and listen to her song, Melusine poses a great risk: perhaps she will carry away the listener. She is not to be trusted, then, just as we do not trust the devil and everything that is dark. This explains both the attraction and repulsion that this female figure has exercised.

Furthermore, Melusine changes shape and transforms what surrounds her by virtue of her powers. She is therefore the great transmuter, she who can possibly re-create the world, which brings her into the ranks of the great goddesses of universal mythology, those primordial deities from whom arises all that is alive and mutable. She is the primal cause. Here we see again the kind of fascination that made Eleanor the great absolute queen, she who was expected to regenerate the world—that is, the aristocratic society of knights and clerks who wished to be acknowledged as such and to have the benefit of an autonomous status. From this perspective, Melusine embodies the forces present in the human being that compel him to transgress taboos in order to attain a new stage of history. Melusine–Eleanor is the transformation of history, the regeneration of old concepts. At the end of the legend, while Melusine is no longer a woman, she is still a siren and has earned the ability to fly through the air, which represents an incredible leap forward in the quest for a profound reality that can be discovered only elsewhere, outside the world of daily life, in a sky that is as symbolic as it is physical and whose fluidity transposes the matter of life.[5]

As we have discovered, this transformation of the world and the individual is reserved for certain privileged people—in other words, those who belong to society, the class of ladies, clerks, and knights. Behind all of this is an entire notion of initiation—indeed, fine amor constitutes a veritable initiatory method intended to push forward men as well as women. Melusine shares certain features with Eleanor in that she is the initiator, the one who helps the knights—and consequently the poets, for even if they are not noble, they are incorporated by right into the privileged class—to discover their identity within the ideal community that woman foresees and tries to install around her. Melusine rules over Poitou in a way that is as secret and marginal as was Eleanor's when she held her court of love in Poitiers. The amorous casuistry of the twelfth century then permitted discovery of the small spark in the world's depths that could set fire to the world and cause it to move from a state of slumber to a waking state. Likewise, Melusine awakens the land of Poitou that is benumbed beneath the winter symbolized by Raimondin. She is the spring that causes the germination of everything that is capable of growing and prospering. One day, however, autumn arrives, exemplified by Raimondin's discovery of Melusine in the cave, and this is followed by winter, which is Melusine's absence— but within this dark time there are glimpses of hope. Melusine returns during the night, and her comforting presence can be felt. Eleanor, the prisoner of Henry, is hardly different on the symbolic plane, which is the imaginal realm and the collective unconscious.

All of this demonstrates the mystery surrounding both Melusine and Eleanor of Aquitaine. Did anyone really know what the queen-duchess was thinking? Do we really know what her actions were? Do we know what her impressions were, what her feelings were? Unless we wish to write a novel, we have to be satisfied to observe Eleanor through her works and her legend. First and foremost, we must restore to this peerless figure her true dimension, which means we must not lose sight of the fact that she can be explained only through the context in which she was fully integrated, for, like all heroes, she is only the symbolic emanation of a defined social group.

Here lies the real problem. Heroes never die, yet they have no real life except to the extent that they represent a mentality, a way of acting, or a lifestyle. So just what did Eleanor represent through her life and legend and her numerous literary incarnations?

First of all, she embodied the concept of woman that had been born during the twelfth century. This notion was revolutionary because up to that time in the Christian West women had only a pejorative image. Eleanor—whether as Iseult, Guinevere, or Melusine—was the woman reborn from her own ashes, she who solemnly asserted her freedom to think and act. Yet she would not have been allowed to lead without profound reason. In the rapidly transforming society of the courts of twelfth-century Europe, it was necessary for a woman to hold a dominant role.

But if she was a woman, she was woman as mistress (as defined in the Latin word *domina* with all its underlying meanings). As keeper of actual sovereignty over Aquitaine and Poitou, she became the image of authority that seduces instead of coldly ordering. As mistress of hearts before becoming a mistress physically, she injected into the society of her time a new sensibility: she became the queen who imposes her will not through creating terror but by casting charm on those around her and those who fall in love with her. This explains her important role in the philosophy of fine amor and justifies the fact that she was used as a model for heroines who had a sacred aspect.

Sacralization was at work here with the figure of Eleanor; that is obvious. In considering Eleanor's behavior and history's perception of her, we may find that she was indeed a horrible shrew who was greedy for gain and infatuated with power and, finally, just as barbaric as her two husbands. No one has ever claimed she was a saint. No one has ever claimed to see her as an angel of mercy. She had to be a strong woman with a dominating nature, for if she was not, she never could have opposed the patriarchal world in which she lived, and it would have succeeded in reducing her to silence. Yet as it happened, she dominated men, even if, at times, she had to temporarily bow before the forces of repression.

It is perhaps because of this that for Eleanor the aspect of mother was added to that of mistress and queen. First, people saw her as the mother of many children. In addition, in correspondence to the cult of the Virgin Mary that was then developing, it was important to present the queen with a maternal image, which could only be reassuring and would gather a number of adherents around her. The mother loves all her children equally—even though we know Eleanor preferred Richard. She then represented the birth of a new society centered around a female who was also a mother.

In fact, Eleanor symbolized sovereignty. She was the sovereign of a society in search of a resolution to the delicate problem of the couple. We know that she wanted to realize the ideal couple in her marriage to Henry II. We know that she was strongly convinced that love could overcome all obstacles—in fact, she advocated a policy of love against the old politics of hate and terror. Here the legendary opposition between *Roma* and *Amor* finds more justification than ever. After all, the main characteristic of Rome was an authority that sought to impose itself by any and all means, including force, and the motto of ancient Rome was "divide and conquer." In opposition to this brutal concept of a society obliged to practice aggression in all its forms in order to secure its own survival, there was another method that consisted of encouraging individuals to love one another within a social group founded on confidence and esteem. This was a dream, of course, another Utopia to add to those that had emerged over the centuries, but this dream, perceived in the courts of the twelfth century, was more than a mind-set; it signified the change taking place at the heart of Western civilization.

Eleanor was much more than the creation of the dreams of her contemporaries; she was a creation of their actual experience of her. During her lifetime, she was surrounded by such an aura of mystery and was in fact so inaccessible that she became the cipher for the crystallization of society's desires—in short, she became the figure in a dream. The people of the thirteenth century, who did not know her, added to this idealization, deliberately transposing to this figure that had been at the very center of a social transformation all the fantasies inspired by woman. Added to this was the impassioned context in which the role women should play was the subject for unprecedented debate. Eleanor had been a free woman, and by virtue of this, through a process of transferring guilt, she became a prostitute—albeit one of high value—in both the popular imagination and the minds of all those who confusedly criticized her. Yet by becoming a prostitute and with the subsequent help of sacralization, she became only more attractive because she was seen as both forbidden and guilty. The beauty of sin requires no demonstration and Eleanor acquired all the aesthetic qualities we could find in transgression. Hence the vision of an ever-radiant and beautiful Eleanor, a solar symbol inherited from the dawn of time, center of the world and keeper of powers that formerly devolved to the god-king, the embodiment of patriarchal society.

This placement of the burden of guilt on Eleanor corresponds to a veritable deification of the queen. It was the style of that era to deify woman, who was both the object of sexual desires and a portal opening into the infinite. Because she was queen, Eleanor already occupied a place in the social hierarchy, and there was no reason to stop at the position she reached; she could acquire other stages and make herself more than the intermediary between men and gods—she could make herself a goddess. All the poems of the troubadours have about them the scent of idolatry. The image left us by Eleanor's contemporaries is one of the queen as a veritable idol. The great harlot of Babylon, Ishtar, who offered herself to Gilgamesh in order for him to uncover the secrets of the Otherworld, was reincarnated in this way for an entire court of admirers who asked nothing more than to see the goddess of former days reappear.

No work describes this frame of mind so well as the Welsh story *Peredur,* written during the twelfth century and based on traditional details. It is an archaic version of the Grail legend and, on numerous points, can be compared to the *Perceval* of Chrétien de Troyes. Throughout his journey studded with initiatory stages, as is customary with folktales, the young hero meets a marvelous woman with whom he falls in love and who emerges on countless occasions to give him aid and counsel. This mysterious woman, whose face is not always identical, is the empress—and it is not by chance that the anonymous author of this tale gives her this title. During the course of the story, Peredur is forced to fight an *addanc,* a kind of monstrous serpent that guards a treasure in a cave, and meets "seated atop a mountain, the most beautiful woman he had ever seen." She speaks to him to warn him against the ruses of the addanc:

> He shall slay you not by valor but by cunning. There, upon the threshold of his cavern, is a stone column. He sees all who come without being seen himself and from the shelter of the column slays them all with a poisoned dart. If you give me your word to love me more than any other woman in the world, I will give you a gift of a stone that will let you see him when you enter without being seen by him.[6]

What this calls to mind is an oath of fine amor: the empress asks the young man to swear fidelity to her, and in exchange for this promise she gives him the means to overcome all danger. The theme is that of both love as salvation and love as a factor in feats of prowess. The mistress of destiny in all this is the empress; she holds all powers, both temporal and spiritual. The hero becomes her liegeman, her knight servant, and it is in this capacity that he is able to perform the different phases of his mission. Furthermore, all of this leads to the creation of a privileged couple, for after performing numerous deeds, Peredur again finds himself in the presence of this mysterious woman. "Handsome Peredur," the empress tells him, "remember the faith you gave to me when I gave you the gift of the stone and you slew the addanc." Peredur responds, "Princess, you speak truly; I have not forgotten." The story goes on to say that "Peredur will govern with the empress for fourteen years."[7]

As this tale shows, power belongs to the woman, and because she is free, she can share it with whom she will. The knight servant is only one who carries out her desires. It is clearly in this sense that the oath of allegiance was sworn to the lady. In contrast with the preceding era in which only the lord counted, in the twelfth century it was the lady who occupied the top of the pyramid. We should not then wonder if Eleanor served as model for the empress in the story of Peredur—although that is not impossible—but instead can conclude that all the authors of the twelfth century were working toward feminizing society.

This does not, however, mean forming a society of women similar to the one that is claimed to have existed during the fabled times of the Amazons. In fact, we have no actual proof of matriarchal societies existing in their pure state. Yet there are moments in history when societies are masculinized to an extreme and other times when, conversely, they are strongly colored by feminization. This was the case in the twelfth century, in which we see coming to the surface all the feminine impulses, both among individuals and in the social groups that reflect these individual mentalities.

Eleanor symbolized this feminization of twelfth-century society in western Europe. The sublimation of her person, which we can observe in both the historical narratives and the simple legends about her, is at the very heart of an attempt to restore to the human race something it had lost long before: its female components—that is, everything having to do with sensitivity, emotion, and intuition. Of course, here again we see developing the eternal quarrel between logic and instinct, with logic being regarded, quite wrongly, as essentially male and instinct being attributed to female mentality.

This is a false quarrel, however, for logic is only instinct that has met and reflected itself. There is no such thing as logic idling like a motor in pure abstraction and there is no instinct that does not extend into the decisions made by the mind. Furthermore, because women have long been removed from the decision-making process and the possession of responsibilities, it is claimed that they are incapable of logic. Yet all must be called into question in a more rational vision of the profound values harbored by humanity. It certainly seems that women are better endowed for all that relates to the emotional domain, but the reason for this is largely biological, for maternity predisposes them to leaps of the heart as opposed to leaps of the mind, and every woman is a potential mother, whether or not this potential is realized. It is always men who wage war and seek to destroy, and it is women who preach reconciliation and seek to build. Unlike women, the attitude of men stems from a constant application of the death instinct. We are compelled, however, to resort to simplification in all classifications: in the twelfth century, after a period in which the death instinct dominated—that is, there was a time of merciless struggle to destroy everything foreign—society arrived at a more feminine concept according to which all living beings had the right to coexist on condition that they had mutual respect for life in all its forms.

Fine amor, so admirably embodied by Eleanor of Aquitaine, can be considered a game, a diversion for the bored aristocratic society that posed problems for itself that the lower classes of society did not have the time to pose. This is true to the extent that the intellectual elite was made up of only members of this caste or those incorporated into it. Yet the phenomenon far outstripped literary acrobatics and pirouettes of erotic casuistry. In fact, emphasizing the fundamental role of love in interpersonal relations, even if they were hierarchized, was akin to realizing that another way could be accessed, one that would lead to the acknowledgment of inner impulses within a society that had too long lived on abstract reasoning arising from disembodied reflection.

In one sense, this realization corresponded to the desire to build a society that would allow the individual to blossom freely in the satisfaction of his deepest and most respectable tendencies. This takes the reverse direction of that of androcratic societies, for this kind of society aims primarily at integrating the human being into an already organized structure governed by mandatory relationships that have always existed and are considered exclusive. In a word, while patriarchal society, like that of feudalism, absorbed individuals willy-nilly into the obedience of the fundamental laws of logic, the society dreamed of by Eleanor and her entourage was created in the measure of human beings and incorporated the satisfaction of instincts.

Here again, we may find Utopia. The Land of Fairy described countless times in Celtic legends and often imagined by the authors of the romances of the Round Table remains a domain of the unreal and of the most intellectual speculation. Yet the fact that so much importance was attached to it denotes a desire to bring this Utopian world out of the imaginal realm and realize it in daily life. The writings of the twelfth century, inspired by Eleanor or testifying to the state of mind she illustrated, show us that this problem was posed in precise terms. Feminizing society—even if it was a fragmentary society of intellectuals, knights, and idle ladies—was the realization of a different world that would replace the vertical one that predominated; a world with one leader who was necessarily a father and thus a man would be replaced with a horizontal system in which all the parties established emotional and tangible relations among them before taking into account the obligatory hierarchy. There was as much difference between the society that existed at Eleanor's time and the one she dreamed of establishing as there is between an excessively centralized state whose orders are laws for all and the lands of the federal type, where various regions administer themselves, based on their regional distinctions.

This is why the history and legend of Eleanor of Aquitaine is important. The concept of this twelfth century in full transformation was not lost. In the twelfth century we can truly witness the birth of a new philosophical system whose emotional components played as important a role as the logical components without which no society can have structure. In some ways, since the moment the troubadours took as goddess the sovereign woman, society became bisexual and thereby made the transition from an abusive patriarchy to an ideal gynecracy.

All roads led to this new world: the role of "our Holy Mother the Church"; the development of the worship of the Virgin Mary, mother of God but also of all men; the recognition of woman as an entirely separate and independent being—these all had an effect on the mentality of the individuals in every social stratum of the twelfth century. In the religious domain, Mary was known as Our Lady. In the mythological domain, always quite close to religion and often blended with it but equally present in the depths of the collective unconscious of the masses, there was Iseult and Guinevere. In the political arena—that is, in the realm of everyday life—there was Eleanor, incarnation of this ancient myth and personification of divine power made woman.

Henceforth, nothing could be as it was. Eleanor marks a turning point in the history of Western civilization. Intentionally through her desire for power and her intelligence, and unintentionally because she was both the emanation of history and the personification of myth, she succeeded in tapping the vital forces of a society that sought a new road to follow. The symbolic images of her that appeared were the manifestations of all the repressed desires of a humanity unsatisfied with its fate. This alone should bring us to consider the figure of Eleanor, for though she was nothing in herself, prisoner as she was of her education and the milieu in which she lived, we cannot help but find a little of that self in her momentous life, stirred by various passions, marked by significant events, hammered by grief, and brightened by the joys of a woman and mother. We should not forget that Eleanor was a woman in every sense of the word. She was the ideal woman for everyone, the ideal mother for all her subjects—and for those who were not.

Perhaps Eleanor's actions were a failure strictly on the political plane. She did attempt to expand then save the Plantagenet empire and she was not successful, for her son, John Lackland, lost it once and for all. But should she be considered one of the great women of history solely for her political role, however it may have failed? Personal failures do not count when we examine the succession of events that transpire across the centuries. Eleanor's mythical role was much more important and much more enduring because it left its influence on the mind-set of the men and women of western Europe and did so long after she had left this life.

The dream for which she was the center in the middle of the twelfth century continues even in our day, and perhaps this dream is like myth: it cannot die even if, at times, it is concealed in such a way that its presence cannot be sensed. Eleanor of Aquitaine, twice the queen of two different countries but the constant sovereign of the troubadours, remains alive in our eyes. Indeed, she was never her own person. It is the fate of history's heroes to be the collective property of peoples and poets.

NOTES

Chapter 1. Twice a Queen

1. Until the sixteenth century, he was honored under the name of St. Guillaume [William] in the breviary of Bordeaux.

2. Originally, both with the Carolingians and the Capets, the monarchy as such was not hereditary. The king was merely the count of Paris and the lord of Ile de France and was thus heir only to this domain, but as king, meaning suzerain or sovereign of the other nobles, he was theoretically elected by his peers. Hence the custom established by the kings to coronate their sons while they were still alive.

3. A variation of this story exists. Saldebreuil, a lazy rascal but spokesman for the scholars of Paris, allegedly gave a welcoming speech to the queen when she was visiting the university. Flattered and content, Eleanor would have given him a fat purse. During the course of the meal that followed, this scholar was brought in on a stretcher, wounded by a companion who was envious of his success. The queen then cared for him with a great deal of solicitude.

4. *Romania,* LXVI, 160.

5. A play on words in Latin between *castris* (camp) and *casta* (chaste).

6. *The Chronicle of William of Newburgh,* I, 92–93.

7. Here is what the era's most impartial historian, John of Salisbury, had to say about the matter. "The prince's (Raymond's) familiarity with the queen and his frequent discussions with her, almost without interruption, made the king suspicious." William of Tyr goes even further in 1180: "Once Raymond saw that nothing would come of it, he changed his position and

started laying pitfalls for the king. In fact, he planned to carry off, either by force or shadowy intrigues, the king's wife, who had agreed to this; she was one of a number of madwomen. Yes, I say, she was a thoughtless woman, as she showed both before and after this in a most obvious way. Contrary to royal dignity, she set little store by marriage and ignored the conjugal bed."

The accusation could not be any more clear. It should be known that William of Tyr, like all the English, hated Eleanor, and by writing this in 1180 at a time when Eleanor was imprisoned by King Henry II, he could not help but please the king. Finally, however, this generally well-informed archbishop could not dare openly to accuse the ex-queen of France and current queen of England of repeated adultery (both before and after this) if Eleanor's conduct was beyond reproach. The later historian Gervais de Tilbury shows more caution, but his prudence speaks volumes. According to him, the rift between Louis VII and Eleanor was a result of "certain things that happened during this journey, and it is preferable to keep one's silence." The mystery that surrounded the rift only excited the commentators and paved the way for all the legends concerning Eleanor.

8. Here is what John of Salisbury says on this subject: "Regarding the quarrel that had arisen in Antioch between the king and the queen, the pope soothed it after having separately listened to the complaints of the two spouses. He forbid them from ever again alluding to any kinship between them and confirmed their union both orally and in writing. He forbid under pain of anathema of hearing anyone use this kinship to criticize their marriage. This marriage could not be broken under any pretext. This decision appeared to be infinitely pleasing to the king. The pope made them [the king and queen] sleep in the same bed, which he had adorned with rich fabrics. During their several day visit he worked, through private audiences, to restore their mutual feelings. He heaped them with presents and when they took their leave, this rather austere man could not keep from shedding tears. At their departure, he blessed their persons and the kingdom of France" (*Historia Pontificalis,* 537). This leads to the conclusion that the disagreement between Louis VII and Eleanor must have been quite serious, as the pope stepped in personally as an intermediary and confirmed their union despite its canonical consanguinity.

9. "The pope swears by God in heaven that you can find no better woman, neither in intelligence nor beauty nor allure. Go then, take your woman, and

may God grant you joy in her" (*Girart de Roussillon,* verse 385–88). For more on this subject, we can read the very interesting thesis by René Louis, *De l'Histoire à la Legende, Girart, comte de Vienne,* vol. 1, 370, in particular.

10. The chroniclers give no date for the birth of Alix. Some have put forth the notion that she could have been the result of an adulterous union, but this opinion does not withstand scrutiny; the pope would not have reconciled Louis with Eleanor if she was pregnant from an illicit affair. A more acceptable answer is that the child was conceived in Tusculum at the time of the reconciliation blessed by Pope Eugene III—a reconciliation that, as we know, had little depth.

11. William of Newburgh writes that, disgusted with her husband, Eleanor began thinking that a union with Henry would be better suited to her temperament.

12. For example, the author of the *Chronicle of Tours.*

13. Before accusing Eleanor of duplicity or venality, we need to remember that the Church plays no active role in marriage; the priest is merely the witness of the sacrament the couple gives each other, records their consent, and blesses their union. This allows the argument to be made for everyone's good faith, but it is primarily a souvenir from the early days of Christianity when marriage was just barely tolerated by the Church.

14. Gervais of Canterbury speaks of a "very specious oath."

15. It is likely that Bernard of Clairvaux was disturbed by the fact that the French king had no male descendant. We might also look to the fears of the Church: According to Robert de Thorigny, abbot of Mont-saint-Michel, who was close to both Louis VII and Henry II, Eleanor had premeditated leaving with Henry. Therefore a scandal had to be avoided at any price.

16. They were determined as legitimate by virtue of the good faith of Louis and Eleanor, who had allegedly married in ignorance of their consanguinity.

17. Thibaud V of Blois was the second son of Thibaud of Champagne, with whom Eleanor had problems concerning the marriage of her sister, Petronella. Here is a titillating detail: later, Thibaud the Cheat married Alix of France, Eleanor's second daughter.

18. Gervase of Canterbury notes: "Eleanor secretly sent envoys to the duke (Henry Plantagenet) informing him of her newfound freedom and pressing him to contract a marriage with her. In fact, it was said that it was her skill that had obtained this repudiation full of artifice. But the duke, enticed by this lady's high birth and especially by lust for the holdings she possessed,

unable to endure love and any delay, took a few companions with him and made the longer journey in short order. Within a brief time, he attained his long-desired union."

19. *Senescallus,* the "ancient one" as opposed to "senior," the oldest; in other words, the "lord." This is a fairly imprecise rank at this time. In fact, it was mainly a mark of honor bestowed upon a noble family.

20. We can note how little she regards the importance of the French king, her legitimate suzerain, for she—like the duke of Brittany—claims to hold her power from God alone and not as the grant of a fief by the sovereign. The rest of the writ is also quite significant. She definitely sought to bury the past and act as a new benefactor. "When I was queen with the king of France, the king made the gift of the Sevre Woods to the abbey, and I, too, gave and conceded these woods. But since I have separated from the king by judgment of the Church, I have taken back this gift, and on the counsel of wise men and at the prayer of Abbot Pierre, this gift I formerly made with regret I renew today with glad heart . . ."

21. The idea was that the abbess should be the mother of all the monks and nuns—consequently, a widow who had children seemed best to materially and psychologically manage this mixed group. The origin of this custom is typically Celtic and reached its peak during the twelfth-century attempt to restore to women their moral authority and full personality. We should not overlook the fact that this century also witnessed the birth of courtly love, a kind of deification of women, and Eleanor was largely responsible for the success of this mentality both because of her personal attitude and because of her encouragement of both troubadours and northern poets.

22. During the course of a crossing from Normandy to England, all of the children of the king of England perished in this shipwreck. Henri Beauclerc never recovered. It was then that Matilda took the veil at Fontevrault, where she had spent her youth.

23. "After having separated by cause of consanguinity from my lord Louis, most illustrious king of France, and having been united in marriage with my very noble lord Henry, Count of Anjou, and moved by divine inspiration, I wished to visit the holy congregation of the virgins of Fontevrault, and by God's grace I was able to realize the purpose I had in my mind. Thus I came to Fontevrault, and, guided by God, crossed the threshold where the nuns where gathered, and there, my heart full of emotion, I approved, conceded,

and confirmed all that my father and my ancestors had given God at the church of Fontevrault, first and foremost the alms of five hundred Poitevin sous that Lord Louis, at the time he was my husband, and I had given."

24. Etienne de Blois had a legitimate son, Eustache, who was a notorious incompetent, and a bastard son who was legally removed from succession to the throne. Eustache died in 1153, and on the intervention of the bishop of Winchester, Etienne's own brother, Etienne reluctantly accepted this solution. He could find none better, for he was sick himself and increasingly abandoned by his supporters.

25. The venerable John of Etampes is supposed to have told Eleanor: "Noble lady, long have people spoken of you and long shall they speak. You are she foretold by the prophet Merlin six hundred years ago, when he portrayed you as a great eagle whose two wings spanned both England and France." Eleanor allegedly replied: "I cannot see my husband, the king, repeating the exploits of William the Conqueror on that isle." The old man then responded: "It is not King Louis. This eagle of Merlin's prophecy is you, beautiful Queen Eleanor." Eleanor then terminated the discussion with a joke: "I need only become a widow to prove Merlin right." Whether true or false, this unverifiable anecdote is certainly based on Eleanor's well-known ambition.

This is not the only time that twelfth-century authors established links between Eleanor and the pseudo-prophecies of Merlin. We know that around 1232, Geoffrey of Monmouth wrote his famous *Prophecies of Merlin,* which were later included in his *Historia Regum Britanniae* on orders or counsel from the Anglo-Norman dynasty but which were based on written and oral traditions from Wales. Geoffrey happily transformed them into literature by giving current relevance to the famous prophecies attributed to the prophet-bard Myrddin, a sixth-century historical figure who had lived with the northern Britons (on the Scottish frontier). It should also be noted that once she was queen of England, Eleanor asked Robert Wace, canon of Bayeux, to provide a French adaptation of the *Historia Regum Britanniae.* This was the famous *Roman de Brut,* the starting point in France and the Anglo-Norman speaking lands for the literary rise of the Arthurian legend. More on this subject can be found in my *King of the Celts,* which examines, in addition to the Arthurian legend itself, the historical circumstances that prevailed—with Plantagenet blessings—over the spread of Arthurian romances throughout Europe.

26. Peter of Blois noted: "Daily in Mass, in counsels, and in other public doings of the realm always from morning until vespers, he stands on his feet. And he never sits, unless riding a horse or eating. . . . In a single day, if necessary, he can run through four- or five-day marches. It is quite difficult to know where he is and what he is doing, because he is ever changing his mind. Thus foiling the plots of his enemies, he frequently mocks their plots with his sudden arrival. . . . [H]e fatigues almost every day the most powerful for the labor. Truly he does not, like other kings, linger in his palace, but traveling through the provinces he investigates the doings of all." In fact, it does seem that no other king of this time was so feverishly active. Henry had no capital and no fixed residence, which might explain the size of his domains. Furthermore, in such a far-flung empire, which spanned from the Scottish border to the Pyrenees, his presence—or that of Eleanor—was required at any price to maintain a unity, which, without their constant effort, would have been purely nominal. No empire was ever as well managed and centralized as the Anglo-Angevin empire.

27. Bernard de Ventadorn was thought to be in love with the chatelaine of Ventadorn (he was only the son of one of the castle servants) and was exiled by the jealous lord of the manor. This is when he formed part of the company of Eleanor, to whom he dedicated numerous poems, which were the basis for the rumor of a possible affair between the two.

28. This earldom was created by William the Conqueror to reward the Britons who contributed assistance to his conquest of England.

29. Giraldus Cambrensis, who always wrote with a poison pen, did not miss this opportunity to make a play on words: he wrote in Latin (*Rosa mundi* in Latin means "rose of the world," but a pun also exists in the name *Rosa Munda,* which means "beautiful rose") and stated that she deserves not her real name, but rather that of *Rosa Immundi,* meaning "rose of impurity" or "rose of unchastity."

30. Later, in order to regain his freedom after the payment of the ransom collected by Eleanor, Richard the Lion Heart swore homage to the emperor of Germany (the Holy Roman Germanic Empire) for England. This was a purely formal homage, however. Even later, the quarrels of John Lackland with his barons, the king of France, and the pope led John to acknowledge the suzerainty or sovereignty of the papacy over his kingdom.

31. Particularly according to Gervase of Canterbury, who depicts Henry trying to bribe the papal envoy.

32. This consanguinity was further removed than the one between Louis VII and Eleanor, but it was quite real. Henry and Eleanor were both descendants of Robert the Pious.

33. Richard had been recognized as duke of Aquitaine and count of Poitou, thus as not only the heir but also the holder of his mother's domains. The situation was unclear, however, and it worried Henry. Hadn't he refused his eldest son, who was also acknowledged and crowned king of England, the power he demanded? Henry felt he was trapped and could do nothing without Eleanor. Furthermore and with good reason, he distrusted Richard's attitude; Richard could very easily restore these titles to his mother, who, we should not forget, regarded Richard as her favorite child. Despite some times of apparent chilliness, Eleanor and Richard were always in collusion.

34. Here is the text by Richard the Poitevin's continuer, in a lyrical and prophetic tome that is crammed with biblical quotes. [Bracketed notes are the author's. —*Trans.*]

> Tell me, two-headed eagle, tell me where were you when your eaglets [Eleanor's sons], soaring away from their nest, dared lift their claws against the king of Aquilonia [the King of England]? It was you, we have learned, who urged them to rebel against their father. This is why you have been torn from your native land and have been borne to a foreign country. Your barons, with their peaceful words, have taken advantage of you with their ruses. Your lute plays only dismal tones now and your flute plays only airs of grief. Once delicate and voluptuous, you enjoyed royal freedom and overflowed with riches, surrounded by young girls accompanied by lute and drum who sang smooth refrains for you [allusion to the court at Poitiers, to which Eleanor invited poets and musicians from all lands]. The sound of the instruments was your enjoyment. You took great delight in the virtuosity of your musicians. I beg you, queen of the two crowns, to cease constantly tormenting yourself. Why allow your heart to be troubled by the tears each day brings? Return, oh captive, to your cities if you can! And if you cannot, weep with the King of Jerusalem and say: Unhappiness is my lot, my captivity is prolonged, I have dwelled among an unknown and crude race! [The Aquitanians never let slip an opportunity to declare their civilization's superiority to the barbaric Anglo-Normans.] Weep ever again and say: My tears both day and night have been my bread while each day I am asked, Where are your servitors? Where are your attendants? Where are your counselors? Some of them have

been torn from their lands and condemned to a shameful death. Others have been deprived of sight [allusion to the cruelty of the repression of Henry II]. Others finally wander in different lands and are regarded as fugitives. You, the eagle of the broken covenant, how long must you protest before your prayers are granted? The king of Aquilonia has laid siege to you. Go, cries the prophet, without truce. Make your voice resound like the trumpet so that your children may hear you! Because the day is at hand when they will set you free and you can return to your country.

35. Each of the three—Richard, Geoffrey, and Henry the young king—claimed that they had been wronged in the division. During this time, John Lackland, too young to take any action, was clearly resolved to do whatever it took to get his share. Geoffrey said one day that it was the fate of the Plantagenets to war against each other. It is true that the sons of Henry II were given encouragement by the king of France, whose policy consisted of weakening his more powerful vassals and neighbors through internal quarrels, as well as by the ever quarrelsome Aquitaine barons, who were never disposed to obey any suzerain authority, be it French or English. In these quarrels, a leading role was played by the warrior troubadour Bertrand de Born, who extolled war in his poems. He spent his life stirring Henry's sons against their father, then reconciled with the king and began stirring up the brothers against each other.

36. Claiming himself an heir to the legendary Arthur, whom he sought to have recognized as an authentic historical figure (mainly through the discovery of the alleged tomb of Arthur and Guinevere in Glastonbury) in order to use this for his own political ends, Henry II, who saw this child as Richard's legitimate heir, wished primarily to show that the Anglo-Angevin dynasty went back to the Celtic origins of English history. For more on this, see my book *King of the Celts,* particularly the chapter entitled "The Political Background," in which is analyzed the Anglo-Norman then the Anglo-Angevin influence on the spread of the Arthurian legends.

37. It is likely that this entire scene at Gisors had been planned in advance. Richard had reached an understanding with the French king so that all would unfold to place Henry II in an inferior position. It was intended to publicly show that all the Continental domains of the Plantagenets were fiefs of the French crown.

38. Giraldus Cambrensis recounts a fairly odd anecdote: In one of the rooms of the palace of Windsor there was a painting depicting an eagle and four eaglets.

Three of these eaglets attacked the eagle's back and wings with beak and claw, and the fourth eaglet, who was the smallest, was perched on the eagle's neck, trying to peck out his eyes. According to Giraldus, Henry would have analyzed this painting as follows: "These four eaglets are my four sons, who will never stop persecuting me until I die. Of them, the youngest, who is my favorite, will be the cruelest to me and will wound me more deeply than the others." It is not known if what Giraldus Cambrensis recorded is exact, but it is certain that Henry II experienced great pain when he learned of the betrayal of his favorite son.

39. According to the chronicler Roger of Hoveden, Richard said one day: "I would sell London if ever I could find a buyer." It should be noted that he sold primarily English domains.

40. Richard had suggested giving in marriage his sister Jeanne, widow of the king of Sicily, to the brother of Sultan Saladin, Malik-al-Adil. The two would then have ruled together over Jerusalem, and arrangements would have been made to end the war with reciprocal cessions of territory. Jeanne, however, categorically refused her brother's plan, which was more dream than reality. Richard drew close enough to see the confines of Jerusalem but never managed to reach it. He eventually reached a compromise with Saladin that allowed the Westerners to keep the ports and the littoral. As reward for his bravery, Saladin offered Richard safe conduct for a pilgrimage to the holy sites. Richard, however, refused, according to the chronicler Joinville: "Good Lord God, I pray you not suffer me to see your holy city, as I am unable to deliver it from the hands of your enemies."

41. In fact, Ireland had been sold to Henry Plantagenet by the papacy. There has been debate as to the authenticity of the 1155 Laudabiliter bull by which the pope charged Henry II with reforming the Church of Ireland and with reestablishing there the denier of Peter [this refers to the annual contribution made to Rome]. Nevertheless, three 1172 letters of Pope Alexander III approve Henry's assumption of power over Ireland. At this time, compared to the fragile Louis VII, the Church viewed the sole valid power in the West as the Anglo-Angevin dynasty. In addition, Henry's power there was a means of removing the secular quarrel between the Church of Ireland—which was always marginal and attached to Ireland's distinguishing features, especially its system of bishopric-abbeys that verged on semiautonomy—and the centralist Church of Rome. In the same way, Henry II had obtained from the

pope the definitive liquidation of the metropolis Dol, in Armoricain Brittany, to the benefit of the metropolis of Tours, a traditionally Roman Catholic denomination, one that (even better) was located on Plantagenet lands. In fact, except for the slight hitch of Thomas Becket's murder, Henry II was always on the best of terms with the papacy.

42. This did not prevent Philip Augustus from being excommunicated a short time later because of Ingeborg's repudiation. His reconciliation was nevertheless easy. Capetian France began its definitive stint as the eldest daughter of the Church, which would last several centuries—to the extent that, starting with Philip the Fair, the papacy was under direct Capet tutelage at Avignon.

43. Peter of Blois was the longtime secretary and close friend of Henry II.

44. Frederick Barberossa, emperor of Germany, at odds with the papacy, did not hesitate to oppose Alexander II with an antipope. It was actually the unwavering support of Henry II, who rallied to Alexander, that prevented a large schism at the time.

45. The play on words exists only in Latin: *ligati potius quam legati*. It is obvious that when writing these letters, Peter of Blois sacrificed Latin redundancies, courtly preciousness, and supposedly intellectual humor to the literary style of the time, with its accumulation of biblical citations. The majority of letters written at this time are in this style.

46. All of these events play a role in the origin of the legend of Robin Hood, symbol of the supporters of King Richard in one of the English regions dominated by John Lackland's minions, represented by the sheriff of Nottingham.

47. This is made evident by this poem written by Richard himself during his captivity:

> No prisoner will ever speak his mind
> fittingly unless he speaks in grief.
> But he can, for consolation, make a song.
> I have many friends, but their gifts are poor.
> It will be their shame if, for want of ransom,
> I remain as prisoner these two winters.
>
> They know well, my men and my barons
> of England, Normandy, Poitou, and Gascony,
> I never had a poor companion
> I would leave in prison for money.

I do not say this as a reproach,
but I am still a prisoner.

Now I know for sure,
a dead man or a prisoner has no friend or family,
because they leave me here for gold and silver.
That's my concern, but even more my people's,
for when I am dead, they will be shamed
if I die a prisoner.

It is no wonder I have a grieving heart,
for my lord keeps my land in torment.
Now if he remembered our vow
that we both took together,
I know I would not long
be here a prisoner.

They know well, the men of Anjou and Touraine,
those bachelors now so magnificent and safe,
that I am arrested, far from them, in another's hands.
They used to love me much; now they love me not at all.
There's no lordly fighting now on the barren plains,
because I am a prisoner.

Tell my companions whom I loved and love—
the men of Caen and Perche—
Song, tell them they are not men to rely on;
the heart I had for them was never false or faltering.
If they turn against me now, they act like peasants,
as long as I remain a prisoner . . .

48. This is what did happen with the Capets. Furthermore, Philip Augustus urged Arthur to claim the crown.
49. John obviously did not swear this oath of loyalty and instead inspired an insurrectional attempt on his part.
50. In Eleanor's charters, Richard is always referred to as *carissimum,* "very dear," whereas John is referred to merely as *dilectum,* a simple, polite word.
51. Upon news of Richard's death, a conversation is also recorded between the always authoritative William Marshal and Hubert Gautier, the all-powerful

archbishop of Canterbury charged with the management of the kingdom:

> "What hope remains to us after this tragedy?" asked the archbishop. "None, for I can foresee no one who can defend the kingdom. I expect to see the French assail us without anyone able to resist them."
>
> William replied, "We should hasten to choose his successor."
>
> The archbishop answered, "In my opinion, we should choose Arthur of Brittany."
>
> "Ah! Milord," said William, "this would be an evil choice. Arthur has had naught but evil counselors and is resentful and proud. If we place him at our head, he will give us trouble, for he has little love for the English. But let's look at Count John. In good conscience, he is the closest heir to the land of his father and brother."
>
> "Yes, it is his birthright. The son is closer than the nephew to the land of his father. Marshal, it shall be as you desire, but I tell you that you will never regret anything you have done as much as you will regret this choice."

52. It is claimed that faced with choosing between her two granddaughters Urraque and Blanche, Eleanor chose Blanche because Urraque's name would be impossible to pronounce in the French court. We know that Blanche of Castile inherited her grandmother's temperament and displayed it on several occasions, particularly in the great struggle she waged against the high vassals of the French kingdom.

53. Since the homage at Tours, Eleanor was suzerain, or sovereign, of John and the Lusignans. It was her duty to resolve the quarrel before the king of France. It should be noted in this regard that if John was able to put together a considerable dowry for his young bride containing, in particular, the cities of Saintes and Niort, he could not have done so without the consent or at least the tolerance of his mother. This does not mean that she approved John's brainstorm, but she could do little else than stand surety for John.

54. We can note that in a deft political move the king of France refrained from giving Aquitaine to Arthur, thereby seeking to show that he still respected the old duchess. Normandy was similarly out of the question; Philip was keeping it for himself.

55. Arthur and Hugh de Challerault were so sure of their prey that they did not take any precautions against an enemy coming from outside. They had

walled up all the gates of the city except for one to prevent the besieged from escaping, and thus they were literally captured in a mousetrap of their own making without even having time to defend themselves.

56. Unless Arthur was a legitimate heir to the Plantagenet domains, as we have seen in the text. In any event, because John had no child, the duke of Brittany was truly his heir.

57. This action has fueled much debate. Efforts have been made to spare John's reputation from the horrible crime by attributing it to his companion. In 1210, however, William of Briouse, who had become a mortal enemy of the king of England, described the scene in its entirety. According to his testimony, it seems there can be no doubt that it was John who personally killed his nephew in one of his fits of bloodthirsty rage, which were common. Modern psychologists would describe John as bipolar, experiencing radical mood swings that carried him from periods of complete apathy to periods of demented agitation.

58. By seeing to the death of Arthur, John lost Brittany for the Plantagenets because the heiress of the duchy legally was Arthur's half sister, young Princess Alix, daughter of Constance of Brittany and Guy de Thouars. The political ambition of Henry II was the union of Armoricain Brittany to England, whatever the cost. Arthur could have achieved this union, as, in large part, he could have saved the Plantagenet empire. (Though Philip Augustus was dead set on obtaining Normandy.) Arthur's murder, then, testifies to the poor political instincts possessed by John Lackland. It is true that John's subsequent behavior was even more insane.

Chapter 2. Eleanor's Strange "Divorce"

1. This concern stemmed from not only the possibility that any child born might not have been sired by Louis VII but also because it was believed during that era that a woman's sexual relations with any man who was not her husband could adulterate his racial purity. Proof of this can be seen in the theory and practice of courtly love: a lady could be loved by a lover—this was even viewed as commendable—but not in just any fashion. There were rules to observe: a lover could love sentimentally and platonically and could practice acts frowned upon by current moral standards, including the most intimate kinds of caresses, but in no case was the sexual act permitted, for fear of its consequences for the purity of the race. This is why a literary text

such as *The Romance of Tristan and Iseult* is fundamentally against courtly love, defending instead total love, whereas Chrétien de Troyes's *Cligés* is truly anti-Tristan and is essentially a courtly work.

2. Generally speaking, in couples, the woman, rather than the man, was always accused of being sterile, for such a claim could be used in the event of repudiation.

3. Of Eleanor and the troubadours who were invited to court, the following anecdote has been told: During a conversation with a troubadour, Eleanor told him she had never lost her reason in a glass. The troubadour responded, citing the authority of Aristotle, whose doctrines were beginning to be all the rage. He said, "Aristotle observed that women do not easily get drunk by virtue of the fact they have very moist bodies, as shown by the sheen of their skin and the periodic purges that free them from superfluous moisture. The wine they drink meets such a large quantity of moisture in their stomachs that it is greatly diluted, and therefore no more than vapors make their way into the brain." Eleanor was said to have added then: "This moisture does not spare women from more formidable intoxications." It is evident that her detractors invented this anecdote. We should note in passing the puerility of the arguments of Aristotle, who was something of a guru to the medieval Church; as recent experiments have proved, biologically speaking, women tolerate alcohol and wine less well than men.

4. For example, after the death of the three sons of Philip the Fair, who had no male heir, the French crown was given after much debate to Philip of Valois, who was the closest relative to the dead king. Interestingly, the daughter of Philip the Fair, Isabel, who was married to the king of England, theoretically could have claimed the throne and then passed it down to someone of English lineage. This solution had been contemplated but was rejected because anything that led to falling under the dominion of the king of England was deemed unacceptable. It was at this time that the Salic Law assumed its full importance. The English sovereigns, however, did not see its validity, in deference to their own customs, and took the opportunity of the death of Philip the Fair to claim the throne of France, which led to the Hundred Years' War. Later, Isabeau of Bavaria, wife of the mad king Charles VI, was won over to the English cause and recognized the king of England as the official heir of the French crown.

5. This is the etymological meaning of the word *vassal,* which comes from the

Gallic term *vassos*, "servitor," and can be seen in the Breton *gwas*, which originally meant "servitor" and now means "man."

6. French civil law, which was inspired by Roman law, retraced the lineage of one person of a couple from the present back to their common root, then came back to the present down the other person's line. In this way, a brother or a sister, who are related on the first canonical degree are related at the second civil degree. First cousins are removed to the second canonical degree but to the fourth according to the civil code.

7. In order to gauge the hypocrisy of all this, it is important to point out that Eleanor and her second husband, Henry Plantagenet, were also descendants of Robert the Pious to the fifth canonical degree.

8. I can offer the following genealogical diagram (the numbers represent the canonical degree of relation).

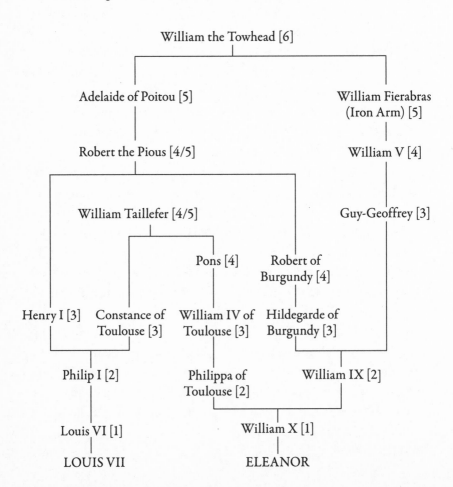

We can see by this that Eleanor and Louis VII were actually related and that it was easy to find any degree of kinship between royal and noble families. By way of comparison, following is a diagram showing the consanguinity of Eleanor and Henry Plantagenet. (As in the previous diagram, the numbers represent the canonical degree.)

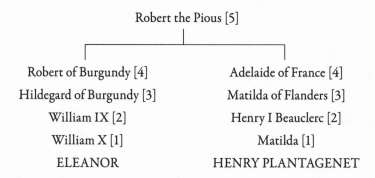

Robert the Pious [5]

Robert of Burgundy [4]	Adelaide of France [4]
Hildegard of Burgundy [3]	Matilda of Flanders [3]
William IX [2]	Henry I Beauclerc [2]
William X [1]	Matilda [1]
ELEANOR	HENRY PLANTAGENET

9. This jealousy is noted by several chroniclers, particularly by the author of the *Chronicle of Tours*.

10. See chapter 1, note 11. In particular, William of Newburgh wrote that, disgusted with her husband, Eleanor felt a union with Henry would better suit her temperament.

11. In particular, it was alluded to by Robert de Thorigny, abbot of Mont-Saint-Michel, whose testimony historians find essential, though we can also cite William of Newburgh and Gervase of Canterbury.

12. Here we find the longstanding quarrel between legality and legitimacy, a quarrel that has never been settled. Indeed, throughout history people have gone to war in the interest of seeing one prevail over the other. The War of Succession in fourteenth-century Brittany offers an illustrative example of this quarrel's futility. Based on the Salic Law, the French monarchy supported Jeanne of Penthièvre—a woman—at the expense of another male heir, John of Mortain, who, conversely, was supported by the English monarchy, which did not recognize the Salic Law. In such domains, the only rule was opportunism.

13. Originally, Gallic territory was divided into three large regions: the Narbonnaise, the area that was under Roman influence longest and that bordered the Mediterranean (Gallia Torgata); the Celtic between the Seine and Garonne Rivers; and the Belgic between the Seine and Rhine Rivers. The

Celtic region of Gaul, by far the largest, had within it the metropolis of Lugdunum, or Lyon (where there currently resides an archbishop bearing the title Primate of the Gauls), but in order for this region to be managed it had to be divided into three parts: First Lyonnaise (metropolis Lyon), Second Lyonnaise (metropolis Bourges), and Third Lyonnaise (metropolis Tours). In the religious arena, this administrative apportionment remains almost intact, but new metropolises were ultimately created. For example, given the importance of the ancient Gallic Senones tribe, the town of Sens became the seat of a metropolis that included the ancient city of the Parisii. During the twelfth century, Paris was only the seat of a bishopric dependent on Sens. Meanwhile, almost all the provinces before they became absorbed into the nation of France after the Hundred Years' War emerged from this apportionment. For example, the earldom of Poitou largely corresponds to the city of the Gaulish tribe the Pictavi, the viscounty of Limonges to the city of the Lemovici, the earldom of Auvergne to the city of the Arverni, Touraine to that of the Turones, Anjou to that of the Andegavi, Maine to that of the Cenomani, and Saintonge to that of the Santones.

In the twelfth century large fiefs, such as Aquitaine, Champagne, and Burgundy (this last was half in the Capetian kingdom and half in the Holy Roman Empire), resulted from the merger of different territories. Normandy and Brittany were two special cases. Normandy was a territory ceded to the Normans [the Norsemen] for them to settle, but the diocesan division remained. Brittany resulted from its occupation by British Islanders on the western part of the peninsula and Carolingian conquests of its eastern territories. Its ecclesiastic organization was largely imported from England, but we can still recognize the former cities of the Gaulish tribe the Veneti (the diocese of Vannes), Redones (diocese of Rennes not including Dol or Saint Malo), and the Namnetes (diocese of Nantes). This apportionment was not the work of chance: economic necessities, various traditions, and the languages used formed the cohesion of these groups and distinguished them from one another. We should also note that this arrangement remained in effect until the French Revolution (for France) and until Bismarck (for Germany), and after these times the ancient states were still respected.

14. *The Song of Apremont,* one of the longest chansons de geste, written in its final form in the twelfth century, echoes this situation. Defied by a Saracen king, Charlemagne summons all his vassals to go to war. To the most power-

ful one among them, Girard de Rousillon, duke of Burgundy and other territories, Charlemagne sends as ambassador Archbishop Turpin. Girard de Rousillon, however, gives the archbishop the rudest of welcomes and refuses to join Charlemagne. The story is quite instructive because of the reason Girard provides in support of his refusal: he holds his realm from God himself and owes nothing to the son of King Pippin. When the archbishop threatens him with an interdict, Girard retorts that he does not care and that he will create a pope to his liking, if need be. Based on what we know, this tale is no caricature but an actual illustration of the circumstances that prevailed in western Europe during the eleventh and the beginning of the twelfth centuries.

15. The counts and dukes of all the large fiefs could also entrust smaller territories to men they trusted. The counts and dukes thus became the direct suzerains of these new vassals, who were no longer dependents of the king. In fact, their domains were now fiefs once removed from the crown, which significantly complicated relations with central authority. For example, the lords of Lusignan, whose domains were quite wealthy, were the direct vassals of the counts of Poitiers and in principle had nothing to do with the king of France, because the fief they occupied had been granted to them by the counts of Poitiers. In practice, however, the lords of Lusignan, who had constant difficulties with their direct suzerain, went above the hierarchy and addressed the king. The strategy of the kings of France was always to help the vassals once removed from the crown (sometimes after causing the problems that required their aid) in order to diminish the influence of the holders of the fiefs.

To complicate matters, there was also the possibility that a vassal was the vassal of another sovereign of a separate territory or was himself the suzerain of another vassal. In fact, no territory was independent, for the feudal pyramid automatically caused the power of every suzerain to flow, and it was possible to be a suzerain or a vassal several times over. This interdependence was certainly no unit for the kingdom. Therefore, theoretically at least, the king was the sole authority able to render justice and to delegate his powers to whomever he liked and to coin money. In reality, however, it was another story entirely: The dukes and counts rendered justice on their own behalf without referring to the king and had individual currencies, which only added to the confusion and did nothing to facilitate exchanges between provinces because these currencies did not all have the same value. In the event of war, when the king requested *service d'ost*—that is, military or financial assistance from his vassals—the vassals contrived pretexts to provide as little as possible. Furthermore, in certain cases, the vassals were obliged to fulfill only forty days of service d'ost; if the trouble dragged on beyond that time, they could abandon the expedition and return home. On the other hand, when a vassal of the king was attacked by one of his neighbors, he never failed to appeal to his sovereign. It is easy to see that in this feudal society, what we now call *patriotism* did not exist. At that time, another mind-set prevailed, one formed by the political divisions of that era.

16. The division of England before the Norman conquest into seven independent kingdoms that were later united is known as the Saxon heptarchy. Yet Saxons naturally resisted centralization and found common cause with Celtic customs. All of this is the origin for the great diversity that can still be seen today within the United Kingdom.

17. Another characteristic (later) example was the marriage of Anne of Brittany to Charles VII (and then to Louis XII). Nevertheless, the duchy of Brittany remained independent of the kingdom of France and not until an actual treaty was drawn up in 1532 did the two countries unite under the same sovereign.

18. This vase is now housed at the Louvre Museum.

19. This charter served as a model for other cities. When we examine these charters, we can note two groups: there are Norman cities such as Falaise, Pont-Audemer, Alençon, Caen, Domfront, Bayeux, Évreux, and Fécamp, which were more or less under the responsibility of Eleanor or Richard; and in the southwest, there are Aquitanian cities such as La Rochelle, Saintes, Angoulême, Poitiers, Niort, Oléron, Ré, Cognac, Saint-Jean-d'Angély, and Bayonne, which formed part of the personal domains of the queen-duchess. Conversely, in the Plantagenet domain of Anjou and in England, which were under Henry's direct domination, no city received a similar charter, which seems to prove that the inspiration for charters was Eleanor and not the king.

20. Similarly in Brittany, upon the abdication of Duke Conan IV, the duchy went to his daughter Constance, who married Geoffrey Plantagenet. On the death of Geoffrey's son Arthur, who was eliminated, as we know, by John Lackland, the duchy went to Arthur's half sister, the daughter of Constance and Guy de Thouars.

21. This political treatise was completed by John of Salisbury in 1159 and fits into a philosophical current running parallel to Aristotelianism. Its inspiration is varied, but the base is primarily biblical. It is a feudal document concerned with the transmission of office and property through heredity. The oath of fealty holds particular importance in the treatise because it was no mere formality but instead involved true commitment on the part of both the one who gave the oath and the one who received it. John of Salisbury, who justifies tyrannicide in certain cases, absolutely denies this right to those who have sworn an oath to the tyrant. In fact, because his basic argument is that a higher, divine, transcendental law has always existed, there would be no need for a king if people obeyed this law. The recognized necessity of having a king is therefore a sort of punishment for humanity's inability to govern itself.

Because of this, the king resembles more an administrator responsible for the proper functioning of the law than humanity's guide. For a man to be king, however, he must show proof of his qualities. Thus, in the last resort, it is the collective, which John of Salisbury divides into *populus* (the people themselves as they exist naturally) and *universitas* (the people organized into a structured body), that decides the king's fate. There must be perfect accord between the populus and the universitas. (We can therefore see that the problem of the nation-state and the state as a body distinct from the nation was not born in modern societies.) Because society is feudal, every property owner is necessarily a prince, thus a kind of king, though on a small scale. Because the idea of community carries the most weight, the prince, as representative of this community, is in some way the owner of all his subjects' property, making them little more than his tenants. For a more detailed examination of John of Salisbury's theories, see my book *King of the Celts,* pages 59–73.

Chapter 3. Queen of the Troubadours

1. We know that the legend of Tristan was known quite early throughout the Occitan world. The allusions made by troubadours are too specific and too many to be the work of chance. The Arthurian legend was known as far as Italy since the beginning of the twelfth century, and we can find evidence of this in the sculptures of the cathedral of Modena. See *King of the Celts,* in which I examine in detail the different origins of Arthurian romances.

2. As I explained in *Women of the Celts,* particularly in the chapter entitled "Iseult or the Lady of the Orchard," in Celtic society women retained both the magic and the moral prerogative that permitted them to choose freely the men they loved. The Irish archetype of Iseult is Grainne. Her name derives from a word meaning "sun," which adds to the radiant power of the woman, heiress of ancient female solar deities who themselves reveal an archaic society with gynecratic tendencies. It is not by chance that the legend of Tristan and Iseult, with all its antiphallocratic content, was developed over the course of the twelfth century although it had been known a long time before.

3. A study of medieval urbanism could form an excellent illustration of this rise of the bourgeoisie at the same time when the provinces of the north were subject to the strong influence of Occitania. Traditionally towns and cities were formed around a sanctuary, and the houses were built to no preestablished plan. As it was for the smallest villages, the active center of these towns and cities remained the church square. In our day, we can see examples in many urban centers, especially in Poitiers, Clermont-Ferrand, Le Puy, Brioude, and Quimper. These are ancient cities in which new neighborhoods were later constructed on the periphery of the active center.

Starting in the twelfth century, however, and initially in Occitania, entirely new towns appeared, particularly the famous *bastides,* which brought together bourgeoisie and serfs seeking employment. These bastides were built in accordance with an entirely different blueprint. The church was no longer the civic center, which was proof of a more secular authority. The active center of these towns was a square (or rectangular space), often with arcades in which were located the stores and homes of the merchants, the masters of these new towns and obviously the most representative of the communes they formed. The church was not removed, but it was no longer the guide for the urban expansion around it. There are typical examples of this plan in Toulouse (Capital Square) and in all the bastides of the southwest, namely in Monpazier and Villefranche-de-Périgord (Dordgone), at Villeneuve-sur-Lot and at Monflanquin (Lot-et-Garonne), and at Villefranche-du-Rouergue (Aveyron). This kind of urbanization is characteristic of the importance given to the merchant guild, which, now free of the tutelage of lord or priest, claimed its own meeting square (the square is the equivalent of the Roman Forum) and distinguished itself from other forms of authority by its more secular nature and a specific kind of administration. This bourgeoisie, solidly established in this way in the heart of the city, formed the core of the rich and active class that would lead directly to the capitalist society of the nineteenth century. La Rochelle, with its numerous arcades, was created by Eleanor's father and built in line with this concept. In Brittany we can note Auray (Morbihan), whose creation goes back to the end of the twelfth century. The original settlement is located on the river of Auray and consists of a simple port and several houses that have taken over the opposite bank around the sanctuary of St. Goustan, but the new quarter is centered around a square and is responsible for the town's size.

This style spread mainly through northern France and Flanders, where the bourgeoisie was richest and most powerful, as is shown by the central squares of Saint-Quentin, Lille, and Brussels. The same model survived for some time and can also be found in the Place des Vosges in Paris, which dates from the seventeenth century.

4. For more on this subject, consult Erich Köhler's book, *L'Aventure chevaleresque* [The Chivalrous Adventure] (Paris: Gallimard, 1974). His analysis of the phenomenon of chivalry is based on its relation to the Arthurian romance, but because the models for the Arthurian heroes can be found in the contemporary life of that time it is simply a study of the caste of Capetian or Plantagenet knights.

5. "La saga primitive de Lancelot du Lac," in Jean Markale, *La Tradition celtique en Bretagne armoricaine* (Paris: Payot, 1984), 119.

6. I have explored this question in depth in my book *Women of the Celts* by introducing an archaic and certainly non-Indo-European notion of the female. The Celts belong to the Indo-European branch of peoples and were thus connected to a patriarchal society, but because, upon their arrival in the West, they subjugated and colonized the indigenous populations whose society was not necessarily patriarchal, there is good reason to deduce that Celtic civilization was stamped with gynecratic influences. As has too often been claimed, the Celts did not have a matriarchal society, which remains to be proved absolutely, but rather had a different mind-set. In addition, characteristic of Celtic society at the beginning of the historical period, both in Ireland and in Britain, is a matrilineal tradition.

7. See the chapter "Iseult or the Lady of the Orchard" in *Women of the Celts*. There is no point in revisiting here the concept of *geis,* the formidable magic spell a woman can use to compel a man's love. The two Irish predecessors

that led to *Tristan and Iseult,* both the story of Deirdre and that of Diarmaid and Grainne, are quite significant and should be taken into consideration upon studying the origins of courtly love.

8. We have two significant examples, one in the *Romance of Tristan,* in which, in the presence of the pine tree, the hero asks Iseult to give him what he needs to recover his equipment that he pawned, and in a lay attributed to Marie de France, the *Lai de Graelent-meur,* in which the future king of Ys, completely ruined, has to borrow a horse and arms.

9. Instead of being a right, it is more a duty that any important figure—king, lord, or even priest—should perform to dispel the curse of the spilling of virginal blood. By sleeping with the young wife of a vassal, even symbolically, as eventually became the practice, the lord did the vassal a service. This may appear paradoxical, but originally it was another bond between the lord and his vassal. What is most curious is that fine amor can be considered as a counterpart of the *droit de cuissage* [also *droit de seigneur,* or "right of first night," which gives the lord of a domain the right to deflower the wives of his vassals on their wedding nights], which determines that because the lord sleeps with the wife of his vassal, the vassal can, under certain conditions, sleep with the wife of his lord. The problem of this so-called courtly love is that it has not been examined with an eye that takes into account the extremely complex social relations that governed archaic societies.

10. Jean Markale, *Epics of Celtic Ireland* (Rochester, Vt.: Inner Traditions, 2000), 86–90.

11. Ibid., 129–35.

12. Jean Markale, *L'Épopée celtique en Bretagne* (Paris: Payot, 1971), 195–96.

13. We can measure how far the *Romance of Tristan* is from the courtly concept of fine amor because Tristan and Iseult's union can only be complete. The legend was incorporated into the courtly opus, but in fact it is anticourtly. The same holds true for the love affair of Lancelot and Queen Guinevere. As exemplified by his *Knight of the Cart,* only Chrétien de Troyes is in accord with the dogma of fine amor. What we know as the *Prose Lancelot* does not arise out of this same fine amor mind-set.

14. In my book *King of the Celts,* I have compiled a list of all the arguments that allow us to attribute the incredible spread and development of the Arthurian legends on the Continent to the Plantagenets. The policy of Henry II essentially consisted of earning recognition for the legitimacy of his author-

ity over England, a land of Celtic origin. (He was, after all, an Angevin.) The myth of an Arthur who was king of the isle of Britain and part of the Continent could only strengthen his position and counterbalance the history of Charlemagne, which served as the mythic screen for the Capetians.

15. *La Poésie des Troubadours* I, 151.

16. Here is the translation of the passage from the *Romance of Troy* that is inserted in the middle of the book: "Of this woman (Briseis), I wish not in truth to be blamed by she who has such bounty, honesty, honor, wealth, measure, wholesomeness, high nobility, and beauty. Thanks to her, all the misdeeds of other women are erased. In her all science rules. There is no other woman comparable to her in all the world. Rich lady of a rich king, without evil, anger, and sorrow, may you always know joy . . ." This could be mistaken for Gawain's description of Guinevere in Chrétien de Troyes's *Lancelot*. This woman is both the inspiration and mistress of all worthy men and surpasses all other women in physical beauty and moral qualities. It is also, on the part of Benoît de Sainte-Maure, a kind of clarification of the reputation of the queen-duchess, who was so often accused of adultery. A little further along, the poet returns to the charge: "Solomon said in his writings, he of such great wisdom, 'who can find a strong woman, the creator should praise . . .' Strong is she who defends herself against capture by mad hearts. Beauty and chastity together are something quite precious, it seems to me. Could there be anything under heaven more desirable?" The strong woman the author mentions can be only Eleanor, if we use the word *strong* in its psychological sense. Furthermore, the allusion to the combination of beauty and chastity is characteristic of those that usually laud Eleanor, an homage to one who had the courage to refuse her suitors, who were great in both number and in persistence.

Chapter 4. The Legend of Eleanor

1. This is particularly in the Irish tale *Diarmaid and Grainne,* which is the archetypal predecessor of *Tristan.* Diarmaid is related to Finn, and Grainne, the king's wife, compels Diarmaid to kidnap her and then have sexual relations with her. Diarmaid refuses as long as he can, and it is quite clear that he is trying to take shelter behind taboos. But obliged by Grainne's superior power, he has no choice but to obey, transgressing these taboos at the same

time. For more details on this legend see my book *Epics of Celtic Ireland*, 139–47 and in *Women of the Celts*, 226 and the following pages. I should also point out the famous tomb of Tristan in Cornwall, where he is described as being the son of Mark-Konomor (see *La Tradition celtique en Bretagne armoricaine*, 22–23).

2. Even animals have this tendency. A cat who is accustomed to sitting on the knees of its owner will often lie voluptuously on an item of the owner's clothing when he or she is absent or cannot put the cat on his or her knees.

3. Another example of this is collecting objects or clothing that once belonged to a famous individual. In the religious arena, the worship of relics is the same kind of phenomenon, although in this case the sexual component is sublimated.

4. The masturbation habits of the young boy attracted to his mother's (or sister's) clothing are well known. There is nothing extraordinary or perverse about these habits, for they form an important biological and physical stage of the boy's growth. The exchange of clothing that is practiced perfectly innocently in some families stems from the same tendency.

5. Contrary to what is commonly believed, transvestism is not homosexual. A man who dresses as a woman first goes through a simple fetishistic stage. Then, because this does not completely satisfy his needs, he seeks to identify with the beloved person and finally with the ideal woman. In one sense, he is personally incarnating femininity. From this stage, a man may go on to become a homosexual through complete identification, but this is not a mandatory consequence of the transvestism.

6. There is a literary exception in *The Chanson d'Aliscans,* in which Guiborc, wife of William of Orange, takes command in the absence of her husband against the Saracens besieging his fortress.

7. Yet toward the end of her life in 1201, Eleanor was obliged to take command of the citadel of Mirebeau besieged by her own grandson, Arthur of Brittany.

8. Jean Markale, *Epics of Celtic Ireland*, 56.

9. *Tain Bô Cualnge* in *Epics of Celtic Ireland*, 91–100.

10. Jean Markale, *The Celts* (Rochester, Vt.: Inner Traditions, 1993), 160–63.

11. Jean Markale, *Epics of Celtic Ireland*, 86–91.

12. Ibid., 129–35.

13. Jean Markale, *L'Épopée celtique en Bretagne* (Paris: Payot, 1971).

14. Tancrede is a Christian knight and Clorinda is a Muslim queen. They love each other, but religion separates them. One day, Tancrede fights a Muslim

knight who is none other than Clorinda cross-dressing as a man, and he fatally wounds his adversary before realizing his foe is Clorinda. The combat of Tancrede and Clorinda, magnificently set to music by Monteverdi, is a masterpiece of black eroticism, the battle of the two lovers acting as the equivalent of amorous foreplay that leads to the sexual act, and Clorinda's death acting as the equivalent of orgasm.

15. Jean Markale, *Epics of Celtic Ireland,* 102.

16. Ibid., 177–83.

17. Jean Markale, *L'Épopée celtique en Bretagne.*

18. Jean Markale, "La Reine des Prouesses" [The Queen of Feats] in *La Tradition celtique en Bretagne armoricaine,* 39–46.

19. Ibid., 148–68, see *La Saga de Yann* [Yann's Saga], of which there are a number of variations.

20. See Salvatore Santangelo, "L'amor lontano di Jauffré Rudel" [The Distant Love of Jaufré Rudel], *Siculorum Gymnasium* (1953), 1–28. It has been shown that Rudel's poems were written before 1148 in honor of the duchess of Aquitaine.

21. This is the argument I developed in *Women of the Celts,* first showing the position held by women in Celtic society and the image of femininity as it appears through tales and legend. Celtic marriage, even under Christian influence in Ireland, was always only a temporary contract between two individuals and was ever open to challenge by one of the two contracting parties. Thus divorce by mutual consent existed and was a complete exception to twelfth-century laws.

22. He stated in his *De Nurgis Curialum* that Henry married Eleanor "although she had, according to what was said privately, relations with his father, Geoffrey."

23. In his *De principis instructione,* he claims that "Geoffrey, count of Anjou, had misused Eleanor when he was seneschal of France, in consequence of which, or so it was said, he warned his son Henry on several occasions, admonishing and forbidding him to touch her in any way as it was not suitable for a son to marry a woman his father had already known." The accusation is serious but unverifiable. It would seem to imply that Henry Plantagenet had the intention of marrying Eleanor during his father's lifetime. What is odd about this story is that later Richard the Lion Heart refused to marry his fiancée Alys of France on the pretext that she had been his father's mistress.

24. In particular, it has been rejected by Zingarelli in his *Ricerche sulla vita du Bernard di Ventadorn*. In her article, "The Literary Role of Eleanor of Aquitaine and her Family" (*Cultura Neolatina* 14, page 18), Rita Lejeune notes that all of Zingarelli's arguments must be revisited in light of the constant movement of Eleanor and Henry, who had no fixed residences. It is highly likely that the poets and musicians of the court followed the sovereigns on their travels.

25. The origin of this belief is easy to determine. It involves unconscious biological reactions that occur during sleep that are sometimes accompanied by erotic dreams. The succubi, or female demons, are creations of the guilt inspired by perfectly unconscious reactions leading to what is called nocturnal emission. Incubi, or male demons, meanwhile, are quite convenient for explaining inopportune pregnancies and births.

26. We should note that Ralph di Diceto completely eliminated the two daughters resulting from Eleanor's French marriage, as well as Matilda, who was the daughter of Eleanor and Henry II and was older than Richard.

27. We can note the abundance of notes and their exactitude. It is almost like reading a detective story.

28. Of course, there are a large number of variations on this story. In the fourteenth-century *Chronicles of London*, Eleanor hurled herself on Rosamond and tore off her clothes before placing her, entirely naked, in a bathtub full of water. She then brought in an old woman who slashed the veins in both of Rosamond's wrists, and while the unfortunate woman bled to death, another old crone came in and placed toads on top of her breasts. We can see that the staging of this melodrama was the result of careful study. Another version portrays Eleanor forcing her rival to choose between the dagger and poison. Rosamond resigns herself to drinking poison. Several more-recent authors take pity on Rosamond though; they maintain that Eleanor was satisfied with the capture of her rival and her imprisonment in a convent, which corresponds more to the historical reality.

29. This refers to Henry II, who suspected his wife of infidelity and sought to profit from the situation to make Eleanor talk.

30. This most likely refers to William Marshal, companion and confidant of Henry II, then loyal servant of Richard and Eleanor.

31. To persuade the count to accompany him, the king swore an oath to take no action despite what the queen might say.

32. The only adultery that can be held against Eleanor is that which took place in

Antioch and which prompted the rift between her and Louis VII. Again, we do not know anything about what actually happened. No other accusation of adultery against Eleanor is based on proof or even a presumption of proof.

33. Conversely, an older man who marries a very young girl is deemed respectable and is respected. During Eleanor's time, many mature men wed princesses of eleven or twelve years of age, yet no one cried scandal. The marriage of Geoffrey Plantagenet to an older Empress Matilda, however, sparked pejorative comment before Eleanor's marriage to Henry. Then, when Eleanor, less than two months following her "divorce," married the younger Henry, it provided an excuse to dredge up all the old rumors.

34. This is the meaning that can be given to the well-known legend of the city of Ys: Intolerably, this city was completely under the dominion of Princess Dahud. Legend then invented nameless debauchery attributed to the princess that would justify the divine punishment inflicted on the city, its inhabitants, and the princess alike. Dahud's (good witch's) guilt led to the residents being swallowed by the waves of the sea—that is, they are symbolically repressed in the unconscious. See my chapter called "The Submerged Princess" in *Women of the Celts*, 43–84.

35. The most characteristic of these stories is certainly *La Saga de Yann*, which appears in my *La Tradition celtique en Bretagne armoricaine*, 148–68. The young hero has absolutely no right to be king. He is really a usurper, but through battle by showing proof of his ability to assume the highest responsibilities—symbolized by the love he inspires in a fairy princess—he has won the right to rule. Legally, it is by marrying the princess that he becomes king of a land whose former king, unjust and incapable, had been eliminated by the princess herself.

36. I have provided a detailed explanation of the Celtic concept of royalty and the horizontal system that characterizes their society in *King of the Celts*, mainly in the chapter dedicated to "The Specific Qualities of the Celts," 221–53.

37. Jean Markale, *Epics of Celtic Ireland*, 91–100.

Chapter 5. From Guinevere to Melusine

1. The invention of the wall chimney dates from the twelfth century. Before this time, if the hearth was not in the center of the room, it was at least in a space away from the wall, and a hole in the roof allowed smoke to exit. The

simplest meal occurred in a gathering around the hearth; the diners sat in a circle and ate the food that was cooking there. This was common procedure with the Celts, according to Irish texts that are quite explicit on this topic. It was probably from this notion of a common meal eaten in a circle around the hearth that the image of the Round Table came.

2. I have provided arguments and texts in *La Tradition celtique en Bretagne armoricaine,* 108–32, concerning this problem. Lancelot does not appear in the Welsh texts preceding Chrétien de Troyes. A German version, whose Breton origin is beyond doubt, tells of the adventures of Lancelot (named Lanzelet in this text) in a context that is totally different from that of the Arthurian legend. Lancelot is an Armorican hero and remains such in romances of the Round Table, in which he is explicitly referred to as coming from Little Britain [Brittany]. It is without doubt Chrétien de Troyes who incorporated Lancelot into the tales about Arthur, as would later be done with Tristan and Iseult or as Geoffrey of Monmouth did with Merlin. In any case, Lancelot never appears in the Triads of the Island of Britain.

3. These sculptures date from the beginning of the twelfth century and prove the age of the Arthurian legend. They allow us to recognize an expedition led by Arthur to bring back the queen who was carried off by a mysterious lover or, quite simply, was in a full-fledged amorous elopement.

4. Chrétien de Troyes, *Perceval le Gallois,* trans. Foulet (Paris: Editions Stock, 1947), 191.

5. In fact, the original context of Melusine is perfectly pagan. It was Jean d'Arras who transformed the pagan goddess into a so-called historical woman-fairy with a Christian stamp. Melusine became a constructor of churches and monasteries and benefactor of the poor and orphans. She replaced the Virgin Mary to perform all kinds of miracles and thereby offered a reassuring image. It should not be forgotten, however, that Melusine had a much more disturbing origin; she was the woman-serpent and because of this was somewhat different from the fairies that the rural storytellers described in their folktales. It was because she was both a woman and a serpent that she could perform magical feats. Her powers came from her dual nature, just like Merlin, to whom she should be compared.

Rabelais, who had a sound knowledge of the traditions of Poitou, tells us in his Fourth Book: "You will find there witnesses of renown, old and solidly built, who will swear to you on the arm of St. Rigomer that

Melusine, their original foundress, had a woman's body down to the prick-purse, and that below that she was a serpentine Chitterling, or perhaps a Chitterlinic serpent." Through Rabelais's cheeky humor, we can get a sense of the reality of the legend in fourteenth-century Poitou, an area still quite isolated from the current of ideas that were then shaking the world. This dual nature makes her dangerous to those who are incapable of supporting the weight of the sacred. The same can be found in the context of fine amor: there, too, is a taboo that should not be transgressed, for the lover should not see his lady before she gives him permission to do so, and the lady is inaccessible, divine, and so terrifyingly beautiful that it is almost impossible to look at her except after a slow initiation through which are acquired habits and habituation—for it is dangerous to contemplate the deity without being prepared. This is the reason for all religious or philosophical initiations, and this corresponds to humanity's desire since the dawn of time: to contemplate that which is impossible to contemplate, and to express what is inexpressible.

6. J. Loth, *The Mabinogion,* volume 2 (Paris: Ernest Thorin, 1889), 94–95.
7. Ibid., 103.

SELECTED BIBLIOGRAPHY

Bezzola, Reto. *Les origines et la formation de la literature courtoise en Occident.* Paris: Champion, 1958–1963.

Chambers, Frank McMinn. "Some Legends Concerning Eleanor of Aquitaine." *Speculum* (1941): 459–68.

Delpech. *Le divorce d'Aliénor d'Aquitaine.* Paris, 1965.

Kelly, Amy. *Eleanor of Aquitaine and the Four Kings.* Cambridge, Mass.: Harvard University Press, 1950–1959. New edition 1991.

Labande, E. R. "Pour une image véridique d'Aliénor d'Aquitaine." *Bulletin de la Société des antiquaries de l'Ouest* (1952): 175–234.

Larrey, Isaac de. *Histoire d'Éléonore de Guyenne.* London, 1788.

Lejeune, Rita. "Rôle littéraire d'Aliénor d'Aquitaine." *Cultura neolatina* (1954): 5–57.

Macheco, Palaméde de. *Histoire d'Éléonore de Guyenne.* Paris, 1822.

Pernoud, Régine. *Aliénor d'Aquitaine.* Paris: Albin Michel, 1965.

Suire, Abbé Alphonse. *Aliénor d'Aquitaine.* Niort, France, 1936.

Vital-Mareille. *La Vie ardente d'Éléonore d'Aquitaine.* Paris: E. Flammarion, 1931.

Walker, Curtis Howe. *Eleanor of Aquitaine.* Chapel Hill: University of North Carolina Press, 1950.

INDEX

BOOKS OF RELATED INTEREST

Women of the Celts
by Jean Markale

Montségur and the Mystery of the Cathars
by Jean Markale

Courtly Love
The Path of Sexual Initiation
by Jean Markale

Cathedral of the Black Madonna
The Druids and the Mysteries of Chartres
by Jean Markale

The Great Goddess
Reverence of the Divine Feminine from the Paleolithic to the Present
by Jean Markale

King Arthur and the Goddess of the Land
The Divine Feminine in the *Mabinogion*
by Caitlín Matthews

Women in Celtic Myth
Tales of Extraordinary Women from the Ancient Celtic Tradition
by Moyra Caldecott

Seduction and the Secret Power of Women
The Lure of Sirens and Mermaids
by Meri Lao

INNER TRADITIONS • BEAR & COMPANY
P.O. Box 388
Rochester, VT 05767
1-800-246-8648
www.InnerTraditions.com

Or contact your local bookseller